A history of the Middle Ages

A history of the Middle Ages

World Events from 500 CE to 1500 CE

Phyllis G. Jestice

SIRIUS

Picture Credits

t = top, b = bottom, l = left, r = right

Alamy: 11, 23, 26, 32, 34, 38, 49b, 62b, 65, 71, 78, 79b, 83, 101, 107, 131, 139, 143 (x2), 147, 156t, 159, 169, 182, 187, 209t, 214, 216, 219, 227t, 233t, 245t

Bridgeman Images: 9, 46, 53b, 76, 86, 97, 152, 173, 184b, 196, 223, 244t,

David Woodroffe: 41, 80t, 87b, 103, 180, 200

Historic England: 51

Library of Congress: 242

Metropolitan Museum of Art, New York: 20, 29, 48, 93, 108t, 114, 118t, 132, 171, 208, 213, 226b, 236t, 238

National Palace Museum, Taiwan: 111t

Science Photo Library: 17b

Shutterstock: 5, 18, 19, 22b, 39, 42, 43, 44b, 49t, 52, 54, 56, 57b, 58, 60, 64, 72, 74t, 75b, 81, 85, 89, 91, 99, 102, 104, 105 (x2), 106, 110, 112, 118b, 121, 125t, 128, 130, 133, 135, 136, 142b, 149, 150, 157 (x2), 163t, 174, 175, 176 (x2), 178, 188, 195t, 202, 206t, 217b, 220, 225 (x2), 227b, 229, 234, 239t, 244b

Smithsonian Institution, National Museum of African Art: 79, 177l

Thuringian State Office for Heritage Management and Archaeology: 204b (B. Stefan)

Wellcome Collection: 144

Wikimedia Commons: 10, 12, 13 (x2), 14, 16, 17t, 20, 21 (x2), 22t, 24, 25, 27, 28, 30, 31, 33, 36, 37, 44t, 45 (x2), 47, 50, 53t, 57t, 59, 61, 62t, 63, 66 (x2), 67, 68, 69, 70, 73, 74b, 75t, 80b, 82, 84, 87t, 88, 90, 92, 94, 95 (x2), 96, 98, 108b, 109, 111b, 113, 115, 116, 117, 120, 122, 123 (x2), 124, 125b, 126 (x2), 127, 134 (x2), 137, 138, 140, 141, 142t, 145 (x2), 146, 148, 151 (x2), 154, 156b, 158, 160, 161, 162 (x2), 163b, 164, 165, 166, 167, 168, 170, 177r, 179, 181, 183, 184t, 185, 186, 189, 190 (x2), 191, 192, 193 (x2), 194 (x2), 195b, 198, 199 (x2), 201, 203, 204t, 205, 206b, 207, 209b, 210, 211 (x2), 212, 215, 217t, 218, 221, 224, 226t, 228 (x2), 230 (x2), 231, 232, 233b, 235, 236b, 237, 239b, 240, 241, 243, 245b, 246, 248, 249

SIRIUS

This edition published in 2024 by Sirius Publishing, a division of Arcturus Publishing Limited,
26/27 Bickels Yard, 151–153 Bermondsey Street,
London SE1 3HA

ISBN: 978-1-3988-4461-2
AD010854US

Printed in Malaysia

Contents

TIMELINE

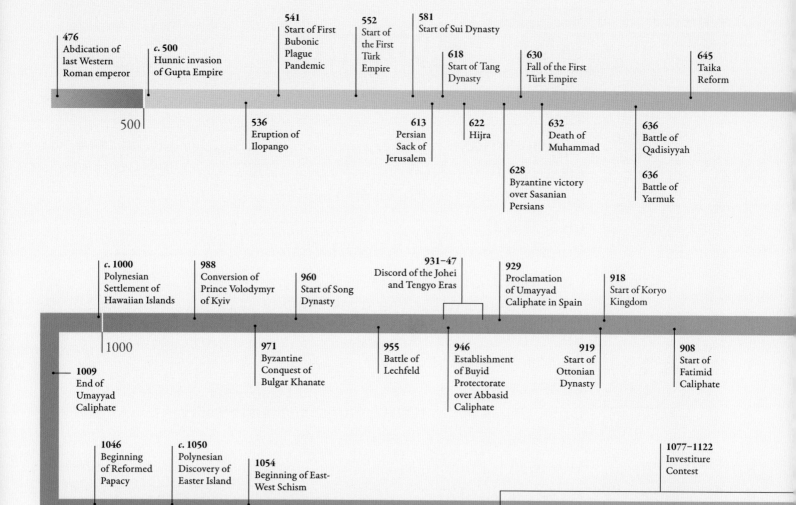

476 Abdication of last Western Roman emperor

c. 500 Hunnic invasion of Gupta Empire

541 Start of First Bubonic Plague Pandemic

552 Start of the First Türk Empire

581 Start of Sui Dynasty

618 Start of Tang Dynasty

630 Fall of the First Türk Empire

645 Taika Reform

500

536 Eruption of Ilopango

613 Persian Sack of Jerusalem

622 Hijra

632 Death of Muhammad

628 Byzantine victory over Sasanian Persians

636 Battle of Qadisiyyah

636 Battle of Yarmuk

c. 1000 Polynesian Settlement of Hawaiian Islands

988 Conversion of Prince Volodymyr of Kyiv

960 Start of Song Dynasty

931–47 Discord of the Johei and Tengyo Eras

929 Proclamation of Umayyad Caliphate in Spain

918 Start of Koryo Kingdom

1000

1009 End of Umayyad Caliphate

971 Byzantine Conquest of Bulgar Khanate

955 Battle of Lechfeld

946 Establishment of Buyid Protectorate over Abbasid Caliphate

919 Start of Ottonian Dynasty

908 Start of Fatimid Caliphate

1046 Beginning of Reformed Papacy

c. 1050 Polynesian Discovery of Easter Island

1054 Beginning of East-West Schism

1077–1122 Investiture Contest

c. 1050 Start of Golden Age of Cahokia

1061 Formation of Almoravid Empire

1066 Norman Conquest of England

1071 Battle of Manzikert

1086 Almoravid Invasion of Spain

1096–9 First Crusade

1085 Conquest of Toledo by Alfonso VI of León-Castile

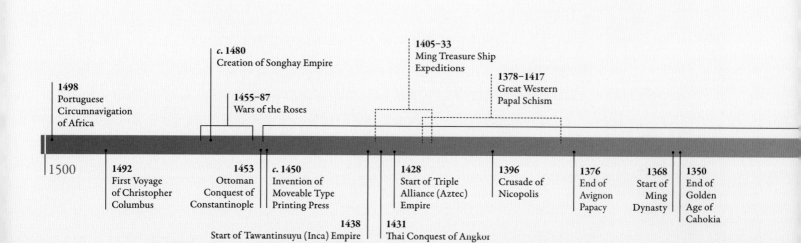

c. 1480 Creation of Songhay Empire

1405–33 Ming Treasure Ship Expeditions

1378–1417 Great Western Papal Schism

1498 Portuguese Circumnavigation of Africa

1455–87 Wars of the Roses

1500

1492 First Voyage of Christopher Columbus

1453 Ottoman Conquest of Constantinople

c. 1450 Invention of Moveable Type Printing Press

1428 Start of Triple Alliance (Aztec) Empire

1396 Crusade of Nicopolis

1376 End of Avignon Papacy

1368 Start of Ming Dynasty

1350 End of Golden Age of Cahokia

1438 Start of Tawantinsuyu (Inca) Empire

1431 Thai Conquest of Angkor

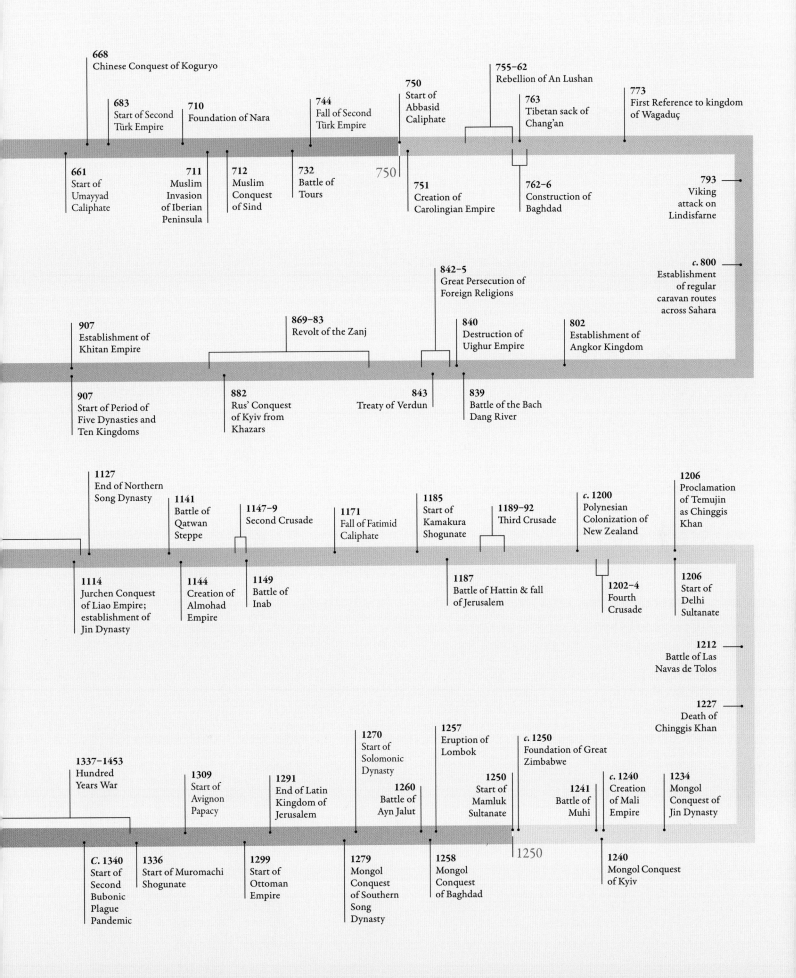

668
Chinese Conquest of Koguryo

683
Start of Second
Türk Empire

710
Foundation of Nara

744
Fall of Second
Türk Empire

750
Start of
Abbasid
Caliphate

755–62
Rebellion of An Lushan

763
Tibetan sack of
Chang'an

773
First Reference to kingdom
of Wagaduç

750

661
Start of
Umayyad
Caliphate

711
Muslim
Invasion
of Iberian
Peninsula

712
Muslim
Conquest
of Sind

732
Battle of
Tours

751
Creation of
Carolingian Empire

762–6
Construction of
Baghdad

793
Viking
attack on
Lindisfarne

c. 800
Establishment
of regular
caravan routes
across Sahara

907
Establishment of
Khitan Empire

869–83
Revolt of the Zanj

842–5
Great Persecution of
Foreign Religions

840
Destruction of
Uighur Empire

802
Establishment of
Angkor Kingdom

907
Start of Period of
Five Dynasties and
Ten Kingdoms

882
Rus' Conquest
of Kyiv from
Khazars

843
Treaty of Verdun

839
Battle of the Bach
Dang River

1127
End of Northern
Song Dynasty

1141
Battle of
Qatwan
Steppe

1147–9
Second Crusade

1171
Fall of Fatimid
Caliphate

1185
Start of
Kamakura
Shogunate

1189–92
Third Crusade

c. 1200
Polynesian
Colonization of
New Zealand

1206
Proclamation
of Temujin
as Chinggis
Khan

1114
Jurchen Conquest
of Liao Empire;
establishment of
Jin Dynasty

1144
Creation of
Almohad
Empire

1149
Battle of
Inab

1187
Battle of Hattin & fall
of Jerusalem

1202–4
Fourth
Crusade

1206
Start of
Delhi
Sultanate

1212
Battle of Las
Navas de Tolos

1227
Death of
Chinggis Khan

1337–1453
Hundred
Years War

1309
Start of
Avignon
Papacy

1291
End of Latin
Kingdom of
Jerusalem

1270
Start of
Solomonic
Dynasty

1257
Eruption of
Lombok

c. 1250
Foundation of Great
Zimbabwe

1260
Battle of
Ayn Jalut

1250
Start of
Mamluk
Sultanate

1241
Battle of
Muhi

c. 1240
Creation
of Mali
Empire

1234
Mongol
Conquest of
Jin Dynasty

C. 1340
Start of
Second
Bubonic
Plague
Pandemic

1336
Start of Muromachi
Shogunate

1299
Start of
Ottoman
Empire

1279
Mongol
Conquest
of Southern
Song
Dynasty

1258
Mongol
Conquest
of Baghdad

1250

1240
Mongol Conquest
of Kyiv

A Global Middle Age?

Producing a global history of the Middle Ages is a tall order for a number of reasons. First and foremost, the term "Middle Ages" for a historical period is a term invented by Italians in the 14th century, a derogatory name for the period between the end of the western Roman Empire and what they perceived to be their own glorious and enlightened time, an "in-between time" that scholars like Francesco Petrarca dismissed as dark and useless. As such, the term does not even describe European history accurately, although in the 19th century it came into common use to describe the period roughly 500–1500 of the Common Era. Other world regions of course experienced different cultural currents, although scholars of many areas have distinguished between an ancient times and modernity, usually with something between them.

RIGHT *A European merchant shop in 1455. Miniature from a translation of Aristotle's* Ethics, *evidence of the long shadow of ancient thought on medieval Europe.*

For China, the "medieval" period most often is regarded as starting in the early 4th century CE. with the collapse of the unified Han state; most end the era with the fall of the Tang Dynasty in 907. Indeed, Chinese scholars sometimes call the Song Dynasty (960–1279) the beginning of modernity, pointing to its elaborate bureaucracy, flourishing market economy, and widespread literacy, all of which form a strong contrast to the European Middle Ages. Scholars of Japan divide the era discussed in this book into three distinct periods—primordial and classical only succeeded by "medieval" in the late 12th century. For the Maya, the classical period endured 250–950; a standard history of "medieval" Africa covers the period 1250–1800. The unique histories of each region have meant that states have developed and declined at their own speeds.

Nonetheless, there are benefits to examining the history of the period 500–1500 from a global perspective. The recent "global turn" in historical study has emphasized a more bird's-eye view of history, examining large processes that have shaped the human condition. Even without contact between population groups, societies over time came up with similar solutions to the challenges of survival. When population reaches a certain point, people have developed agriculture, and throughout the world the difficulties of assuring cooperation between humans led to the rise of chiefdoms and kingdoms. Whatever the continent, rulers and their subjects created a religious underpinning to stabilize governments, running the spectrum from rulers approved by a god or gods to the belief that they were themselves divine. But although patterns of human development can be seen clearly in a global perspective, local experience—whether geographical, social, or historical—assured variation in the solutions people found depending on where they lived. A comparative look can aid our understanding, for example when examining

LEFT *Mural of Francesco Petrarca in his study from the Hall of the Giants, Padua (last quarter of the 14th century).*

the similarities and differences between "feudalism" in Japan and Europe.

We are conditioned to think of the modern world as global, the Portuguese and Spanish voyages of exploration of the late 15th century ushering in a new age of interconnectedness between world regions. Very few regions developed in complete isolation during the medieval millennium, however. An enormous amount of evidence exists for interaction between populations on a global scale in the period 500–1500. Great trade networks had already been established in the ancient world and rose to new heights in our period, including the Silk Roads by both land and sea, caravan routes across the

Sahara, transit along rivers and coasts wherever possible, or the Mediterranean as a vital hub for commerce since the 2nd millennium BCE. The only novelty of interconnectedness after c. 1500 is that the vast networks already in place in the Americas for the first time were linked to the vast exchange networks of Europe, Africa, and Asia. Throughout the medieval millennium, contact between eastern and western hemispheres had been almost nonexistent, limited by the enormous expanse of ocean to a few encounters, such as the Scandinavian "discovery" of North America in c. 1000 and limited Polynesian contact with South America. Where there was interregional contact, exchange almost inevitably led to

ABOVE *A water mill from Song-Dynasty China. Note the convenient water transport for the processed grain.*

La royne
Le roy
Labour

ABOVE *An idealized portrait of the orders of society from late medieval France, with king and queen at center stage.*

conflict, and conquest is a vital part of our story. Everywhere there were people, there was at least regional exchange, and everywhere populations had to deal with foreigners in their midst, whether they came as merchants or as conquerors.

This volume explores a number of large themes that hold true globally during the medieval millennium. The first is the fragility of human populations in face of the natural world's challenges. Societies dependent mostly on human and animal muscle rather than machines did not have the means to control their natural environment to the extent that humankind has developed in the 19th to 21st centuries. When weather patterns changed, they prospered or suffered accordingly, and although strong governments could ameliorate the situation (for example by creating irrigation systems), such solutions were fragile and difficult to maintain. Above all, with no understanding of microbes, there was no way to limit epidemic disease besides quarantine and in time building a natural immunity in the population.

A second theme of this book is the quest for stability. States had to deal with the consequences of natural disaster or the unnatural disaster of foreign invasion, rising and falling as conditions shifted. Even without catalysts like climate change or belligerent neighbors, every state of the millennium also had to come to grips in some way with the problem of ideal versus reality. Central governments developed often-imposing ideologies of jurisdiction and sovereignty, claiming the right and duty to control every aspect of their subjects' lives. No state, however, not even the massive bureaucracy of China, had adequate means to enforce the rulers' will. Communication with peripheral areas was limited to the speed a horse or man could run, forcing rulers even of states with well-developed postal systems to rely heavily on the skill and integrity of regional officials. And a perennial difficulty was how to pay for government. This was a world of subsistence farming. Although many regions found means to increase surpluses—whether by terracing hillsides, introducing new plows, or introducing new and improved crops—the lack of artificial fertilizers and insect control limited both population growth and the government's ability to collect taxes.

As a third distinguishing feature of the era, most civilizations investigated in this volume were marked in a way that makes it more plausible to define them as living in a "middle" era—their societies were shaped by a reverence for the past. Almost everywhere, something had come

LEFT *A 15th-century European market, from Nicolas Oresme's translation of Aristotle's* Ethics.

before, an earlier society that was regarded with wistful nostalgia or ardent longing. China during the medieval millennium constantly harkened back to the glory of the Han Dynasty, as Europeans invoked the long shadow of Rome. Mesoamericans venerated the ruined remains of earlier civilizations at places like El Tajín or Teotihuacán, crafting legends that they were the home of gods, while the rajahs of India honored the memory of Asoka even though nobody could read his inscriptions any longer. Rulers asserted their legitimacy by claiming descent from ancient rulers (such as in Ethiopia claiming descent from Solomon and the queen of Sheba) or even deities. The 12th-century French scholar Bernard of Chartres proclaimed that we are dwarfs perched on the shoulders of giants, a statement that would have rung true around the globe.

Finally, an apology is due to the hundreds of millions of ordinary people who lived and died in the medieval millennium, who hardly appear in the pages of this book. Medieval societies were very much like icebergs, the visible part supported by a submerged 90 percent whose stories are largely unrecoverable. The literate elite was only rarely interested in writing about non-elites, and even archaeology serves us poorly in this regard because the poor lived in flimsy dwellings and could not afford to be buried with grave goods. Nonetheless, we should never forget that without the farmers, artisans, builders, and performers of myriad tasks, both women and men, the civilizations we study could never have existed, much less achieved the heights they did.

BELOW *The career of a Chinese civil servant. On the left, scholars are taking the civil service examinations; on the right, the successful candidate has become a high government official.*

CHAPTER 1

Ripple Effects: The Global 6th Century

In the period immediately before the dawn of the medieval millennium, two of the greatest empires of Eurasia had undergone radical transformation. In China, the Han Dynasty had collapsed in the early 3rd century CE and repeated efforts to reunite its territories under a single ruler had all ended in failure. Much further to the west, the precocious Roman Empire had fragmented. While the Eastern Empire (which historians much later dubbed the "Byzantine Empire") remained largely intact, Rome's Western Empire— including Rome itself—had fallen under the rule of Germanic warlords, leaders of the peoples that had overrun Rome's frontiers in the 5th century. As a result, the 6th century in Eurasia and northern Africa was dominated by the struggle for stability and the restoration of earlier greatness. The task of rulers was, however, complicated by shifts in the natural environment, which also had a deep impact on political organizations in the Americas and the Indian subcontinent, and of course on the daily lives of millions of people around the world.

RIGHT *The Byzantine emperor Justinian, surrounded by courtiers, makes an offering at the Church of San Vitale in Ravenna, Italy.*

MAXIMIANV

THE END OF THE "CLASSICAL OPTIMUM"

A number of civilizations around the world had benefited from a period of good weather, with warmer temperatures and longer growing seasons, known as the Classical Optimum. That era of increased solar radiance and climate stability gradually ended between 300 CE and 600 CE, giving way to the Late Antique Little Ice Age. The first half of the 6th century in particular suffered heavily from climate instability, with very cold winters and major regional famines. The climate decline was aggravated by very high volcanic activity in the 530s and 540s. Most important was the massive eruption of Ilopango (in modern El Salvador) in 536. Its dust cloud cut solar input to Earth for

BELOW *Ruins of the Great Marib Dam, Yemen. Maintained for over a millennium, it was never repaired after a final breach in the late 6th century.*

as much as a decade. The Byzantine historian Procopius describes a dust cloud that endured an entire year, and the haze was recorded from Britain all the way to Korea, as well as China, where handfuls of yellow dust could be picked up from the streets.

Changing weather patterns led to drought in some regions and massive flooding in others. Floods in particular have left a visible archaeological and geological record. We know, for example, that sea levels rose in Northern Europe in the late 5th and early 6th centuries, and that the northern German coast was especially hard hit. The result was the widespread abandonment of coastal settlements (which

How We Know about Early Medieval Climate Change

Piecing together the evidence for climate change in Earth's history is a complex business, but over the past 20–30 years environmental historians and scientists have reached near consensus on the ebbs and flows of world climate, although not always on what the sociological impact of climate change has been. The evidence for climate change takes many forms. Most traditionally, historians have always known from written texts about periods of exceptionally bad weather, as chroniclers complained about floods or cattle plague. Comparative study of written sources can build a composite picture of climate change over longer periods—as long as there are written sources.

For much of the world, however, we do not have written sources, whether because the society was preliterate or, in the case of the Maya, because later conquerors purposefully destroyed most of their written culture in infamous book burnings. In those cases, and to deepen understanding everywhere, we rely on science. Archaeology can reveal the destruction of water conveyance systems, the changing size of domesticated animals, and, sometimes, when land passed in or out of cultivation. Beyond that, examination of core samples from glaciers and bogs shows us what plants grew in an area at a given time (thanks to pollen deposits), volcanic activity (ash), and the like. Perhaps most exciting is the science of dendrochronology—figuring out historic climate based on trees. If a piece of wood is found in a site that can be dated by other means (for example the rafter supports of a medieval cathedral), dendrochronologists can trace the weather back to the time the tree was a sapling, based on how well-developed tree rings are for each year. The final result is a complex map of periods of greater and less solar radiance, of El Niño and La Niña effects, of North Atlantic Oscillations, and of monsoons that have allowed scholars to reconstruct climate in history.

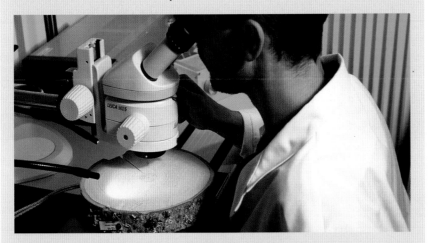

A dendrochronologist at work. The thickness of tree rings reveals weather in each year of the tree's growth.

ABOVE *Gold dinar of Chandragupta II, one of the last strong rulers of India's Gupta Dynasty.*

earlier scholars attributed to mass migration to England). In far-away Yemen, massive floods destroyed the great Marib Dam, the centerpiece of Saba's complex irrigation system. Both regions were very slow to recover.

In India, highly dependent on seasonal monsoon rains for agriculture, the end of the Classical Optimum brought a long dry spell. Most of the subcontinent had been united under the Gupta Empire, but by the early 6th century the problems inherent in holding together a large, multilingual and multicultural empire had been magnified by a series of droughts that encouraged regional rebellions, although the arrival of invading Huns in c. 500 certainly did not help matters. The Hun leaders Toramana and his son Mihirakula were especially famed for their atrocities, including the targeting and torture of Buddhists, which began that religion's decline in its homeland. The Gupta hegemony had collapsed by the middle years of the century and the economy as a whole declined with fewer coins minted and less evidence of trade guilds.

Probably the most significant, but least-understood, effects of the 6th-century climate turn were felt in the Americas. The Maya had developed a highly complex culture in Mesoamerica by the 2nd and 3rd centuries. Although they never formed a unified empire, individual city-states had urbanized to an impressive degree, with populations that in some cases numbered as many as 100,000; the multicultural Teotihuacan further north probably exceeded 200,000 at its height. Maya rulers, enjoying status as descendants of gods, had created societies rich with monumental architecture and ritual, profiting from extensive coastal canoe trade, agriculture, and frequent wars. The Maya culture was seriously undermined by a series of droughts by the latter 6th century, however, and a number of significant urban centers had been abandoned by the 580s. Thanks to the resources of strong central governments, a number of city-states survived, especially by creating large irrigation networks. The whole was not ultimately sustainable, though, and all the surviving great Maya cities declined over the next two centuries. It was only slightly later, in the first half of the 7th century, that Teotihuacan in what is now Mexico collapsed, although initially the city-state had been able to take advantage of others' climate woes to expand southward. Archaeologists have attributed the burning of palaces and ritual centers to a rebellion of peasants or enslaved people rather than a foreign invasion. That the destruction occurred at the time of a major drought suggests that elite demands on the workers had become intolerable. In Peru, the Moche and Nasa cultures also collapsed in the late 6th century, devastated first by massive El Niño flooding and then a major drought.

BELOW *Pyramid of the Sun, Teotihuacan, Mexico, surrounded by lesser temples.*

THE EURASIAN STEPPE

Perhaps no region was as heavily hit by the climate instability of the Late Antique Little Ice Age as the steppe of Central Asia. This region was home to a sparse population of pastoral nomads and semi-nomads, very reliant on rainfall to provide fodder for their animals and in some cases to sustain limited agriculture. They also depended heavily on hunting to supplement their food supply. These pastoralists had little margin against disaster, and failure of the grasslands even for a single year could be catastrophic. And catastrophe for the nomads of the steppe spelled disaster for their sedentary neighbors.

The reason for fear among the sedentary peoples was simple. Although there were never many nomads per square mile on the steppe, there are a great many square miles. So, when the pastoralists united they were a formidable force. While normally divided into mutually antagonistic population groups, speaking a range of Altaic languages including many Turkic dialects, in times of crisis strong leaders could rise and unite the peoples. Once united, the steppe nomads were extremely hard for sedentary peoples to fight. While settled farming populations relied heavily on large infantry formations, nomads fought almost exclusively on horseback. Their tactics were based more on the hunt than what "civilized" people recognized as warfare, the pastoralists relying heavily on ambush and shooting their strong compound bows from a distance rather than engaging directly. Repeatedly in the medieval millennium (and before, notably with the Parthians and Huns), the peoples of the steppe proved to be an irresistible force.

The 530s and 540s saw a major reconfiguration of power across the steppe that spilled over into the sedentary lands of both Asia and Europe in a vast ripple effect. A leader named Tumen, who claimed descent from a she-wolf and the only survivor of a massacred tribe, created a confederacy of Turkic peoples, rebelling against the overlordship of their fellow pastoralists, the Avars. The rebellion marked the beginning of the First Turkic Empire (552–630), an ethnically and linguistically diverse state that stretched from the Caspian Sea to Manchuria, its khagans ruling over agricultural areas as well as pastoralists. Although inherently unstable, since any member of the royal family could claim the right to rule and succession fights were the norm, this empire deserves to be better known than it is. The Turks were the first Inner Asian nomads to leave native written sources, creating their own script for the purpose, suggesting a new desire to emulate sedentary-style government. The khagans proved to be skilled diplomats, too. They took advantage of the weakness of a divided China even before unifying their own empire, with a first known attack against the Northern Wei in 542, looking for the products of sedentary lands, especially silk. Under the khagan Muhan (555–72), the empire played the warring dynasties of northern China against each other, threatening attack or alliance with enemies and trading horses for luxury goods; Muhan reportedly received 100,000 rolls of silk per year in this way. When China finally reunited under the Sui Dynasty late in the century, though, the Sui administration recognized the Turk threat and encouraged the steppe empire's internal divisions, igniting a series of civil wars

BELOW *Turkic* balbal *statues, Kyrğyzstan. These anthropomorphic statues were produced for several centuries.*

ABOVE *The Sogdian merchant An Qie welcomes a Turkic chieftain, from a Xian tomb (579 CE).*

that weakened and ultimately destroyed the Turkic Empire as an independent state.

The Turk khagans were deeply concerned to revive the northern branch of the Silk Road, the ancient caravan route that stretched from China to the Mediterranean and was a major source of wealth. They tried to persuade the shah of the Sasanian Persian Empire to open up more trade in Persia, but the shah refused and had the second Turk emissary killed. In retaliation, in 569 the Turks invaded Persia, although they made little progress because a massive Sasanian system of fortifications based on Merv protected their core lands from assault from the steppe. The Turks crossed the Amu Darya (the river bordering modern Uzbekistan, Turkmenistan, Afghanistan, and Tajikistan) in 588–9, only to be crushed by a Sasanian army. Much more successful was their approach to the Byzantine Empire. The Byzantine emperor was happy to encourage trade that bypassed his empire's ancient enemy, so direct trade was developed, Sogdian merchants serving as the middlemen and making Samarkand a boom town.

The effects of the First Turkic Empire were felt far into Europe. Tumen's rebellion had begun after he had helped his Avar overlords suppress a revolt, then requested an Avar bride as reward, only to be rebuffed. Tumen's confederation then

destroyed the Avar Empire, and the remnants of the Avars were driven west into Byzantine lands, where, incidentally, they introduced the stirrup to Europe. When a Turk embassy demanded the return of their "fugitive slaves" in 568, the Avars moved on yet again and eventually settled in Pannonia, again causing a ripple effect that pushed Slavic peoples into the Balkans and the Germanic Lombard people into Italy. For several generations they took what advantage they could from the Byzantine Empire's preoccupations, at times imposing tribute in return for military assistance and frequently raiding Byzantine territory. By the end of the 6th century, Byzantine annual payments had nearly doubled, from 900 to 1600 or more pounds of pure gold.

The Slavs, too, became historically visible in the early 6th century, first appearing as they exerted pressure on the Balkan border of the Byzantine Empire. Unlike the Avars and Turks, the Slavs were agrarian, practicing a shifting agriculture that worked a field for a few years, then moved to fallow land nearby; also unlike the Turkic peoples, they waged war as infantry. They were not united into kingdoms or major chiefdoms; instead, the Greek sources suggest the Slavs were at least somewhat democratic in their political structure. The Slavic push into the Balkans and Greece, reaching Athens by c. 580, exerted yet another strain on the recovering Byzantine state. Emperor Justinian (527–65) held them back by restoring the fortresses of the Balkan and Danube frontier on an unprecedented scale, only to have the dam break after that dynamic emperor's death.

BELOW AND LEFT *Avar belt fittings. Avar tombs attest to the wealth of the short-lived Avar state.*

THE GREAT BYZANTINE REVIVAL

Although never overrun by Germanic migrations like Western Europe, the Eastern Roman Empire had suffered its share of disruptions in the 5th century. It was in the 6th century that the eastern regions, now severed from Rome and most of Europe, began to develop into a distinct culture that led 16th-century historians to relabel it as "Byzantine," a name derived from the original name of Constantinople. It is important to remember, however, that the inhabitants of the Eastern Roman Empire always regarded themselves as Romaioi—the Greek word for Romans—until the state's final destruction in the 15th century. By the 6th century, "Byzantium" was regaining stability. German threats had been largely shunted to one side, in part by steering Germanic kings like the Ostrogoth Theodoric to fight other "barbarians" in Western Europe. Rulers sat more securely on the throne, in part thanks to the institution of religious coronation by the patriarch of Constantinople, which began with the coronation of Leo I in 457. When Emperor Anastasius died in 518 with no clear successor, the imperial guard chose one of its officers, the poorly educated and administratively inexperienced Justin, as their new emperor. Fortunately for the Byzantine state, Justin had already adopted his clever nephew, Justinian, who did the real ruling long before he succeeded his uncle in 527.

One of history's most fascinating marriages is that between Justinian and the former circus performer Theodora. Their rule was a true partnership until Theodora's death in 548, as the couple aimed to restore the empire's greatness as well as its geographical scope. Part of their plan was to unify their people under the banner of Christianity. Unlike most religions in existence at the time, Christianity as a monotheism found it difficult to tolerate other faiths, and persecution of non-Christians and of different interpretations of Christianity had begun soon after the conversion of Emperor Constantine in the early 4th century, although the persecution of dissenters had usually been half-hearted at best. That changed under Justinian and Theodora, with attacks on Greco-Roman polytheists, who were banned from public teaching in 529, as well as the persecution of Manichaeans and Samaritans. Active attacks on doctrinally different Christians, however, caused more division than unification, as even within the imperial family the emperor believed Christ had a dual nature (human and divine), while the empress held, with most Egyptians and Syrians, that Jesus had a single, or monophysite,

ABOVE *Facing the mosaic of her husband Justinian (pp.14–15), Empress Theodora makes her own offering at the altar of San Vitale, Ravenna.*

ABOVE *A 6th-century Visigothic tremissis, imitating the coinage of Emperor Justinian. The reverse shows a stylized Victory with crown and palm.*

ABOVE *Fresco of the Nativity, one of the many fine paintings decorating the Nubian cathedral at Faras.*

divine nature. Oddly, both Justinian and Theodora seized an opportunity to send rival missionaries to Ethiopia, where the empress's monophysite views won general acceptance.

In 529, the Byzantine legal code also received a substantial overhaul, the Code of Justinian aiming to include every valid law of the empire and eliminate obsolete legislation. A second commission then codified the legal commentaries,

producing a complete *Code of Civil Law* in 534. An important purpose of this work was certainly to enhance the standing and authority of the imperial family, especially after its public image had taken a severe beating in the Nika riots of 532, when rioting gangs combined to demand a pardon for two murderers and almost caused the emperor to flee as they tore a path of destruction through Constantinople. Plucking opportunity from near disaster, however, Justinian proceeded to rebuild the great church of Hagia Sophia destroyed during the disturbances on an enormous and innovative scale, using it and other building projects around the city and beyond to enhance imperial prestige.

The centerpiece of rebuilding the empire was war. Early in Justinian's reign, his generals achieved major victories over the Sasanian Persians, the Bulghars (an ethnically diverse grouping of Hunnic and Turkic peoples whose very name means "mixed ones," and part of whom later moved westward and formed the core of modern Bulgaria), and the Slavs, securing Byzantium's frontiers. The emperor wanted more than security, however; his goal was no less than regaining the western provinces of the Roman Empire, over which no emperor in Constantinople had held more than a shadowy authority since the abdication of the last Western Emperor in 476.

RIGHT *Hagia Sophia, Istanbul, completed in 537 CE. The great church of "Holy Wisdom," designed by Isidore of Miletus and Anthemius of Tralles, is one of the masterpieces of world architecture.*

The unpopular rule of the Vandals in North Africa presented an opportunity. The Germanic Vandals had arrived in Africa in 429, becoming a political elite that replaced and expropriated the Roman aristocratic landowning class. Massive efforts by the Romans to retake the wealthy province had failed in 441, 460, and 468. But the Vandals had alienated the province's Roman and Berber populace with a major push to convert them to the Arian version of Christianity, which held that Jesus is not equal to God the Father. In their fear of rebellion, the Vandal rulers had also destroyed the walls of all the region's many cities, except their capital Carthage. The Byzantine attack in 533, led by Justinian's general Belisarius, caught the Vandal king Gelimer by surprise. With little popular support for the Vandal rulers, the entire Byzantine campaign of reconquest took less than a year.

The ease of reconquest in North Africa certainly encouraged Justinian to pursue a new campaign of a region less profitable but certainly more central to the identity of the empire he ruled: Italy. In the hands of Germanic rulers since 476, and even well before that as a series of Western Roman emperors had effectively been puppets of their Germanic generals, it had been to the advantage of both the Gothic rulers in Ravenna and the Byzantine emperor in Constantinople to pretend that the area was still part of the greater empire. The deposition and murder of Amalasuintha, however, gave Justinian a justification to invade. But the Ostrogothic rulers of Italy were a much greater challenge than the Vandals of Africa had been. While they too were Arian Christians, the Ostrogoths had not attempted to impose their beliefs on the Nicene Christian populace. Indeed, they had troubled the native population very little, Theodoric the Ostrogoth creating parallel legal and administrative systems for the Romans and the Germanic military elite. For their part, Byzantine leadership challenges and heavy financial commitments elsewhere led to massive difficulties paying troops, followed by riots. The result was nearly 20 years of war, from 535 to 554, before Italy was finally restored to imperial hands. In the process, the peninsula suffered much greater destruction than it ever had during the Germanic migrations, especially the city of Rome, which was besieged by Byzantines or Ostrogoths no fewer than seven times during the struggle, a process that breached the major aqueducts that had enabled Rome to support a large population throughout Late Antiquity.

BELOW *From Vandal-ruled Carthage, this 5th- or 6th-century mosaic shows a hunter roping a stag.*

The Unhappy Tale of a *casus belli*

Theodoric, king of the Ostrogoths, had been sent to Italy with the Byzantine emperor's blessing and had defeated and killed the unauthorized ruler Odoacer by 493. Theodoric proceeded to rule very successfully until his death in 526. Then came a problem, however: Theodoric had no son to succeed him. He had arranged for his daughter, Amalasuintha, to marry a noble who would rule (the Germanic peoples had no tradition of independent female rule) and provide dynastic continuity. When her husband died, Amalasuintha attempted to rule on behalf of her young son.

The queen soon ran into difficulties, however. Not because of her biological sex, but probably because she had become too culturally Roman to suit the tastes of Ostrogothic nobles, especially after her son died. She appointed her cousin, Theodahad, as co-ruler, hoping to strengthen her position, but he rapidly deposed her and seized the throne for himself in 534. Amalasuintha was imprisoned and soon strangled. Because the queen had officially acted in Italy only as deputy for the Byzantine emperor, her murder was a pretext for Justinian to declare war against the Ostrogothic usurper.

Marble bust from the Capitoline Museum, Rome, thought to depict Queen Amalsuintha.

Justinian died at the age of 83 in November 565. He is often blamed for bringing the Byzantine Empire to the brink of extinction with his overreach and financial exactions. It should be noted, however, that the reconquests almost certainly paid for themselves. Byzantine armies were relatively small, usually amounting to fewer than 25,000 men, well within the empire's economic means at the time. What really overbalanced Justinian's careful equilibrium were circumstances beyond his control. The mid-6th century saw a series of earthquakes that devastated the eastern seaboard of the Mediterranean, including the destruction of Beirut. Worse, plague struck Constantinople in 541–2 and returned to ravage Europe and the Near East for generations to come. Bubonic plague reached the Egyptian port of Pelusium from Ethiopia in October 541, perhaps originating in India and spreading thanks to flourishing Red Sea trade. Scholars differ on how great mortality was, noting how frequently contemporary chroniclers exaggerate disasters (for example, one contemporary writer claimed the plague left 230,000 dead in Constantinople, about half the city's population at the time), but it was certainly significant. There is, though, no evidence of a general population collapse in the Byzantine Empire, comparable to the second plague pandemic in the 14th century. In Western Europe, population decline had begun in the 5th century, well before the plague, although the disease would certainly have worsened the situation. Whether a massive or only a moderate disaster, however, the plague pandemic would have strained the Byzantine economy at the worst possible time considering Justinian's expenditures for war and building.

After Justinian's death, Byzantium rapidly fell into decline, with poor leadership adding to economic woes. Ironically the hard-won Italian peninsula was lost only a few years after the great emperor's demise, as the Lombards overran the region. Two significant new external threats also rose to new significance: the Slavs and Sasanian Persia. The Slavs renewed their raids into Byzantine territory in the 570s, and when they returned they were a much larger force, often under a single chief. They were also bolder—as when they took Thessalonica by storm in the 580s—and bloodier, their passage marked by massacres and the enslavement of much of the populace. Byzantium's renewed war with Persia is harder to understand. When the Lombards invaded Italy in 568, Emperor Justin II sent no significant help, instead choosing to attack Persia. Khusrau I responded vigorously, sacking Dara, Byzantium's chief fortress on the frontier, in retaliation. The situation did not improve when Justin had a nervous breakdown upon hearing the news. Persia was the more significant threat. A centralized state already, Khusrau I (531–79) had instituted major economic reforms, rationalizing the tax system and greatly improving the roads and urban infrastructure of his empire. He was also a great patron of learning, giving refuge to polytheistic Greek scholars after Justinian closed Athens' famed Academy in 529. It is hard to understand why the Byzantine emperor chose to pick a fight against a shah so great he was known as "the immortal soul."

LEFT *Perhaps depicting Justinian, the 6th-century Barberini Ivory shows a Byzantine emperor triumphing over barbarians.*

EUROPE FINDING ITS FEET

The Lombard migration into Italy was the last significant invasion of Western Europe for several centuries, and Europe gradually came to a new balance after the dislocations of the invasion period. The new reality in most regions included a rather small Germanic military elite that gradually melded with a native aristocracy and over which a Germanic king ruled. Only the former Roman province of Britain saw significant enough Germanic settlement—by Angles, Saxons, Jutes, and other opportunistic adventurers—to gradually make a Germanic dialect the spoken language of the region. Borders were fluid well into the 6th century as Franks battled Burgundians, Visigoths struggled for supremacy against Vandals and Suevi, and so on.

Germanic rulers very much wanted to enjoy the fruits of Roman government rather than disrupt it. The new regional kings were quite amenable to Christianity, which by then was the exclusive religion of at least the elite classes in Western Europe, although their adherence to Arianism caused tensions. They imitated Roman ways, keeping Roman tax systems in particular intact and were content to let bishops rule over cities, which had been in decline since the 4th century. Over time, however, the Roman tax system faded away, kings relying more on personal estates and perhaps not always understanding how taxes worked (one Frankish king burned his tax rolls, believing that God was punishing the sin of taxation by making his son dangerously ill). The long-term result was weaker states in Europe for centuries, since tax-raising states are inherently more stable than those that offer land in return for military or political loyalty; salaried officials can

LEFT *A Visigothic votive crown, offered to a church; the hanging letters say "King Reccesuinth offered this" in Latin.*

be dismissed easily, while nobles strongly resist any effort to take away *their* land.

Besides Theodoric's Ostrogoths in Italy, the two European success stories of the 6th century are the Franks and the Visigoths. The gifted military and political leadership (not to mention utter ruthlessness) of Clovis (481–511) made the small kingdom centered on Tournai into a major state, as his Franks defeated other Frankish polities, the Alamanni, and, in 507, inflicted a major defeat on the Visigoths at Vouillé. Clovis's sons went on to capture the region ruled by the Burgundians, and by the 530s invaded Italy. The whole process was aided by Clovis's inspired or expedient conversion from polytheism to catholic Christianity, which won him the influential support of his kingdom's bishops. Those bishops were willing to preach war against the Visigoths as a holy endeavor, since the Visigoths were Arian Christians. The Visigoths, forced out of their holdings north of the Pyrenees by the Franks, only gradually consolidated their hold on the Iberian Peninsula, in large part thanks to Reccared's conversion to catholic Christianity in 587 and the subsequent outlawing of Arianism. Both states gave promise of future greatness, Visigothic kings being the first

ABOVE *Baptism of the Frankish king Clovis by St. Remigius, along with other scenes from the saint's life (9th-century ivory plaque).*

Germans to wear crowns and sit on a throne and Reccared's predecessor, Leovigild, even founding two small cities. Both fledgling states were, however, impeded by succession disputes and unruly nobles that they did not have sufficient infrastructure to control.

CHINESE RENEWAL

The last emperor of China's Han Dynasty was killed in 220 CE, an episode in the civil wars that had already wracked his empire for a generation. For nearly three centuries, no ruler was able to reunite the Chinese lands, although many tried and short-lived dynasties were created in both the north and the south. At least in elite culture, this era of division was regarded as lamentable and unnatural. Deeply imbued in Chinese culture was the sense that China *ought* to be united under a single ruler, the *huangdi*, whose very title (usually translated in English as "emperor") means "celestial magnificence." While not personally divine, the *huangdi* ruled with the mandate of heaven, with sweeping rights and duties as supreme ruler, sole legislator, and highest judge.

Many tried to effect a unification in China's highly militarized society, a world in which heavy cavalry had become the key striking force of armies thanks to the introduction of the true saddle and stirrup, in addition to heavy armor for both rider and horse. Many military innovations came from the steppe, and indeed a steppe people, the Tabghach (called the Tuoba in China), came to control all China north of the Yellow

The Worm that Changed History

The silkworm, native to China, is an extraordinary creature. Feeding exclusively on the leaves of the mulberry tree, the worm grows rapidly, in time spinning a cocoon of fine silk thread. The Chinese people early recognized that the cocoons could be processed into a very fine, lustrous, resilient fabric, crediting the invention of sericulture to Leizu, wife of the mythical Yellow Emperor. Making the cocoons into a usable product is very resource- and labor-intensive. Five tons of silk cocoons produce about 150 pounds of finished silk cloth, each cocoon producing about a mile of thread after it has been softened in hot water and unwound. Several threads must then be spun together to create thread strong enough for weaving.

Silk production was a carefully guarded Chinese monopoly for many centuries, a highly desirable luxury product that admittedly only gave its name to the "Silk Road" trade route across Asia in the 19th century, but a name that nevertheless accurately reflects the most significant trade good. Eventually, however, the silkworm reached the Byzantine Empire, thanks to the improved trade connections facilitated by the First Turkic Empire. In 552, two Nestorian Christian monks smuggled silkworm eggs out of China, enclosing them in a hollow walking stick, and brought them to the West. While Chinese silk remained the most desirable, Byzantine craftsmen were soon competing against what Chinese weavers could make with their own fine silk fabrics.

Chinese Emperor Huizong was a noted painter and poet. In this work he depicted court ladies preparing silk.

River, creating a dynasty known as the Northern Wei (386–534). Their ruling class soon adopted the Chinese language and ways, although they maintained a separate administration for their pastoral subjects on the steppe. At the end of the 5th century the Northern Wei emperor Xiaowen even banned the Tabghach language and practices at his court. Xiaowen relocated his capital to Luoyang, south of the Yellow River, and by 495 had forcibly moved about 150,000 northern warriors to the south. The border elites were relegated to second-class status, so it is not surprising that frontier revolts broke out in 496 and again, much more seriously, in 523. The Northern Wei ended in violence when a general marched on the capital and took control of the court, on the pretext that the empress dowager Hu had poisoned the young emperor to seize control for herself. The general proceeded to kill more than a thousand officials who had come to welcome and submit to him. He also drowned the dowager and the three-year-old puppet emperor in the Yellow River. The general himself was soon killed in a palace ambush orchestrated by his own puppet ruler, and much of China descended into anarchy.

The situation changed in 568 when a man named Yang Jian became duke of Sui. Working in close partnership with his wife—they were very close and, on their marriage, Yang vowed never to take a concubine—the duke began to plan and then execute a series of conquests.

RIGHT *Statuette of a Northern Wei soldier. Such figurines of the warlike Tabghach people are quite common.*

RIGHT *Emperor Wen of the Sui Dynasty; a portrait of the later Tang period.*

In 581, the successful war leader proclaimed himself emperor, taking the reign title Wendi, and unification was complete by 589. The process of unification had not been easy, as rulers of other Chinese states felt they had just as much claim to heaven's mandate as the duke of Sui. The final stage, the conquest of the state of Chen in 588–9, was a particularly massive enterprise. It was preceded by a year of shipbuilding for a Yellow River attack, including the construction of great "Five-Banner" warships, towering five-deck vessels that could hold 800 men. Wendi committed eight armies totaling 518,000 men to the attack, versus perhaps 100,000 soldiers in the Chen army. Even after Chen submitted, parts of China were slow to acknowledge Wendi's rule. The year 589 saw an extremely violent rebellion in the south, apparently sparked by local elites spreading a false rumor that the emperor was planning to relocate hundreds of thousands of southerners to the north. The desperate rebels targeted Sui officials, even dismembering and eating some of them.

Wendi and his successor soon established an impressive level of control, however, and a decree issued in 595 disarmed Chinese private citizens and banned the private manufacture of weapons. The Sui rulers also successfully reimposed the long tradition that every able-bodied male owed the state one month of labor per year. They employed millions of workers to restore border walls and construct new ones, and hundreds of thousands to dig the Grand Canal. The finished water channel stretched 1,200 miles (1,931 km). Forty paces wide, it could accommodate up to 800-ton ships, transporting grain from the south to the grand new capital of Chang'an. The first Sui emperor also worked to enhance his authority through religion. A devout Buddhist in a century when Buddhism was becoming popular throughout the Chinese lands, Wendi presented himself to the people as a divinely ordained Buddhist ruler. He established many Buddhist temples and monasteries, keeping tight government control over the Buddhist clergy.

In an interesting parallel to the Byzantine Empire of the time, the Sui longed to revive the glory of the Han Dynasty, and that meant restoring China's borders from the time of

BELOW *China's Grand Canal, a crowning achievement of the short-lived Sui Dynasty.*

ABOVE *The tomb of Muryeong, who ruled Baekje, one of Korea's three early kingdoms, from 501 to 523.*

Han greatness. That meant retaking northern Vietnam and the Korean peninsula, which had gained independence in the chaos of divided rule. As we will see in the next chapter, however, Korea strongly resisted reintegration in the Chinese Empire, and the Sui emperors' stubborn refusal to abandon their plans led to the fall of the dynasty.

More successful was the cultural imperialism that began to penetrate Japan deeply in the 6th century. Japan had been undergoing a long process of unification, starting with the establishment of the Yamato Kingdom in the late 3rd century. The state developed spectacularly in the 5th and 6th centuries. Economic prosperity was leveraged to support a more ambitious central state with the massive conversion of land to rice fields. A series of innovations were introduced from northeast Asia, including horses and iron weapons. Chinese culture also arrived, at first mostly by way of the Korean kingdom of Paekche, starting when a Korean scholar came to tutor the Yamato crown prince in *c.* 400. In the early 6th century, Paekche began sending experts in the classics, music, divination, and medicine on a regular basis. Particularly influential was the introduction of Buddhist sutras from Paekche in 552. The religion quickly caught on, thanks to the patronage of the imperial family and aristocratic clans.

Japan suffered some growing pains in the 6th century, especially an extended crisis from 529–540. The problem was overreach. Loyal to its ally Paekche, the Yamato government sent troops to the Korean Peninsula to combat the power of the rival state of Silla, only to suffer disastrous defeat. Rebellions at home and succession disputes ensued, crowned by a second failed expedition to aid Paekche in 539. Nonetheless, Japan's government at the end of the 6th century was confident in its divine right, the ruler proclaimed as *tenno*, the "heaven [-descended] luminescence." Japanese pretensions shocked the Sui court when the Japanese empress (half of Japan's known early rulers were women) sent a letter with a mission to China that addressed the Sui emperor as a fellow

The Long Reach of the Silk Road

One of the most fascinating archeological finds of the 20th century is the tomb of the Northern Zhou general Li Xian (died 569) and his wife Wu Hui, discovered in Guyuan, China, in 1983. The couple were interred in a large brick chamber, the walls of which were decorated with paintings of courtiers and officials. Among the grave goods was found a silver ewer, decorated with a scene from the Trojan War. Very far from the Greek cultural home of the story, this ewer demonstrates well the longing for exotic luxuries that underpinned the Silk Road. For the story of the Trojan War to reach a Chinese tomb, a series of cultural connections had to occur. The ewer itself was probably crafted in Bactria, in Central Asia, and then transported, perhaps on camelback, to a market where Li Xian could purchase it in China. But how did a Bactrian silversmith know the story of the Trojan War and become familiar with the Greco-Roman style he employed? He must have seen similar work, brought from the West and sold in markets in Bactria and Sogdia. We know that Sogdian merchants traded regularly with Constantinople in the 6th century, serving as international middlemen for a booming trade in luxury goods.

Silver ewer from the tomb of Li Xian.

child of Heaven. Such a claim expresses perhaps better than any other the sublime self-confidence of the new and rising states of the world by the end of the 6th century.

CHAPTER 2

Empires Old and New in the 7th Century

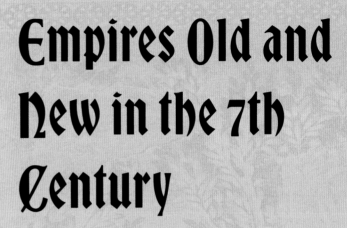

At the dawn of the 7th century, a prophet might have felt confident predicting the course of the next hundred years: the long stalemate between Byzantium and Persia would continue, China's reunification was unlikely to last, European kings would continue to squabble for power, and interregional trade would continue unchanged. Of those, only the European squabbles had come to pass. Instead, one of history's great imponderables—the rise of a new and militantly expansionist religion—rapidly reshaped the geopolitical realities of the Middle East and northern Africa, destroying the Sasanian Persian Empire and bringing Byzantium to its knees. The ripple effects of Islam's rise had a major impact on Eurasian trade as well. In time, all of Asia might have fallen under Muslim rule, had it not been for the other false prophecy: China's Sui Dynasty did in fact fall, but after only a brief struggle a new, strong Tang Dynasty began raising China to ever greater heights. It was an era in which great empires rose, but in which others failed to face the new challenges of the age.

LEFT *A mosaic from the Great Mosque of Damascus, Syria, one of the oldest and largest mosques in the world.*

THE BYZANTINE-SASANIAN WAR

In the year 600, the Sasanian Empire of Persia and Byzantium were strong and stable states, each with a long history and considerable governmental infrastructure to support strong rulers. Surprisingly, the two states were even friends at the time. The Byzantine emperor Maurice had been instrumental in restoring Shah Khusrau II to his throne, and the result was a long-term alliance. The situation changed in a heartbeat, when Maurice's army mutinied after he ordered them to spend the winter north of the Danube during the course of a very successful campaign against the Slavs. Led by a particularly brutal officer named Phocas, the troops executed Maurice and most of his family. Professing outrage at his ally's murder, Khusrau declared war, doubtless thinking it an ideal opportunity to win the wealthy cities along the eastern seaboard of the Mediterranean that Persia had coveted for centuries. Phocas proved to be as incompetent as he was brutal, engaging in purges of the Byzantine aristocracy rather than mounting an effective defense against the Persians.

Phocas was in turn overthrown and killed in 610, when the Byzantine governor of North Africa sent his son Heraclius to Constantinople with an army.

Heraclius took the throne himself, but it took years to turn the tide of the Persian advance. About half of Byzantium's territory was lost in the 610s. The situation stabilized only slowly, as Heraclius borrowed money from the Church and overhauled the army by recruiting new soldiers, hiring mercenaries, and paying back wages; he even melted down Constantinople's bronze statues to mint coins to pay troops. In 613, Heraclius also made desperate efforts to restore peace, only to be rebuffed by the Persian shah, so the war continued, including Khusrau's conquest of Alexandria in Egypt in 619. In c. 620, the emperor withdrew all Byzantine troops from the Balkans to fight the Persians, rightly regarding the Sasanians as the true existential threat. The Avars, the most unified of Byzantium's enemies in Europe, tried to take advantage of Heraclius's

RIGHT *This 7th-century bronze steelyard-weight probably represents the Byzantine emperor Phocas.*

Who Ruled the Slavs?

While Slavic raiders frequently probed into Byzantine territory in this period, they did not unite into a single state that could plan large-scale conquests. Instead, much of the Slavic populace of the Balkans suffered the harsh overlordship of the Avars, until the Avar defeat in 626 gave many of them a chance to break away. They found a very unlikely leader in their revolt, a Frankish merchant named Samo.

Samo was a trader who apparently operated in the northwestern Slavic lands, probably shipping furs, amber, and other luxury items to the Kingdom of the Franks. A major Slavic group, the Wends, chose the foreigner as their king (the Slavs had no tradition of kingship at that time, but this was the title given to him by the Frankish chronicler, Fredegar). Samo united a number of Slavic communities, leading their rebellion against Avar oppression. He proved to be an able leader, also leading them to victory over a Frankish army in 631. The merchant continued to rule until his death, sometime between 658 and 669, adopting Slavic ways, including taking 12 Slavic wives. His state, an artificial construction that answered a particular need, collapsed on Samo's death. The first true Slavic states did not form until the 10th century.

Modern statue of King Samo, Náklo Hill, Czech Republic.

preoccupation with the Persian war. They pulled together an army of Avars, Slavs, Bulghars, and Gepids, launching a full-scale attack on the Byzantine capital, Constantinople, in 626 when the emperor himself was far away on the Persian frontier. That the attack was beaten off after a 10-day siege was attributable to the imperial fleet, but above all to the Virgin Mary, who reportedly protected the city. The siege's failure ended Avar domination of the Balkans, giving Byzantium a breathing space on that front.

That the Byzantines believed that the mother of Jesus Christ took a hand in their rescue raises the inevitable question: was the Byzantine–Sasanian War a "holy war" fought for ideological reasons as well as territorial advantage? At first sight, the Persian sack of Jerusalem in 613 and massacre of its population suggests animosity against Christianity, as did the fact that Jerusalem's conquerors carried off the relic of the True Cross (believed to be the actual cross of Jesus's crucifixion) with them in triumph. The truth is more complex, however. Jerusalem had surrendered to the Persians, but then expelled its Persian garrison, so the Persian general returned and took the city by storm. Jerusalem then suffered the usual fate of those who reneged on a surrender. Khusrau was not opposed to Christianity; Nestorian Christians played important roles in his administration and his wife, Shirin, was a Christian. The True Cross, while a war trophy, was treated with respect and entrusted to the care of Christian administrators.

While Khusrau would not have seen the conflict as a holy war, the reverse was probably true for the Byzantines. When Jerusalem was sacked, Byzantines were quick to accuse the Jewish population of the region of helping the Persians, leading Heraclius to begin the forcible conversion of his Jewish subjects. The perceived attack on Christianity also gave Heraclius's calls to unify in face of the threat a new force, as churches voluntarily gave up their wealth and the emperor himself took the field. The clearest sign that it was a holy war for Heraclius came in 624, when a Byzantine army totally destroyed the great Zoroastrian fire temple of Adur Gushnasp in Media in revenge for the Persian damage to Jerusalem. His failure to protect the holy place cost Khusrau the support of many of his nobles and priests.

Thanks in large part to an alliance with the Turkic peoples of the steppe, Heraclius finally inflicted a decisive defeat on Khusrau in 628. The humiliated Persian shah was then imprisoned and soon executed by his own son, sparking a major civil war; the years 628–32 saw at least ten rulers and would-be rulers in the Sasanian lands. The Byzantine Empire fared better, but the great city of Constantinople suffered a massive population decline, from a high of about 500,000 under Justinian to under 100,000, in large part because the financially strapped government ended free grain distributions in 618. The massive costs of war stretched the Byzantine economy to near-breaking point, as it did that of Persia. The rigors of war can also help explain a deep decline in Byzantine education and scholarship that lasted through the 8th century, with literary production far reduced and knowledge of Latin fading away.

BELOW *In this 12th-century enamel plaque, Emperor Heraclius gives the Persian Khusrau II his deathblow.*

THE COMING OF ISLAM

Given breathing space, Persia and Byzantium may well have been able to recover. Instead, a new and unexpected threat soon engulfed both empires.

Patterns of life on the Arabian Peninsula, a region little known or considered by either great empire, had been shifting for several generations by the early 7th century. At the heart of the shift was international trade. Mariners had long discovered the monsoon patterns that propelled commerce in the Indian Ocean, creating a Silk Road by sea as well as by land. In the late 6th century, though, with Byzantium and Persia so

frequently at war, the land route for luxury goods was unsafe, as was a sea route that ended at the Persian Gulf. The Arabian Peninsula was ideally situated to step in as the new transshipment hub. Since navigation in the Red Sea is hazardous, much Indian Ocean commerce was offloaded in southern Arabia, then carried overland to Syria, along with frankincense and myrrh from Arabia itself. Mecca developed as the hub of the new trade network, benefiting from the presence of a great shrine, the Ka'ba, a pilgrimage site and sanctuary for the polytheists of the peninsula. A tangle of religions—polytheists mingling with

BELOW *The Ka'ba in Mecca is Islam's holiest site; the current structure was built after the original was damaged in 683.*

Jews and Christians—and of frequently rival extended kinship networks, as well as both sedentary peoples and nomads, the peninsula and arid lands around it had few clear governmental structures. And, as was inevitable in a society dominated by the merchant class, the rich got richer while the safety net of clan membership failed many of the poorest.

There were many prophets in the medieval millennium; indeed, there were many prophets among the Arab populace in the 7th century. Only one, however, articulated a message that led to the creation of one of the world's great religions: Islam. The prophet Muhammad was a native of Mecca, orphaned when young but able to establish himself by marrying the widow of a caravan owner and taking over the dead husband's business. Keenly aware of the stresses within his society, Muhammad frequently went to the desert to pray and meditate. It was there, probably in the year 610, that he began to experience a series of visions and revelations, asserting the absolute singularity of God and a message of submission to God and social responsibility. After three years, Muhammad began preaching the messages he received, which were later assembled into the Qur'an, and he gradually gathered followers.

Muhammad's monotheistic message was unpopular among the Quraysh, the merchant clan that dominated Mecca and relied on pilgrimage to the Ka'ba for trade. Under increasing threat, in 622 the small Muslim community, about 70 people altogether, fled from Mecca, migrating to Yathrib (which soon became known as "the city of the prophet," Medina). With this event, the *hijra*, Islam marks its beginning as a faith community. The people of Medina welcomed Muhammad and his disciples, accepting the prophet as arbitrator. The Meccans refused to back down, though, and in 624 a superior Meccan force attacked Medina, only to be defeated. The Meccans tried—and failed—again in 627. Finally, in 630 the triumphant Muhammad was able to enter Mecca, where he destroyed the images in the Ka'ba and

rededicated the shrine to the one God. By the time he died in 632, Muhammad had united the clans of the Arabian Peninsula, some embracing his religious message and some simply following Muhammad as a charismatic leader.

The movement Muhammad had launched was in danger of dying in infancy. The Arabs had no generally accepted authority structures to provide a framework after Muhammad's own demise. While the Muslim community close to the prophet immediately chose one of Muhammad's early followers, Abu Bakr, as his successor or deputy (*khalifa*), the new caliph could not claim Muhammad's prophetic status. Many of the clans saw no reason to accept Abu Bakr's authority, considering Muhammad's alliance at an end. Muhammad's followers refused to accept this fragmentation, and the result was a series of short, sharp campaigns in 632–4 known as the Ridda ("apostate") wars, although in fact many who broke away from the alliance established by Muhammad had never professed their faith in Islam.

What ultimately convinced waverers and reconciled the defeated to the caliph's rule was the extraordinary success of the Muslim community. Muhammad had already won significant victories against superior forces; now Abu Bakr and his successors looked beyond the Arabian Peninsula to other lands with significant Arabic populations. They began to launch raids into both Byzantine and Persian lands, quickly demonstrating that, when Arabic nomads joined forces, they were every bit as formidable as their counterparts on the steppe of Central Asia. Including a high proportion of nomads, the early Arabic attackers were experienced raiders, using the desert as a communication route and refuge in emergencies. Highly mobile, the armies of the first wave of conquest consisted only of fighting men and necessary support staff; families and herds were left behind. While the forces were of moderate size, probably about 24,000 for the conquest of Syria, they were attacking lands already weakened by a generation of war. The conquest of Egypt began in 639 with a

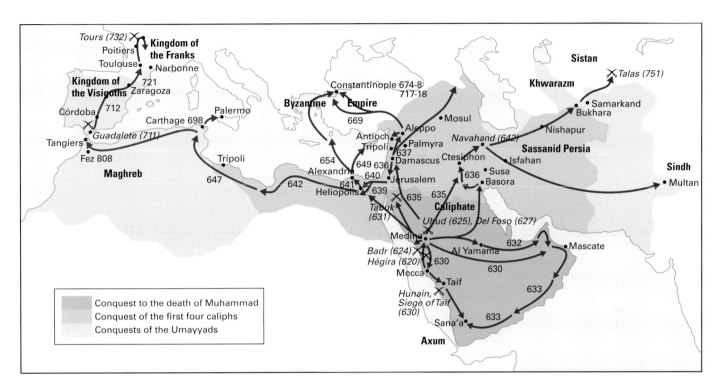

ABOVE *The Islamic Conquests.*

mere 4,000 men. Once they started racking up victories, the conviction that God smiled on the conquests made future victories ever more likely.

The Muslim expansion erupted in 633, when Abu Bakr dispatched four small Arabic forces into southern Palestine. With help from fellow Arabs of the border area, the Muslim force crushed a regional Byzantine army early in 634. Emperor Heraclius immediately recognized the danger and sent his brother to counter them with the Byzantine Army of the East. The Arabs, however, received reinforcements in time and soundly defeated the Byzantine army at Yarmuk, Syria, in 636. The annihilation of the Byzantine force allowed the newcomers to take major cities, including Damascus, Antioch, and Jerusalem. Pressure on the empire continued with few pauses. By mid-century, Emperor Constans II was able to take advantage of a lull during an Islamic civil war to reorganize the Byzantine army, settling soldiers on land grants to support themselves. Nonetheless, the situation was so critical that, in 662, he

relocated to Syracuse in Sicily, believing he could no longer hold Constantinople despite its outstanding natural and man-made defenses. After the emperor was assassinated in an army plot in 668, his successor moved back to Constantinople.

The surrender of Jerusalem demonstrated the way the wind was blowing. The second caliph, 'Umar, came in person to accept the holy city's surrender. The terms were generous, as spelled out in the Pact of 'Umar, which was purportedly issued at the time. Islam accepted Judaism and Christianity as true "religions of the book," regarding the revelations to Muhammad as the final chapter in a sequence of divine revelation. Therefore, both Jews and Christians—including those who had been persecuted as heretics by their coreligionists—were welcome as subjects. These *dhimmis* were of course regarded as inferior to Muslims, but payment of a special tax secured them legal protection. Far from trying to convert subjugated peoples by force, in the early conquest period the Muslims emphatically

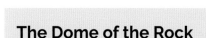

The Dome of the Rock

One of the crowning achievements of the early Islamic caliphate is the Dome of the Rock in Jerusalem, constructed in 691–2 by order of the Umayyad caliph 'Abd al-Malik. Jerusalem is not mentioned in the Qur'an, but from the beginning Muslims paid the city special reverence, viewing it as one of the key sites in the belief system that Muslims traced from themselves back through Christians to God's revelations to the Jews. In the generation after Muhammad's death, the legend evolved that the prophet had been miraculously transported to Jerusalem and from there ascended on a spiritual visit to heaven known as the night journey.

The Dome of the Rock celebrates Muhammad's night journey, but also serves as a bold declaration of Islam's superiority. The building is situated on the site of Judaism's destroyed Temple, meaning that the Dome of the Rock represents a physical and symbolic claim by Muslims of this older holy space as their own. The splendor of the building proclaims the greatness of Islam, as do the mosaics of the interior. The work of Byzantine artists, the decoration avoided figural imagery in accordance with Muslim beliefs, instead setting a number of inscriptions in stone. Those texts were chosen to emphasize the oneness of God, a direct confrontation with the Christian belief that God is a trinity.

The Dome of the Rock.

did not desire non-Muslim conversion or the assimilation of conquered peoples. Arabic women were discouraged from marrying non-Arabs, even if they were Muslim, and non-Arabic converts did not receive full equality.

Muslim moderation as much as fiscal exhaustion explains why nearly three-quarters of the Byzantine Empire's population did not put up much of a fight. Once the state armies had been neutralized, the bulk of the populace, civilians untrained in warfare, settled down quietly to Muslim rule. Many Jews, barely tolerated by their Christian rulers, saw the Islamic invasions as an absolute godsend. The bulk of the population of Egypt and Syria, monophysite Coptic and Eastern Orthodox Christians respectively, who had suffered persecution as heretics, probably agreed. Except for an end of persecution as long as they paid the *jizya*, a head tax on non-Muslims, little had changed. The conquerors kept the administrative systems intact in the lands they conquered, even using many of the same administrators. The Arabs themselves were content to establish garrison towns in newly conquered regions, such as Fustat in 641.

The Muslim conquest of the Sasanian Persian Empire was even more dramatic. In Emperor Heraclius, Byzantium had an experienced, decisive leader who resisted as much as his means allowed; by contrast, Persia had little clear leadership after Khusrau II's death. The last Sasanian shah, Yazdegerd III (632–51), came to the throne aged only eight, the central government in ruins around him. Arab raids into Persia had probably already begun in Muhammad's lifetime, climaxing in a crushing Muslim victory in the Battle of Qadisiyyah in November 636, followed by the sack of the Persian capital, Ctesiphon. Conquest continued inexorably over the following decade, the last Sasanian prince, Peroz, eventually fleeing to China, where he failed to gain military support and settled down as a state pensioner in Chang'an. Muslim forces probed on into Afghanistan in 664, and by 711 a Muslim army had crossed the Amu Darya, seizing the great mercantile cities of Samarkand

and Bukhara. Although at first willing to allow the townspeople of the great Silk Road centers of Central Asia to maintain their cosmopolitan and religiously diverse lifestyle unchanged, later generations destroyed the Zoroastrian fire temples of the region and encouraged conversion to Islam.

After a brief breathing space, conquest continued in the west as well. Efforts to invade Nubia in 641/2 and 652 failed, the Nubians agreeing to pay a tribute of 470 slaves, which continued annually for centuries. West of Muslim-ruled Egypt, 'Abd al-Malik pushed into the Byzantine province of North Africa, taking Carthage in 698 and, as we will see, a further force pushing into Spain in 711. Simultaneously, an eastern regional governor, Muhammad ibn Qasim, pushed into the Indian kingdom of Sind. King Dahir of Sind was killed in battle and Islam gained its first toehold in Hindu lands.

BELOW *The great arch of the Sasanian royal palace at Ctesiphon hints at the glory of Persia's golden age.*

CREATING THE CALIPHATE

BELOW *Gold dinar of Abd al-Malik, 696 CE.*

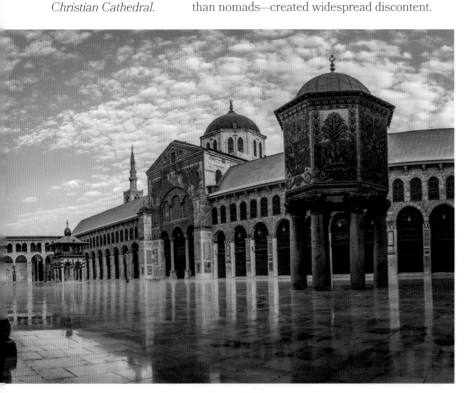

BELOW *The Umayyad Mosque, also known as the Great Mosque of Damascus, was constructed by order of Caliph al-Walid (705–15) on the site of Damascus' Christian Cathedral.*

Despite their military successes, the first generations of Muslims faced enormous challenges creating a durable central government. The first four caliphs, dubbed the "rightly guided" (*rashidun*), were elected, rather than inheriting their position. That the second, third, and fourth were all assassinated speaks volumes about the tensions that threatened Islamic cohesion. The second caliph, 'Umar, was killed by one of his enslaved men, apparently in a personal rather than political action. But then a great rivalry between 'Uthman (who was dedicated to maintaining the Quraysh clan's control) and 'Ali ibn Abi Talib (who, as Muhammad's cousin and son-in-law, claimed a blood right to rule) erupted into violence. 'Uthman's claim won, but his preferential treatment of the first converts to Islam—almost entirely sedentary people of the Hijaz rather than nomads—created widespread discontent.

Matters came to a head in 656, when Arabic settlers in Egypt marched on Medina to present their grievances. They felt betrayed when 'Uthman called for their punishment and besieged the caliph's home, finally assassinating him. 'Ali then succeeded as caliph, but 'Uthman's kinsmen, honor-bound to avenge his death, refused to acknowledge the new caliph's authority until he punished the murderers. After a three-month confrontation between the two factions' armies, 'Ali agreed to arbitration—which cost him the support of many of his own supporters. The complex civil war only ended in 661 when 'Ali in turn was assassinated, by a member of the faction that had turned against him.

'Uthman's kinsman Mu'awiya, who was already governor of Syria, succeeded as caliph (661–80), 'Ali's son Hasan renouncing any claim to the office. The caliphate became a hereditary possession of the Umayyad Dynasty, as Mu'awiya nominated his son as successor. Mu'awiya established his capital in Damascus and took steps to consolidate central authority, including minting the first Islamic coins. Many actively resented and resisted Umayyad rule, however. Mu'awiya continued his family's policy of marginalizing both non-sedentary Arabs and converts of other ethnicities, favoring a small Arabic elite. Especially as they took on ever-more trappings of kingship, critics denounced members of the dynasty as fundamentally un-Islamic, a problem aggravated by the fact that most were in fact poor rulers. Disgruntled Muslims rallied to the kindred of the prophet Muhammad. His daughter Fatima and 'Ali had produced two sons, Hasan and Husayn. In 680, Husayn led a rebellion in Iraq, but he and his followers were massacred in the Battle of Karbala. Deep outrage at the affront to Muhammad's bloodline helped unite the opponents of the Umayyads as the *shi'at 'Ali*—the partisans of 'Ali—who gradually became distinct from the majority Muslim community not just in politics but in theology as the Shi'ites, who still account for about one-tenth of the world's Muslims.

THE DAWN OF CHINA'S GOLDEN AGE

China had reunited under the Sui Dynasty in the late 6th century, but the Sui suffered a number of problems that made it one of the shortest-lived dynasties in Chinese history (581–618). Some difficulties were out of any ruler's control, including strong monsoons and major flooding—but even these events were taken as evidence that heaven did not favor the ruler. The more immediate cause of the dynasty's fall was a series of disastrous wars against Korea. Yangdi, the second Sui emperor, was determined to bring the Korean kingdom of Koguryo back under Chinese authority, and launched massive attacks on the Korean Peninsula in 612, 613, and 614. Committed to fighting in a harsh and unfamiliar climate, the Chinese armies were plagued by poor planning and intelligence. To pay for it all, the emperor massively increased taxes, refusing to accept the dishonor of defeat by an "inferior" foe. Even after widespread rebellion broke out in 613—when the emperor, unusually, was personally commanding the campaign— attacks on Koguryo continued.

The future founder of the Tang Dynasty, Li Yuan, was a garrison commander who rebelled and gradually gathered support. Sui exactions were deeply resented, and many rebels targeted all members of the educated class as the tools of their oppression, making a point of killing anyone who could quote from the histories or Confucian classics. By 615, the empire was in shambles and disaffected guardsmen killed the Sui emperor in the spring of 618. It took another five years of fighting, spearheaded by the new emperor's dynamic second son, Li Shimin, to consolidate the rule of a new dynasty, the Tang. Li Shimin usurped the throne himself in 626, killing his two brothers and forcing his father to abdicate; he is known to history as Emperor Tang Taizong.

Under the Tang, China enjoyed a period of glorious flowering. We know about it in considerable detail thanks to two great inventions: paper and woodblock printing. Paper, a Chinese invention, had existed for centuries, but by the late 6th century was common enough for everyday use. Cheap writing material enabled a great increase in the availability of books and thus of

ABOVE *Yang, second emperor of China's Sui Dynasty, as depicted on the* Thirteen Emperors Scroll *by the artist Yan Liben (d. 673).*

LEFT *Mural of Tang Taizong, surrounded by court officials (642) from the Mogao Caves, near Dunhuang, western China. Also known as the Caves of the 1000 Buddhas, this site is a system of 500 temples, in use from the 4th to 14th century.*

literacy, which was no longer restricted to a tiny elite. The invention of woodblock printing in the late 6th or early 7th century also massively increased the circulation of the written word; Chang'an's Institute for the Advancement of Life was said to have had more than 200,000 books in the 7th century.

Major agricultural innovations, including better plows and harness, better rice varieties, and better water control were able to support a rapidly growing population as well as a vast bureaucracy. The Tang could afford to pay salaries to their officials in more than three hundred prefectures, which allowed a high degree of central control. They also maintained a vast postal system that included 1,297 waystations at intervals of about 10 miles (16 km), equipped with teams of horses and trained runners. Messages could reach anywhere in the empire in under two weeks from the capital Chang'an; there were serious penalties for delay, starting with 80 blows with a rod if the messenger was one day late up to two years of penal servitude for six days' tardiness. The state was also strong enough to enforce a militia system, requiring military service from all able-bodied men 20–60 years old. We can also see the great reach of the imperial government in Tang Taizong's comprehensive legal code of 653, its 500 articles spelling out punishments that varied by social status. With a brief interlude from 690 to 705, when Empress Wu declared herself the only female emperor in Chinese history, the only ruler of the short-lived Zhou Dynasty, the Tang state endured until 907.

LEFT *Mural from the Qianling Mausoleum, burial site of Tang emperor Gaozong and the unique female emperor Wu Zetian.*

CHINA'S FLIRTATION WITH THE FOREIGN

The early Tang emperors oversaw one of the greatest military expansions in Chinese history. Between 628 and 683 they established hegemony over much of Southeast Asia, and finally succeeded in bringing down Koguryo in 668 with the help of the Korean Silla kingdom. In that case, however, Chinese forces soon had to be withdrawn because of other threats, leaving Silla to rule most of the Korean Peninsula until 935.

The Tang also defeated a number of Turkic coalitions, expanding into Central Asia and taking control of the eastern termini of the Silk Road. The Eastern Turkic Empire, sometime called the Eastern Turkic Khaganate, had assisted the Tang in their seizure of power, but the Tang returned the favor by promoting rebellions among the subjects of the ruler, or khagan. The last khagan of the First Turkic Empire, Xieli, was captured and died in captivity; over a million surrendering nomads were settled on China's northern frontier. A second Turkic Empire came into existence 683–734, when a group abandoned the sinicized Turks and returned to the Mongolian steppe, soon reconquering most of the land of the earlier eastern khaganate. The other major challenge the Tang faced was the establishment of a Tibetan empire in the early 7th century, which competed for control of Silk Road markets. From 670 on, the Tibetans pushed into China, inflicting a major

BELOW *Envoys from the Korean kingdoms of Baekje, Goguryeo and Silla, bringing tribute to the Chinese court (7th century).*

RIGHT *Sui Dynasty statuette of a court musician playing the pipa.*

defeat on a Chinese army in 695. The Chinese emperors also engaged with Tibet diplomatically, sending at least two Tang princesses to marry Tibetan emperors.

With the expansion came a fascination among Chinese elites for the "barbarian" cultures to their west. Emperors and bureaucrats alike adopted Turkish and Sogdian fashions, military practices, foodways, games, dancing, and music. Emperor Xuanzong (713–56), for example, learned how to play the Kuchaean "wether drum," popular on the steppe, and his notorious concubine Yang Guifei performed salacious Sogdian dances. Even the

distinctive pear shape of the pipa, the musical instrument most identified with traditional Chinese music today, was most likely introduced from Persia in this period.

Fascination with the foreign extended to religion. In 635, the Persian Christian priest Aluoben convinced the emperor to recognize his religion as an "approved cult" and allow the building of the first church in the Chinese capital. Christianity did not take deep root, but Buddhism did, fitting much more easily into China's existing belief systems. Already in the 5th century Chinese Buddhists traveled to India to study their faith in its homeland. By the 7th century, Buddhist influence in China was massive. Thousands of Chinese Buddhists studied and collected texts in South Asia, patronizing major educational centers like the Buddhist temple complex at Nalanda in northwestern Bengal, which flourished from 400 to 1200, attracting students from all over Asia. A side effect was that trade between China and India flourished, and in the 7th and 8th century no fewer than 40 Indian missions came to the Tang court to arrange trading privileges. Early in the century, the Sui emperor, Wen, ordered distribution of the Buddha's relics throughout China, constructing a series of reliquary stupas to house them in imitation of Indian practice; one Tang envoy paid an Indian monastery 4,000 bolts of silk for a small parietal bone of the Buddha. The Chinese even "discovered" a number of their own Buddhist holy places. They decided for example, that Manjusri, a particularly revered bodhisattva (a type of enlightened holy man) had lived at Mount Wutai, which became a major pilgrimage site.

ABOVE *The Wild Goose Pagoda, Xi'an. Originally constructed in the mid-7th century, it was rebuilt by Wu Zetian before the year 704.*

A Pilgrim to India

One of the most famous Chinese pilgrims to India was the Buddhist monk Xuanzang (602–64). Xuanzang traveled around China searching out and comparing sacred texts, apparently concerned about conflicting Buddhist traditions and misunderstandings based on poor translations. At the age of 27, he decided to resolve these issues at their source, setting out for India, despite the ban against foreign travel in place at the time. The monk spent 17 years abroad, returning with a pack train that contained 657 Indian Buddhist texts, many of which were unknown in China. The Wild Goose Pagoda, constructed to house the monk's manuscripts, still stands in Xian. Xuanzang translated a number of the texts he had brought home. Today, he is mostly known for the account of his travels that the emperor encouraged him to write after his return, the *Great Tang Records on the Western Regions*, the source of much valuable information about both India and Central Asia in the period.

LEFT *The 180 ft (55 m) tall Western Buddha, Bamiyan, Afghanistan, constructed in c. 618 and destroyed by the Taliban in 2001.*

STATE-BUILDING IN SOUTHEAST AND EAST ASIA

The rise of two vastly wealthy and expansionist empires was good news for trade, especially maritime commerce based on the Indian Ocean. While Muslim Arabic merchants were happy to join preexisting Persian trade networks, China was more concerned to control trade rather than participate in it directly. The Chinese government had an ambivalent attitude toward trade, welcoming foreign merchants, but treating native Chinese merchants as a degraded, parasitical class. Still, the profitability and desirability of trade could not be denied, and the Tang emperors increasingly established state monopolies over key goods. Muslim entrepreneurship, Chinese desire for the profits of trade, and everyone's longing for the exotic spices of Southeast Asia as well as goods moving from both east and west, led to rapid state development in Southeast Asia, where the Strait of Melaka controlled access to all trade with China.

Indonesian mariners had played an important role in Indian Ocean trade, including the colonization of Madagascar (c. 350–550), but increasingly they faced competition from Muslim trade networks, whose individual merchants enjoyed the caliphate's protection. Islamic involvement in trade had many benefits, including introduction to the Islamic lands of oranges and lemons from China, sugar cane and cotton from India, as well as other foodstuffs. They were highly active, establishing direct trade with China and establishing a community of Muslim merchants in Guangzhou that probably numbered in the thousands.

By contrast, the Tang government lent its support to foreign merchants rather than natives, concerned above all with encouraging states in the southeast that were strong enough to protect trade, yet willing to accept at least token subordination to China. The Tang, therefore, engaged diplomatically with the rising states of Champa (central and southern Vietnam) and Srivijaya, which dominated the Strait of Melaka after its establishment in 670. The Cham people were more attuned to cultural influences from India, however, and its rulers did their best to control China's trade with Southeast Asia. Chinese influence was stronger in Srivijaya, whose kings dominated Indonesia by c. 700. Srivijaya became a center of Buddhist scholarship, attracting monks from both India and China, its people combining Buddhist faith with a firm belief in the magical powers of its kings. In the period 619–756 no fewer than 125 tributary missions made their way from Southeast Asia to the Chinese court, offering token submission and gifts in return for trade benefits.

The 7th century also saw massive Chinese influence on Japan, which coalesced in this period into a strongly centralized state. It was perhaps in 604 that Empress Suiko issued the *Seventeen Injunctions*, laying out how the government should be run on Chinese Confucian principles. It is not a coincidence that she also sent the first official Japanese embassy to the Chinese court. The next generation went

LEFT *A rare survival: a wooden statue of the Buddha from the Funan era of the Mekong Delta.*

much further, with the Taika Reform that began in 645; the Great Reform created a centralized monarchy with a legal code, military system, and taxes, all modelled on Tang practices. The Japanese also adopted the Chinese writing system, and the century saw a burst of literary production. Although the government did not have the power to implement the reforms fully, the state's accomplishments were impressive, and by the end of the century Japan had a national tax system that included labor duties from all adult commoners and the creation of a true capital at Fujiwara in 704, modeled on China's capital.

THE SMALL AFFAIRS OF EUROPE

By comparison to the Near East and Asia, the 7th century was not a great age for Western Europe. The Germanic successor states struggled, more or less successfully, toward greater stability, especially seeking ways to enhance royal authority and curb wayward nobles. The chief impediments to success remained foreign invasion and the lack of clear rules for succession. For example, no king of the West Saxons in England was more than distantly related to his predecessor for over two centuries. While the Frankish kings of the Merovingian Dynasty accepted the special charism, or God-given nature, of the royal lineage, the fact that children often inherited the crown as a result placed ever more power into the hands of great nobles.

The most promising of Europe's early medieval kingdoms was Visigothic Spain. After Reccared's conversion to Catholic Christianity in the late 6th century, the kings forged a highly effective alliance with Spain's bishops. This is especially apparent in the 13 councils held in Toledo between 633 and 702, meetings of both secular and ecclesiastical dignitaries that legislated on all aspects of life under the king's leadership. The Visigoths also began to anoint their kings in a religious ceremony modeled on Hebrew Scripture, beginning with King Wamba in 672.

RIGHT *Artist's reconstruction of the Great Hall at Yeavering, Northumberland, a palace used by the kings of Bernicia in the 7th century.*

The Visigothic alliance with the Spanish episcopate highlights one of the most enduring features of European history: the semi-independence of the Christian Church. Elsewhere in the world, rulers exerted clear authority over religious figures and institutions; even in the Byzantine Empire the emperor almost always dominated the patriarch of Constantinople. In Western Europe, however, bishops had stepped into the vacuum as Roman power waned, and Germanic kings were usually content to leave episcopal power intact, although they soon began to assert themselves in episcopal elections. The language of literacy remained Latin, for the most part the province of the Christian clergy, making Christian clerics essential for government.

While it took a brave bishop to confront a king head-on, another development served to make Europe unique: a largely independent Roman papacy. The church in Rome was the only western Christian community founded by an apostle, St. Peter, giving Peter's successors special authority as transmitters of true doctrine. Historic accident then made the bishops of Rome, the popes, the

RIGHT *The Sutton Hoo ship burial in East Anglia was probably the final resting place of King Raedwald. The treasures discovered include this helmet, modeled on a Roman parade helm.*

The Asian Archbishop of Canterbury

After Augustine's initial missionary work in the English kingdom of Kent, reinforcements came from Rome several times to help spread Christianity on the island. The most striking of these reinforcements was Theodore, from Tarsus in what is now Turkey, and his companion, the North African Hadrian. In 667, the archbishop-elect of Canterbury, who had come to Rome for consecration (the English regarding Rome as their mother church), died. Pope Vitalian took advantage of the situation by choosing his own archbishop. He tried to convince the North African scholar Hadrian to take the appointment, but Hadrian recommended his friend Theodore, who was living as a monk in Rome at the time. Hadrian and Theodore traveled together to Canterbury. Archbishop Theodore and his friend Abbot Hadrian had a massive impact on the fledgling English Church, organizing its dioceses, establishing a school at Canterbury, and even teaching sacred music. By the time Theodore died aged 88 in 690, the infrastructure of Christianity in England was firmly established.

A Victorian-era depiction of Theodore of Tarsus from the Church of St. John the Evangelist, Knotty Ash.

effective rulers of the city and of great estates elsewhere in Italy, besides serving as heirs and transmitters of Roman culture. In this period, popes rarely exerted much influence outside central Italy, but their position as Peter's heirs gave them latent authority. Nowhere was this more visible than with Gregory the Great, pope from 590 to 604. His sense of duty as the "Vicar of Peter" led him to engage with the ruling classes of both Western Europe and Byzantium. It also inspired him to dispatch missionaries, led by Augustine, who in 597 began the conversion of southern England to Christianity. Although for more than a century the popes continued to be very cautious in their dealings with the Byzantine emperors, waning Byzantine power in Italy soon allowed them to proclaim their independence.

ABOVE *Pope Gregory the Great gave this charming depiction of motherly love to the Lombard queen Theodolinda (d. c. 627), who in turn donated it to the cathedral of Monza, where it still remains.*

CHAPTER 3

The 8th Century: The Quest for Stability

Large states at one level must have seemed utterly natural to medieval thinkers: Christians embraced the notion of a Christendom, as did Muslims the concept of *Dar al-Islam*, a universal empire that united all Muslims under the rule of a Muslim caliph. In the case of Europe and China, there was also a moral imperative to live up to the legacy of an earlier great empire, whether Han or Roman. Nonetheless, great empires rarely held together long. Ethnic and linguistic diversity, resentment by peoples who had been forcibly subjected, and the sheer distances involved militated against strong central control of a large state. The discontents of imperial powers are particularly visible in the 8th century. The Umayyad caliphate was replaced by a new ruling Dynasty in a bloody civil war, while in China An Lushan's rebellion nearly brought down the Tang Dynasty. It was only in Europe that the Carolingians achieved a bloodless coup, which led to the great Frankish Empire.

LEFT *Maya musicians from the Temple of the Murals, Bonampak, Mexico.*

ROUNDING OUT THE ISLAMIC CONQUESTS

Muslim elites saw no reason to halt their conquests, especially as the first great expansions of Islamic rule had been so successful. Their most important target was Constantinople, the strength of whose defenses was sometimes the only thing that prevented Byzantine extinction. A magnificent natural site, Constantinople (modern Istanbul) had been protected since the early 5th century by an impressive series of both land and sea walls. Arab determination to possess the city can be seen in two great sieges, in 674–8 and again 717–18. The 717 attack was said to have included 120,000 men and 1,800 ships. The Byzantine Empire was saved by a combination of a very harsh winter that weakened the besiegers, skilled deployment of Greek fire (the Byzantines' secret weapon), and of course the assistance of the city's patron saint, the Virgin Mary.

The Byzantine Empire survived, but under near-perpetual threat. Under those circumstances, it is not surprising that Emperor Leo III (717–41) came to believe his people had angered God, especially after a great volcanic eruption in the Aegean in 726. His answer was iconoclasm, the destruction of images of Christ and the saints in the belief that they were the "graven images" banned by the Ten Commandments. Iconoclasm was official state policy from 730–87 and again from 815–43, causing considerable dislocation and even providing an opportunity for a woman, the dowager empress Irene, to seize the throne for herself in a coup in 797; Irene captured and blinded her incompetent son, winning support with her pro-icon stance. In part because of its internal religious tensions, Byzantium continued to shrink. Its last territory in northern Africa was lost to the caliphate in 698 and Lombards seized

BELOW *Restored section of the Theodosian Walls of Constantinople, a massive double system of walls and moats built in the early 5th century by Emperor Theodosius II.*

the Byzantine territory in northeastern Italy, known as the Exarchate of Ravenna, in 751. By 780, the emperors ruled over lands only about one-third the size of the empire in 600, before the Persian war and Islamic conquests had begun.

Other Islamic advances achieved greater success. With the Muslim defeat of Persia, the caliphate's border had been established at the Amu Darya, with occasional raids into Transoxiana. In 705 the frontier governor, Qutaiba ibn Muslim, turned from raids to outright conquest. Skillfully exploiting Sogdian and Turk rivalries, his army quickly seized Bukhara, Khwarazm, and the great trade city of Samarkand. The expansion into Central Asia was brutal, provoking serious rebellions. But the Islamic army crushingly defeated the Turks in the 730s. Soon, they thrust as far as China's border region, where the Tang were also eager to control the wealth of the Silk Road, lured by the riches of Merv, Bukhara, and Samarkand as well as lesser centers. In the first Arab–Chinese encounter the Muslims won a major victory, the Battle of Talas River of 751. In time, large numbers of Arabs settled in the conquered territories, but, as we will see, political events prevented further expansion.

ABOVE *A Byzantine iconoclast whitewashing an image of Christ.*

Although baulked in their efforts to reach Europe via the Bosporus, Muslim rule pushed into Europe by another route, across the Strait of Gibraltar and into the Iberian Peninsula. In 711, Tariq ibn Ziyad, a freedman in the service of the Arab governor of Ifriqiya (North Africa) probed into Visigothic Spain, where a succession

BELOW *The Ark of Bukhara, Uzbekistan, a large earthwork fortification that served as a fortress until 1920, when it was taken by Russian troops.*

dispute had divided the Christians. Tariq won a major victory at Guadalete in July and quickly seized Córdoba and Toledo. After the governor of Ifriqiya reinforced Tariq, Visigothic resistance soon crumbled, although Muslim control never reached as far as the Pyrenees. Both Muslim conquerors were recalled by the caliph in 714; he had never authorized the invasion in the first place. The result was a highly atypical Islamic province. Central government was limited from the start, in part because the Visigoths had maintained only a very fragmentary tax system for the new rulers to adopt, so Muslim fighters were settled on the land rather than salaried.

Tension among the Muslims—between Arabs and Berbers—also limited government effectiveness. The term "Berber" for one of the major ethnic groups of northern Africa actually originated as an insult term related to "barbarian"—Arabs regarded them as people who babbled nonsensically, illiterate and brutish. After submitting to Muslim rule in the 7th-century conquests, the Berbers rapidly converted to Islam, but were still forced to pay tribute, especially in the form of slaves. They were also recruited for the conquest of Spain but continued to be treated as second-class citizens. The result was a great Berber revolt in 740 that affected both Ifriqiya and Spain. Caliph Hisham had to send Syrian armies to Spain in 742 to pacify that region, settling them on the peninsula to increase the Arabic presence. Nonetheless, resentment continued to seethe.

RIGHT *This 1965 statue created by Gerardo Zaragoza depicts Pelayo of Asturias, who is credited with beginning the reconquest of the Iberian Peninsula from the Muslims in the 8th century.*

RESHAPING THE CALIPHATE

Berber–Arab tensions were only one of many problems besetting the Umayyad caliphs. Protests against their rule—too "royal" and too "un-Islamic" in the eyes of many—came to a head in the 740s. Caliph al-Walid II, who ascended the throne in 743, was an irresponsible spendthrift. His murder by rebels in 744 gave an opportunity to a conspiracy that had been nearly 20 years in the making. The Muslims of Khurasan, in the far east of the caliphate, were prone to rebellion but were experienced fighters, since Arabic settlers had integrated well with local converts to battle frequent Turkish raids. The rallying cry that drew them together was their longing for a caliph from the house of the prophet Muhammad, although the architects of the Umayyad overthrow were vague on *who* the new caliph ought to be, with their choice remaining quietly behind the scenes for years. The actual military leader of the planned takeover was the talented Iranian Behzadan, better known by his pseudonym Abu Muslim. He raised the black flags of his rebellion in eastern Iran in 747, winning over many, both Persians and Arabs, who hated Umayyad rule and the dominance of the Syrians. Doubtless to the surprise of most of the rebels, Abu Muslim then declared a complete unknown, a man without reputation or a following, as caliph. This man, Abu'l-Abbas, was not even a descendant of Fatima and 'Ali, instead tracing his descent from Muhammad's uncle Abbas, who had never converted to Islam. This first Abbasid caliph took the regnal name al-Saffah.

Marwan, the Umayyad caliph, personally led an army against the rebels, but was soundly defeated in February 750 in the Battle of River Zab, south of Mosul. Marwan was forced to flee and was caught and killed several months later in Egypt. Only one member of the Umayyad clan survived. His name was 'Abd al-Rahman and he made his way to the Islamic province of Spain. In 756 his supporters defeated the 'Abbasid governor and captured

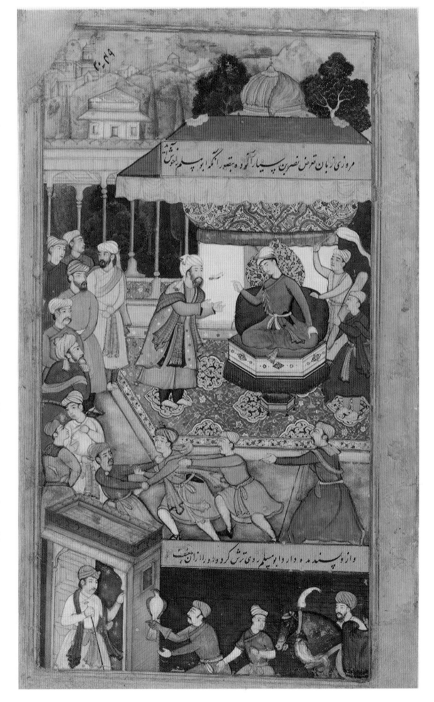

RIGHT *Abu Muslim sitting in judgment, page from the* Ethics of Nasir *(16th century).*

ABOVE *Now a Catholic cathedral, the Great Mosque of Córdoba was constructed beginning in 785 by order of Emir Abd al-Rahman I and expanded several times in succeeding centuries.*

Córdoba. At first simply ruling as independent emirs, the Umayyads of Spain eventually proclaimed themselves as caliphs in 929.

Fervent supporters of the claims of 'Ali's family to the caliphate especially resented the new Abbasid rulers; there were major Alid revolts in 762. Only gradually were the Alids pacified, especially by Caliph al-Mahdi (775–85), who took care to demonstrate his piety and concern for sound religious practice. It was particularly crucial that a ruler visibly defend orthodoxy in this period, as the first Muslim mystics (Sufis) began charting their highly independent and often

idiosyncratic path through the Islamic world. A good example of the problematic nature of Sufis is the 9th-century poet and mystic Mansur Hallaj, who danced around Baghdad, shouting, "I am the divine truth"; he was eventually executed for blasphemy. Sometimes such charismatic religious figures actively rebelled against caliphal authority. Most famous was the so-called "Veiled Prophet of Khorasan" (d. 785/6) who claimed to be an incarnation of God, covering his face lest it dazzle his followers. His anti-Abbasid revolt succeeded in creating an independent state that survived 14 years before the Abbasids could defeat it.

When the first Abbasid caliph died in 754, his brother al-Mansur succeeded; he is regarded as the true founder of the new dynasty. With the exception of the breakaway Shi'ite Fatimid caliphs who seized control of Egypt in the 10th century, all caliphs until the year 1517 were al-Mansur's descendants. Al-Mansur proved to be an obsessive administrator and political genius. Turning away from the Syrian favoritism of the Umayyads, al-Mansur and his successors introduced a very strong Persian influence in both government and court ceremonial. They also made the important decision to make the office of caliph less dependent on Arabic tribal levies: al-Mansur created a standing army on the Persian model, paying for it with more efficient taxation and immense agricultural development, especially in southern Iraq. Administrative oversight was tightened, with professional salaried clerks keeping careful financial records; the caliphs themselves were literate, and many were highly educated. The dynamic al-Mansur also created a new capital, much more centrally located than Damascus. The administrative core of this new city, Baghdad, was constructed in only four years, between 762 and 766, at massive expense. It was located only a few miles from Ctesiphon, the home of the Sasanian Persian shahs' greatest palace. Ideally located for trade, Baghdad expanded rapidly, attaining a population of at least 400,000 by 800 and probably around a million by 930.

The second Abbasid caliph was ruthless in his efforts to concentrate power in his own hands. His most prominent victim was Abu Muslim, architect of the Abbasid takeover. He was acting far too much like an independent ruler in Khurasan, so al-Mansur lured the general to whom his family owed so much to court and murdered him. After a brief hiatus during the rebellion, al-Mansur and his successors also resumed and increased the ongoing Muslim campaign against the Byzantine Empire, making war on the border practically an annual ritual.

What rendered the new caliphate insecure was the lack of a clear rule for succession to the throne. Muslim rulers were polygamous, and the ruler could designate any son he pleased as his heir, or even decree that several should rule in succession. The consequences of this were serious in the 8th century and became catastrophic in the 9th. Al-Mansur's successor, Caliph al-Mahdi, declared that his two sons Musa and Harun should rule in succession. Musa, taking the name al-Hadi, did succeed in establishing himself when his father died in a hunting accident in 785. He then turned against al-Mahdi's plans, declaring his own son as heir to the throne. The displaced brother Harun—and Zubayda, the formidable mother of both—had cause to feel aggrieved. Al-Hadi died mysteriously after 13 months of rule; most likely his mother arranged for a slave woman to smother him. Zubayda's favorite son, Harun al-Rashid (786–809), then became caliph. He honored his mother for the rest of her life, showering her with wealth, which she devoted to the largest civil engineering project of the early Islamic period, the creation of a good road from Iraq across the Arabian Desert

BELOW *Scholars working in an Abbasid library, from the Maqamat of al-Hariri, painted by Yahya al-Wasiti in 1237.*

LEFT *Interior of the Abbasid palace of al-Ukhaidir, Iraq, erected as part of a large fortress complex in 775.*

to the holy cities of Mecca and Medina, complete with cisterns, wells, and guard posts along the way.

The reign of Harun al-Rashid is regarded as the golden age of the Abbasids, although the caliph himself focused on ceremonial, leaving daily government in the hands of powerful viziers of the Barmakid clan. The caliph was perhaps more for show than for rule, for example making the pilgrimage to Mecca eight times in flamboyant expeditions that took about two months each. Ultimately, however, power was still in the caliph's hands, as the Barmakids learned when Harun, probably alarmed at the extent of the power they had garnered, imprisoned and killed his most important servants.

An Astronomer at the Caliph's Court

Arabic elites rapidly embraced the intellectual achievements of the lands subjected to Islam. They learned Indian astronomy and mathematics, including so-called "Arabic" numerals, which actually originated on the Indian subcontinent. From the Byzantine and Persian empires, besides administrative practices, Arab intellectuals drank deeply from the heritage of ancient Greece, including works on philosophy and science. The caliphs welcomed scholars at court, providing generous support and making Baghdad into one of the world's greatest intellectual centers.

An example of how cosmopolitan this educated environment could be is the career of a Christian monk named Theophilos, who served as Caliph al-Mahdi's chief astrologer (no distinction being made between the science of astronomy and the art of astrology in the Middle Ages). Besides benefiting from advanced Indian astronomical observations, Theophilos was clearly fascinated with the heritage of Greece. He was responsible for translating many ancient Greek works into both Arabic and Syriac, making the revered ancient learning available to a much larger audience. Theophilos was only one of many translators and interpreters who flourished in the golden age of the Abbasid caliphate.

Astronomers and geometers at the Abbasid court.

THE CAROLINGIANS AND THE MAKING OF EUROPE

The strongest polity of Western Europe was the Kingdom of the Franks, but almost since its founding in the 5th century it had been plagued by succession disputes, divisions of the kingdom among members of the Merovingian Dynasty, and child rulers. Ultimately, conditions allowed the rise of an extraordinary noble family, known to history as the Carolingians from the fact that several of its greatest representatives were named Charles (in Latin *Carolus*). The Carolingians manipulated alliances and curried favor, gradually becoming indispensable as "mayors of the palace," the official who, rather like a vizier, ran the government on the king's behalf. In time, the Merovingian kings were relegated to a merely ceremonial status, as the Carolingians seized the real power first in part and then in the entirety of the Frankish kingdom by the late 7th century. By the time Charles Martel ("the Hammer") served as mayor of the palace (717–41), he was secure enough to rule several years without bothering to appoint a king. His victory over a large-scale Arabic raid into Francia in 732 also gave Charles the opportunity to present himself as a savior of Christendom against the forces of Islam.

Among the tools the Carolingians employed as they consolidated their power was a highly visible support of Christian institutions, touting their descent from St. Arnulf of Metz. They also identified themselves with ecclesiastical reform, especially supporting missionaries like Boniface,

LEFT *This 14th-century illustration depicts Charles Martel dividing the rule of the Frankish kingdom between his sons. Fortunately for the history of Europe, the older brother Carloman decided to become a monk, leaving Francia undivided.*

who came from England to convert the polytheists on the frontier and restructure the Frankish Church. The alliance with English missionaries bore unexpected fruit. Since England had received Christianity directly from Rome thanks to Pope Gregory the Great's initiative, English churchmen setting out for the mission field in the 8th century felt it was only natural to visit the reigning pope and seek his blessing. The popes were probably surprised but happy to comply, and the missionaries then carried their special reverence for the vicars of St. Peter to the Frankish kingdom with them. It was this budding papal alliance that finally gave the Carolingian leader Pippin the authority to overthrow the last Merovingian king.

In 751, Pippin needed legitimation to usurp the throne. He had himself elected king by an assembly of Frankish nobles, but it was hard to set aside the notion that only someone of Merovingian blood could rule the Franks. Pippin therefore sent an embassy to Pope Zachary, asking the pregnant question of who should rule—the man who actually did all the work of government or the figurehead king. Zachary responded, *ordering* Pippin by apostolic authority to assume the crown. In return, Pippin provided the pope with invaluable military assistance. The Lombards had overrun one of the few remaining Byzantine provinces in the West, the Exarchate of Ravenna, and were threatening Rome itself. In two campaigns, Pippin soundly defeated Lombard pretensions and turned the Exarchate over to the pope. He then spent the rest of his reign consolidating his power.

Pippin's son Charles the Great, or Charlemagne (768–814), built on his father's and grandfather's achievements, creating a state that exerted a massive impact on European history, the Carolingian Empire. Taking sole rule after

BELOW *Charlemagne constructed a great palace at Aachen, of which only the Palatine Chapel survives. Modeled on Roman architecture, it stands as a symbol of Charlemagne's commitment to the restoration of Rome.*

ABOVE *The martyrdom of St. Boniface. The English missionary monk spent most his career in Frankish lands, reorganizing the Frankish Church and finally dying with 52 companions at the hands of the pagan Frisians in 754.*

his brother died in 771, Charlemagne brilliantly deployed the governmental tools he had inherited. The Frankish army was an impressive force. It was not a standing army (the Carolingians did not tax and could not pay for such a thing), but rather a levy of fighting men who brought their own equipment and food, following the tradition of all free male Germans as warriors. Charlemagne ordered a total of 53 campaigns in his reign, personally commanding more than half of them. Some of the wars were those of consolidation, as when Charlemagne secured more effective control of his vassal duchies of Bavaria and Thuringia. Also, in German-speaking

lands, counter-raids against the Saxons on his eastern frontier soon turned to a long, bloody war of conquest that added much of modern Germany to the burgeoning empire. Northern Italy was also subjugated early in the reign, after the Lombard king Desiderius attacked Rome in 772. Charlemagne, holding firm to the papal alliance, invaded Italy in 773–4, deposed Desiderius, and took the Lombard kingdom for himself. Campaigns across the Pyrenees gained a swathe of territory in Spain. Most profitably of all, Frankish armies targeted the Avar lands to the southeast of Francia in the 790s. The Avars, apparently no longer nomads by this period, had for the most part settled peaceably, but occasional raids into Carolingian lands gave a pretext for conquest. When Charlemagne sacked the fortress known as the Ring, the Avar royal residence, the wealth the Franks found there was enormous.

Charlemagne was much more than a warlord, however. He rewarded his followers well with the proceeds of conquest, but also used his share to further a massive overhaul of both Church and state known as the Carolingian renaissance. The king sponsored education, ably assisted by imported scholars like the English Alcuin of York. Monasteries and cathedrals received generous donations, but were also expected to maintain schools, both for their own people and for future government administrators. A massive project of book-copying was carried out around Francia; about 7,000 manuscripts survive from the period, and most of classical Latin literature only survives thanks to Carolingian copies. There was a strong moral imperative behind Charlemagne's educational reform; he wanted priests to have at least a rudimentary education and monks to be able to please God by praying in good Latin. The king further legislated moral reforms, for instance insisting that priests did not hunt. There was also a more secular reason for the government's sponsorship of education. Charlemagne issued orders in writing and expected administrators to be able to read them, and also had the laws of each region copied and demanded that his judges operate in accordance with them. He even

LEFT *A late medieval depiction of Charlemagne (declared a saint by an antipope in 1165) supervising the construction of Aachen's Palatine Chapel.*

instituted a system of inspectors, the *missi dominici*, to oversee the work of administrators.

Charlemagne's achievements were literally crowned on Christmas Day 800, when Pope Leo III elevated him to the rank of emperor. It was the pope's boldest move yet to claim the authority of the ancient Roman emperors and his right to confer that dignity on whoever he pleased. The Byzantine court naturally responded with outrage, but Charlemagne clearly delighted in his new authority as emperor and fought a war to compel the Byzantine emperor to recognize his title in 812. It is not clear of what Charlemagne was actually emperor; his territories, while broad, were certainly not those of the old Western Roman Empire. Nor was Charlemagne happy at receiving the imperial title from the pope, as he demonstrated by personally crowning his son as emperor before his death. Since the son, Louis the Pious, immediately went to Rome for the honor of a papal coronation, the precedent of reliance on the papacy was set, however, with major implications for the future.

Charlemagne's Elephant

Charlemagne and Harun al-Rashid exchanged embassies several times, as the Frankish ruler was eager to protect Christian pilgrims to Jerusalem and established a hostel in the holy city. In 802, a very special present arrived for the emperor from the east: the elephant Abulabaz. The elephant caused a great sensation in Francia; his coming (and unfortunately his drowning death in 810) was covered in considerable detail in several chronicles.

While Abulabaz's story is relatively well known, few historians are aware that the person who brought the elephant west was Charlemagne's emissary, Isaac the Jew. Isaac had gone with several Carolingian nobles on the mission to Harun, but his fellows had died on the journey. Who was Isaac, who only appears in the pages of history with an elephant in tow? It seems likely that the unusual choice of envoy—a Jew for an overtly Christian mission, and a commoner for a high-level diplomatic exchange—came about because Isaac understood long-distance travel. In the 9th and 10th centuries, there is tantalizing evidence of Jewish long-distance merchants, the Radanites, whose networks reached from Francia to China. It was probably the Radanites who inspired the Khazars to convert to Judaism. It is pleasant to think that the cameo appearance of Isaac the Jew is a rare glimpse of the Radanites in action.

A **12th-century fresco of Abulabaz**, from San Baudelio, Spain.

STIRRINGS OF ECONOMIC RECOVERY IN EUROPE

Europe had suffered a severe economic downturn even before the end of the Western Roman Empire, with population decline exacerbated by the plague pandemic of the 6th and 7th centuries. Urban centers had shrunk; the largest city of Christian Western Europe in the 8th century was Rome, with a population of barely 50,000. Nonetheless, conditions were ripe for economic revival. The wealth released into circulation with Charlemagne's conquests certainly played a role. Three other factors were also significant in the revival: greater stability in a number of Western European states; agricultural changes that increased productivity; and private enterprise by traders who hoped to cash in on that growing prosperity.

The stability the Carolingians provided encouraged trade, as the government took rapid action against robbery and piracy, as well as standardizing the Frankish coinage in 793. Francia was not the only state to benefit from stronger central governments in this period. Most notable was the rise of the large, strong kingdom of Mercia in central England. Mercia's King Offa (757–96) was the first ruler of England's many independent states known to have received the religious consecration of unction, which helped protect rulers from rebellion and assassination. Like Charlemagne, Offa aimed to rule more thoroughly, even issuing a small number of gold coins rather than the monometallic silver currency that had been the norm in the West since Rome's fall. And Offa could mobilize resources, most notably in construction of a defensive wall along the entire length of the Mercian–Welsh border, almost 150 miles (241 km). This great earthwork with a stone wall atop at least some of it, known as Offa's Dyke, took at least 5,000 workers laboring for several years to complete.

Agricultural changes were also improving crop yields. Three changes are most notable, and all can be dated to about this time. A new type of plow was gradually introduced, with a moldboard that cut deeply and turned the earth, rather than just furrowing it. Increasingly these new, heavier plows were pulled by horses, the invention of the horse collar and standardization of horseshoes making it possible for equines to pull heavier loads without strangling as they did when yoked. Some areas also began experimenting with three-field agriculture, which involved periodic planting with crops that would replenish the soil, instead of leaving half the land fallow each year to restore fertility. Milder, wetter winters and warmer summers in Northern Europe would have

BELOW *A section of Offa's Dyke, now a popular walking trail.*

been greeted with relief as the climate became more settled for well over a century. The actual farmers—in this period both free peasants and slaves settled on individual plots of land—probably saw little improvement in their lives, but their landlords reaped increasing profits that could be spent on luxuries.

Mediterranean trade in the early 8th century was the lowest it had been in a millennium, but began to rise by about 750, driven in large part by the slave trade as the Carolingians exported their war captives to the Islamic world. More important was North Sea trade, as Frisian and Scandinavian mariners supplied furs, walrus ivory, amber, and other products to a Europe and Islamic world eager for luxuries. Trade emporia were established, such as Quentovic and Dorestad. Most important for long-term trade, Swedish traders established a mercantile hub in the eastern Baltic at a place now known as Staraya Ladoga, the first wood buildings of which were constructed no later than 753. The site gave them access to the Volga River, which led them to both Byzantium and the Islamic lands.

CHINA'S FAILED GREAT COUP

China too faced rebellion and the attempted overthrow of the dynasty in the mid-8th century. Although An Lushan's rebellion ultimately failed, it changed the course of Chinese history. The early Tang emperors had been very open to foreign influences and had also increasingly relied on foreigners from the west—Turks and Sogdians for the most part—for their military. By the early 8th century, China had largely abandoned its old system of conscripted farmer-soldiers, in favor of a standing army largely recruited from the steppe. By 742, a list of Tang frontier forces reports more than sixty garrisons occupying nearly 500,000 soldiers, the larger commands headed by military governors.

One military governor, the Turkish-Sogdian general An Lushan, became especially powerful thanks to court influence—Emperor Xuanzong was infatuated with his concubine Yang Guifei, granting her every wish, while she in turn was

BELOW *The Longmen Caves near Luoyang China are a vast system of 2,300 caves, home to about 110,000 Buddhist statues, carved over several centuries.*

enamored with the handsome general. An Lushan served the empire loyally, until a new prime minister plotted to strip An of his power. He raised the flag of rebellion in 755. At first unstoppable, rebels destroyed the Tang army sent against them. The emperor was forced to flee the capital and his own escort mutinied, leading him to order the death of his favorite concubine Yang and her kinsman whose interference had caused the rebellion. Xuanzong's son soon pressured him to abdicate, however, and the crisis was gradually managed. An Lushan's own followers killed him in early 757, and internal dissension split the rebels. The new Tang emperor made an alliance with the Uighurs that allowed them to triumph in a final great campaign in 762, but in return had to stand by and allow his Uighur allies to sack the Chinese rebel stronghold Luoyang, killing over 10,000 citizens in the process and burning most of the city.

Although imperial rule was reestablished, it had been deeply shaken. To quell the rebellion, the government had been forced to pull troops from the west; as a result, China's westernmost provinces were lost and never recovered. The Tang ruler also surrendered much power to the remaining military governors for the sake of peace; after the major rebel leaders were killed, junior commanders were allowed to remain in their military governorships with near autonomy. Tax rolls were reduced by two-thirds, as many peasants had fled their lands during the fighting. Desperate governmental efforts to make ends meet led to a major decline in Silk Road trade, as the government seized 20 percent of every merchant's assets. Many Sogdians, the key

ABOVE *The journey of Emperor Xuanzong to Sichuan, painted by Li Zhaodao (d.741).*

middlemen of the long-distance trade, were also massacred as supposed allies of the rebels. In general, this is the point at which the Chinese elite decided they did not trust foreigners.

The empires of Central Asia took advantage of the chaos in China. The Uighur khaganate had overthrown the Second Turkic Empire in 744, pulling together a coalition of steppe peoples that endured until 840. Although the Uighur khagan assisted the Tang Dynasty in suppressing An Lushan's revolt, the price extracted was high. The Chinese court had to accept the khagan as the emperor's equal, and on three occasions Chinese princesses were sent to wed khagans in humiliating marriage alliances. Fortunately for China, the Uighurs soon had their own internal dissent, after the khagan Tengri Bögu converted to the Manichaean religion and tried to force his people to convert as well. The khagan and hundreds of members of his family were assassinated in 779, a cousin usurping the throne. The Tibetan Empire also took advantage of Chinese disorder, invading and looting the capital Chang'an in 763. The Tibetan ruler Khri Srong Ide brtsan (756–c. 800) oversaw the expansion of his empire to its greatest extent. He threatened the caliphate along the Amu Darya, and also pushed into Kashmir and beyond, aiming to control trade from India to the west.

LEFT *Sogdian musicians on a camel, an example of the often whimsical art of the Silk Road.*

The Panjikent Murals

Panjikent in modern Tajikistan was an important mercantile city of medieval Sogdia. Sogdian merchants dominated the land Silk Road. Their homeland was wealthy and cosmopolitan, drawing influences from both east and west. Nowhere is the international nature of the region clearer than in the murals of Panjikent. Wealthy merchants began the custom of decorating the walls of their homes with murals starting at the end of the 5th century; the practice continued until the Muslim conquest of the region in 722. The murals display Greek and Turkic influences, and various scenes supported their owners' Zoroastrian, Christian, Buddhist, and Hindu beliefs. They also demonstrate how wealthy Sogdian merchants could become, their fine homes demonstrating the luxury in which they lived.

A Panjikent merchant in all his finery.

A DAWNING GOLDEN AGE IN THE INDIAN OCEAN

Although the manipulations of great empires had caused a decline in trade along the Silk Road land route by the end of the 8th century, the sea route flourished. Every land that faced the Indian Ocean prospered (at least the ruling classes), benefiting not just kingdoms but autonomous merchant communes. We can see that prosperity in a variety of ways.

On the Indian subcontinent itself, no single great state dominated, but the Pala realm that controlled Bengal and Bihar from the 8th to the 12th century was particularly well-positioned to take advantage of trade with Southeast Asia. Its founder, Gopala, was a local chief who consolidated power over northeastern India beginning c. 750. Gopala's state had the resources to maintain not just an army with a large elephant corps but a navy, which engaged in both trade and defense. The Pala rulers actively encouraged maritime trade, establishing diplomatic relations with the Srivijaya Empire of Indonesia, Tibet, and the Abbasid caliphate. Some of their wealth was devoted to monumental temples and to creating a major study center at Somapura.

Smart rulers, though, have always understood that the best way to profit from mercantile activity is to allow merchants a considerable degree of autonomy, simply skimming some of their profit in the form of duties and tolls. Merchant autonomy became visible to a high degree throughout India in this period. Merchant guilds, consisting in large part of migrants, won rights of self-government and even maintained their own mercenaries to protect trade routes and settlements. The most

RIGHT *The Kailasa Hindu Temple at Ellora, India, was carved from the face of a cliff; its excavation is attributed to the Rashtrakuta king Krishna I (d. 773).*

powerful of these guilds, such as the Ayyavolu, formed what was in essence an independent state within the states where they were based. Merchants sometimes got out of hand, however, as in 758 when Arabic and Persian merchants in Guangzhou, China, took advantage of the Tang government's weakness. They drove out the unpopular governor, then sacked the city and fled by ship.

Java in Southeast Asia saw a similar blend of royal control and merchant networks. One important thing a state can do to facilitate trade is to provide a standardized unit of exchange, and Java in the 8th century began to mint coins. Apparently, the coinage was used at first only for major donations and hoarding rather than in trade, although the state did standardize weights to encourage exchange. Smaller-denomination coins gradually developed, their use at first limited to the two major population centers in central and eastern Java.

The merchant communities of eastern Africa also began to flourish. Africa had highly desirable trade goods, from timber to gold to the high-quality steel produced at a number of sites along the coast. The annual monsoons made East Africa as far south as Madagascar a vital component of Indian Ocean trade. Arabic merchants began to move down the coast to take advantage of trade opportunities, joining with the Indigenous people to produce the unique Swahili culture of the region.

Bringing Tea to China

Most people associate tea with China, but *Camellia sinensis*, although native to southwestern China, only first caught on as a beverage in India. Buddhist monks popularized its use, the caffeine content helping to keep them attentive while meditating. Tea became a common drink in China itself only in the latter part of the Tang dynasty. By *c.* 750 it was a major item both in internal trade and in Indian Ocean commerce. The first great work on tea cultivation and preparation was Lu Yu's *Tea Classic* (*Cha jing*), published in the 760s. The widespread drinking of tea brought a double health benefit, both because of the properties of the tea itself and because it was made with boiled water. Thus tea-drinking helped contribute to China's swelling population in the later Tang.

SEPARATE BUT EQUAL: DEVELOPMENTS IN THE AMERICAS

The peoples of the Americas developed many of the same solutions to communal life that defined their counterparts in the eastern hemisphere. Everywhere with sufficient population density required governmental structures to manage ownership and distribution of resources; everywhere it was necessary to unite resources for defense to keep the neighbors from encroaching. And everywhere that developed a strong centralizing authority soon devised methods to enhance the ruler's authority.

Although the Maya never united into a single empire, individual city-states developed all these features to a high degree. The lowland city-states for the most part suffered serious collapse in the period 750–900, climate change increasing warfare as the cities competed for resources and in some cases oppressed their own people to the point of rebellion. The Classic Maya period was coming to an end, but a number of states were still able to flourish for generations. Two in particular stand out, Tikal and Copan.

LEFT *Jade burial mask of Pakal the Great, who ruled the Maya state of Palenque 615–83, one of the longest recorded reigns in world history.*

ABOVE *The Great Plaza at Tikal. To the left is the North Acropolis; the large structure on the right is Temple I, the tomb of Jasaw Chan K'awiil I.*

RIGHT *Stele of Lady K'abel, queen regnant of the Maya city-state of El Perú, who died early in the 8th century.*

Tikal was a great Maya center for over half a millennium (200–800); by the end of the 3rd century it dominated surrounding chiefdoms. At its height, in c. 700, the city was home to more than 60,000 people. After some decline, Tikal enjoyed a great resurgence under King Jasaw Chan K'awiil I (d. 734).

The city's central urban space was re-designed, with a new palace complex and two stepped pyramids around a great plaza. The whole complex was a statement of royal authority; Temple I in the complex was the great king's funeral monument, its nine terraces referring to the nine levels of Xibalba through which a ruler must pass after death before his rebirth as a god.

Whole Maya cities are still being discovered in the jungles of Mesoamerica, but in our current state of knowledge the other great Maya center of the 8th century was Copan. In 695, Waxaklajuun Ubaah K'awiil became king of Copan, ruling for 43 years over a very large territory of vassal cities. He too carried out great projects of urban renewal in his capital, and again an important goal was glorification of the ruler. It is thanks to this king that we have the longest extant Mayan hieroglyphic text. The monumental Hieroglyphic Stairway consists of 62 steps with 2,200 glyph blocks telling the history of the dynasty along with three-dimensional portraits of past rulers. Also a sign of the times, however, Waxaklajuun Ubaah K'awiil met his end when he was captured in war and ritually executed in 738, ending the dominance of his lineage, which had endured nearly 500 years.

Finally, one should note that evidence from North America also demonstrates that communities were organizing. A notable site is Chaco Canyon, in what is now New Mexico. By the 8th century, the Ancestral Pueblo population had developed to create a complex society; elite burials in the region date to as early as this period. By the 9th century, they had begun to create a true city, a site that eventually boasted eight very large masonry pueblos, besides many smaller blocks. The whole was home to perhaps 25,000 people. The site, in semi-desert condition,

probably owes its existence to the Cerillos turquoise mines, the populace trading the semi-precious stone through much of the Americas. The 8th century was also the beginning of the Late Woodland period in the American Midwest. The landscape of several states is dotted with large-scale burials known as effigy mounds. These are impressive earth sculptures depicting different types of figures, especially animals; the largest is a bird whose outspread wings stretch over 600 feet (183 m). One or more people was buried at the heart or head region of each of these figural mounds, clearly people of importance to the culture that expended so much labor to honor them. But there our knowledge fails us. Except the Maya, no American culture developed a full written language able to convey the entire range of human thought, and left with limited (such as Aztec glyphs) or no writing we are left to guess at the social structures, dreams, and aspirations of these peoples.

ABOVE *The Princeton Vase, a masterpiece of the classical Maya period. It depicts an aged deity, known only as "God L," surrounded by female attendants. Below, a rabbit records the scene in a book.*

BELOW *The remains of Pueblo Bonito in Chaco Canyon, New Mexico.*

CHAPTER 4

An Age of Centrifugal Pull

T he medieval millennium was an era of great states, with rulers claiming a religious mandate or even personal divinity. Since historical sources show these larger-than-life figures clearly, it is easy to forget the millions of ordinary people who got on with their lives, often scraping a bare living, hoping the powerful elites of their cultures would not harm them. There were also dynamic peoples who, because they were not literate, have largely vanished from history. A good example of these peoples, whose course can be traced only through archeological, linguistic, and DNA studies, were the populations of Oceania. Originating in Tonga and Samoa, Polynesian mariners systematically discovered and colonized every habitable island in the South Pacific. It was probably in the 9th century that they first made contact with South America as well. Another dominant theme of the 9th century is trade, especially the tension between private entrepreneurship and rulers' efforts to control the wealth that trade generated. Trade, which frequently descended into piracy if the moment presented itself, was both a challenge and an opportunity to centralized states.

LEFT *The Tjängvide image stone, Gotland, Sweden. Carved in the 8th or 9th century, it depicts a Scandinavian longboat under full sail; the obvious weapons suggest the mariners are Vikings.*

TWO TRADE WORLDS: STATEHOOD AND TRADE IN AFRICA

Burgeoning trade on the African continent helps illustrate the variety of possible approaches toward commerce. Some parts of the continent rendered all but regional trade very difficult. This was true of much of Africa's central and southern interior. South of the equator the tstse-fly was prevalent in much of the highland savanna, making it impossible to rely on beasts of burden; the lack of navigable rivers further hindered mercantile development. Nonetheless, even areas only accessed with difficulty were engaging in some long-distance trade by the year 1000, for example in the region of the Kalahari and modern Namibia, where livestock-raising societies came to share the territory with foragers, the proceeds of pastoralism enabling trade with the coast.

Along the coast of East Africa, by contrast, long-distance trade flourished and by the 9th century commerce-oriented city-states had emerged. These had a largely African, Bantu-speaking populace, but with an admixture of Muslim traders who helped to connect East Africa with broader Indian Ocean trade routes. It is likely that these trade centers also attracted merchants from Southeast Asia, like the Malaysians who had settled Madagascar and who introduced an important new crop—the

banana—to Africa. The merchants developed a Bantu-based *lingua franca* with significant Arabic elements, which was known as *Kiswahili*, "the language of the coast," from which the culture of the region came to be known as Swahili. Early Islamic settlers in the region were humble, many of them dissenters fleeing religious persecution. By the 9th century, however, a number of Swahili towns—with hinterlands that provided necessary foodstuffs—were flourishing. Swahili merchants explored the African coast southward, seeking new sources of trade goods. By the late 8th century they had reached the southern part of modern Mozambique, where the availability of gold caused them to set up a seasonal trade entrepôt—Chibueni.

Over time, eight full-scale Swahili cities were established, each occupying more than 15 hectares (37 acres) of land, with at least 28 smaller towns and many walled villages that supported the trade centers; over 400 settlement sites are known. The two largest, Shanga and Manda, each had a population of 15–18,000 at its height. Both of these urban centers were constructed on islands in the Lamu Archipelago, where they were well placed to cash in on international demand for African ivory and rock crystal. Most of the towns were established on islands or at river mouths for convenience. By the 11th century, the most important city-states, such as Manda, Shanga, and Kilwa, had begun to mint their own silver and copper coins.

Kilwa, which reached its peak in the 14th century, is a good example of the prosperity of the Swahili coast, at least for the merchant class. It was the southernmost harbor that could be reached dependably by the time the monsoon season started, and was thus an ideal transshipment point for goods from points

LEFT *Copper coins minted at Kilwa, an important city on the Swahili coast.*

further south. Kilwa came to control the gold trade from the interior of south-central Africa to the Indian Ocean. The gold, mined in the high plateau of modern Zimbabwe, was then carried overland to ports for shipment to the Islamic world and beyond.

The Swahili city-states were centers established by merchants for the benefit of merchants. While most of them had kings, the rulers' authority was limited by a council of "elders," an oligarchy of senior merchants representing the established old families. Although they did not have powerful kings, the Swahili states were far from egalitarian. Commoners were prevented from hunting large animals, whose hides were valuable as export commodities. The elite also jealously guarded their monopoly on harvesting large trees, so commoners could not build their own boats and organize new trading ventures that might challenge the established merchants. And while commoners lived simply, the merchants, by contrast, enjoyed lives of conspicuous luxury, their homes—many constructed from harvested coral—decorated with exotic wares such as Chinese porcelain.

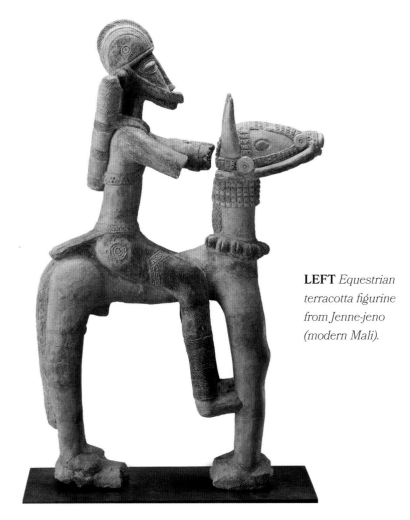

LEFT *Equestrian terracotta figurine from Jenne-jeno (modern Mali).*

LEFT *The ruins of Kilwa. Most of the city was constructed of wood and thatch, so little sign of its former importance remains.*

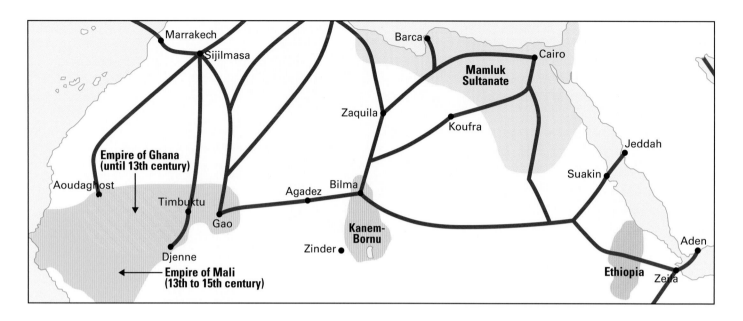

Muslim merchants were also a catalyst for the development of trade in West Africa. Regular caravan routes across the Sahara had been established by the early 9th century. Trade was beneficial for people on both sides of the Sahara, the Muslim world craving the gold mined in the south, but also copper, manufactured goods such as carnelian beads, and slaves; the peoples south of the Sahara needed the salt that was mined in desert oases. Unlike East Africa, however, foreign merchants never constituted more than a small minority of the population, so trade there developed within a pre-existing context of highly ritualized kingship. Cross-Saharan trade also evolved in the context of inter-regional trade that had existed for centuries, for example at trade entrepôts like Jenne-jeno, in present-day Mali.

By the 9th century, a number of city-states had developed, taking advantage of the Niger River to expand trade networks far into the interior. Ife was the most important of the Yoruba city-states,

in what is now southeastern Nigeria. Ife was a center of production, as was the kingdom of Gao, which controlled the salt trade from the Sahara. Above all, Jenne-jeno was a densely-populated urban site by this time, and its 33 hectares (81 acres) were protected by a clay city wall. Soon, however, cities came to dominate whole regions. The earliest large kingdom known around the confluence of the Niger and Benue Rivers was the Nri state, its core population Igbo. The Kanem Empire developed in the Chad Basin about the same time. Both were wealthy, the latter's location making it a major transshipment

ABOVE *The main caravan routes across the Sahara in the Middle Ages.*

RIGHT *Nri ceremonial vessel, 9th century. The kingdom of Nri occupied part of what is now Nigeria.*

point for goods exported as far as Libya, Tunisia, Nubia, and Egypt. Both were also ruled by priest-kings, the accepted intermediaries between the populace and the spirits of the land and their ancestors.

The strongest state of West Africa in this period was the Wagadu Empire, often known as Ancient Ghana (the ruler's title was *the* Ghana). Wagadu dominated the entirety of the western Sahel zone. It was probably founded in the 3rd or 4th century as a key transshipment point for the gold trade. It was also an important center for iron-working, creating a system of indigenous trade upon which Muslim mercantilism was superimposed as an additional layer. An oral tradition written down in the 17th century reports that Wagadu had 22 kings before the arrival

of the first Muslim traders and 22 after. This land of Ancient Ghana was already important in 773, when an Arabic source first refers to it; it was known as the "land of gold" to Arabic geographers of the 9th century. The ruler, who was also known as *kaya maghan*—"lord of the gold"—was precisely that. The rulers of Wagadu kept a careful monopoly on the gold they imported from the interior to keep its value stable on the international market. Clearly, this was a centralized state with kings who could command resources. A much later legend tells that one king named Kanissa'ai maintained a stable of 1,000 horses, who slept on carpets and wore silk halters, each attended by three grooms. By the 12th century the power of the Ghana was legendary in Europe.

BELOW *Ruins of Ouadane, which served as an important staging post for the trans-Saharan trade during the Ghana Empire.*

THE MASSIVE SCOPE OF 9TH-CENTURY TRADE

States and merchants alike certainly kept detailed records of transactions, but almost none of that paper trail has survived from the early Middle Ages. No matter the country, few chroniclers were interested in something as mundane as commerce; their pages are filled with war and religious foundations, with only occasional references to the activities of non-nobles. As a result, scholars are left to reconstruct the patterns of medieval trade through means such as archeology. Two examples illustrate how much can be learned in this way.

The last 50 years have seen great strides in underwater archeology. Shipping in the Middle Ages was hazardous, and many sailors and their ships succumbed to pirate attack, sudden storms, poor vessel design, or even badly loaded cargo

that led boats to sink. A particularly interesting find was a wrecked ship off the coast of the Indonesian Belitung Island in 1998. The vessel, which sank for unknown reasons in c. 830, was a common Arab dhow, a trading ship 50 ft by 21 ft (15 m by 6.4 m), its wooden planks sewn together with coconut fiber, as was common for vessels operating on the Indian Ocean at the time. Although the ship was Arab in style, its timber was not; at least some of the wood of its hull came from trees native to southeastern Africa. The contents of the ship demonstrated that it was on its return voyage from China when disaster struck; it was filled with over 70,000 pieces of Tang porcelain, as well as goods including star anise. Thus, in one shipwreck we can see a great triangle of trade, stretching between East Africa,

RIGHT *Gold cup recovered from the Belitung shipwreck. It was probably manufactured in Yangzhou, China.*

the Islamic Empire, and China. By the 9th century China was engaged in large-scale porcelain export to the Islamic world; the largest kilns in use at the time could fire 12–15,000 pieces at a time.

Rather than a single find, the second example of the scope of trade that archeology has uncovered is cumulative: the vast amount of Islamic silver that made its way into Scandinavian, Slavic, and Khazar hoards starting in the 9th century. Already in the 8th century, Scandinavian traders and raiders had pushed beyond their coastal waters, exploring the potential of sails and improved ship design. By c. 750 there is archeological evidence of Scandinavians raiding along the Baltic coast and by the end of the century they were pushing up the Dnieper, Don, Volga, and lesser rivers to establish trade with both Byzantium and the Islamic world. These eastward-looking Scandinavians, for the most part Swedes, became known as the Rus'—the "rowers"—because of their skilled use of ships. The trade emporium Staraya Ladoga, in northwest Russia, had been established in the 8th century, followed by Gorodishche, much further south, in the 9th; in 882 the Rus' seized control of the Khazar outpost Kyiv. The goods they offered included luxury items such as furs, walrus ivory, and amber, but above all they flooded the Islamic lands with enslaved people, many of them captured

by their fellow Scandinavians in Viking raids throughout Western Europe. Islam's elites were eager for these luxuries, and two extraordinarily productive silver mines in Tashkent and Pendijhir allowed them to spend money like water. The Rus' trade brought back some luxuries to Europe (for example, there are more than a hundred silk fragments in the Oseberg ship burial), but for the most part the traders were paid in cash. There are an estimated half-million extant silver dirhams minted between the 9th and the 11th century, and fully three-quarters of them have been found in Northern Europe, especially in coin hoards in Sweden. Islam was gradually drained of its silver, and as the mines failed in the latter part of the 10th century the caliphate fell into severe economic depression.

The Khazars, who formed a large state covering what is now the southern parts

RIGHT *This delicate, finely crafted silver stag bears witness to Khazar craftsmanship in the 8th and 9th centuries.*

of European Russia, Ukraine, Crimea, and Kazakhstan, were actually more important to the trade between Europe and Islam until their final defeat at the hands of the Rus' in the 10th century; future excavation is likely to discover at least as much Islamic silver in their territories as in Scandinavia. The Khazars were a Turkic people, originally nomadic but in time partially becoming settled. The khaganate was formed in the mid-7th century and became a major supplier of enslaved people for Muslim markets, dealing in captured Turkic nomads and so many Slavs that the ethnic group gave its name to the condition of enslavement in many languages— the disunited Slavs were ill-equipped to resist the oppression of more centralized states. The Khazars are mostly known today as the medieval millennium's sole Jewish state. Their khagan converted to Judaism in the early 9th century, perhaps inspired by contact with Jewish merchants. While the khaganate remained a multi-religious state, Judaism spread widely in the elite and merchant classes.

The Swedish Buddha

In the 8th and 9th centuries, Scandinavians established a number of trade emporia in the North Sea and Baltic. One of these was on the island of Helgö on Lake Mälaren in Sweden. Extensively excavated, the site has revealed workshops as well as evidence of shipping. What has most interested scholars, however, is a silver statuette of the Buddha, crafted in the 4th century in northern India. We will never know how it traversed the thousands of miles from its place of origin; perhaps an Arab merchant had picked it up in a Sogdian marketplace, and at some point it was further traded to a Rus' dealer for its silver content. Rather than being melted down, however, it was kept. Perhaps as a trophy of an adventurous life? Further enhancing the mystery, the Kashmiri Buddha had been buried near an Irish crozier, a Carolingian Frankish sword pommel, an Egyptian Coptic ladle, and a Mediterranean silver dish. Probably deposited in the ground for safekeeping, the Swedish owner did not survive to dig it up again.

The Helgö Buddha.

THE VIKING AGE

As we have seen, Scandinavians began participating in significant inter-regional trade in the 8th century, taking advantage of improved ship keels and beginning to make use of sails. Scandinavians were interested in more than just trade, however. Living in a fragmented world of minor chieftains competing for power, warlords needed both to show their own prowess and to reward their followers. Taking advantage of nautical improvements, they were quick to expand the raiding that had been endemic in northern Europe for many years. Significant attacks on lands bordering the Baltic were well underway by the mid-8th century, as archeology reveals, since we have no written records yet for that region. These Vikings, one of the names given to Scandinavians when they engaged in piracy, soon

BELOW *After repeated Viking attacks, Lindisfarne was abandoned for a time, but recovered and survived until the Dissolution of the Monasteries in the 16th century.*

ABOVE *This Viking-age sword, crafted in the 9th century, was discovered in Oppland, Norway.*

discovered that the more settled lands of Western Europe had much greater accumulated wealth and were ripe for the plucking. Many historians give a very specific date for the start of the Viking Age: 8 June 793, the day Viking raiders attacked the great English monastery of Lindisfarne, on an island off the coast of Northumbria.

Monasteries accumulated wealth, as the pious donated generously to the monks in return for prayers being said for their souls. The monasteries were rich with gold and silver altar adornments, precious book covers and vestments, and were usually storehouses packed with produce and other valuables. As icing on the cake, they were undefended. Monasteries did not need walls because Christians knew they would be damned for attacking them, and monks (and nuns) were forbidden to bear arms. We can only imagine the sensation when the first raiders returned home with the loot of Lindisfarne; that they had an impact is clear from the fact that ever more Viking ships set course for the coasts of

Western Europe—and soon far up rivers—to try to emulate their success.

It was hard to fight Vikings. The first warning of their approach was usually someone spotting their ships from the shore, far too late to send for the armed, trained fighters of a king or local lord. At best, villagers could hope to flee into forests or mountains with some of their goods; if there was no time or place to escape, their goods would be taken, young and attractive people would be seized for sale as slaves, and anyone who resisted would die. Some rulers took strong measures to curb this piracy, Charlemagne in particular creating garrisons along the northern coast and campaigning in the north himself several times. The Vikings, though, simply went elsewhere, opportunistically moving between the British Isles and the Kingdom of the Franks, wherever resistance was weakest.

Vikings returned in large numbers to the western Kingdom of the Franks beginning in 834, when civil war had distracted the nobles

and king who should have been defending their territory against them. Like the Turkic peoples of the steppe, Scandinavians were opportunistic in their approach. They raided, but were perfectly willing to trade their loot. They were also happy to serve as mercenaries for one or other of the warring factions within Francia. An early example of this was in 841, when the west Frankish king Charles the Bald granted the town of Dorestad as a benefice to the Viking Harald and then his brother Rorik. The latter controlled much of Frisia for 30 years, defending it from other raiders on behalf of the Carolingian king. Charles also tried to limit Viking incursions, notably by constructing fortified bridges over the Seine in 862 and the Loire in 873, making it much harder for raiders to push into the interior of his kingdom. The Viking response was to target the kingdoms of England instead.

ABOVE *Excavation of the Gokstad ship, the largest Viking-age vessel yet found, in 1880.*

BELOW *Viking and Magyar invasions of the 9th and 10th centuries.*

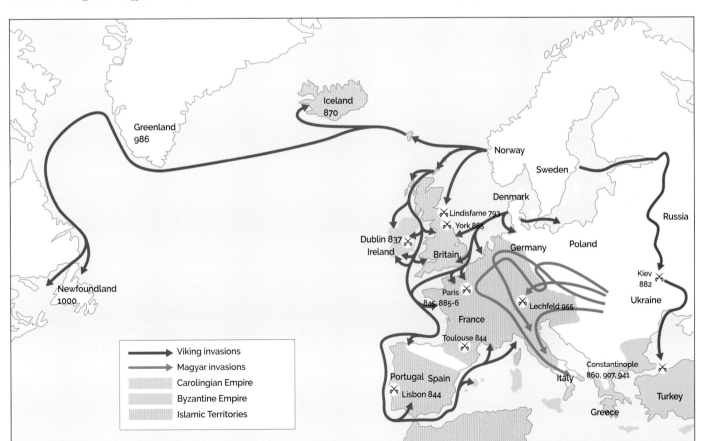

CHRISTENDOM'S RESPONSE

As long as Charlemagne was alive, Viking raiders would make little headway in his empire, despite the temptation of its great wealth. After the great emperor's death in 814, however, the Frankish political situation declined rapidly. Louis the Pious, Charlemagne's sole surviving legitimate son, was able to take power for the most part peacefully, although the tradition of partible inheritance assured that his nephew would rebel against Louis and grab the entire empire. Louis was able to build for a number of years on his father's achievements, continuing to centralize the administration and pushing ahead with a much further-reaching program of moral reform. Naturally, many nobles resented central encroachments on their autonomy, and Louis himself soon gave his discontented subjects a pretext to resist imperial power. Louis played into their hands when, with great formality, he declared how his empire would be divided between his three sons upon his death. But then the widower emperor married again, and Judith, his new wife, soon produced a son. Naturally, Louis wanted the new son, Charles (later nicknamed "the Bald"), to have a share of the Frankish lands, and naturally Charles's older half-brothers resented any effort to steal *their* territories. Noble factions skillfully played the young princes, and, in 829, Francia descended into civil war, sons rebelling against their father and then fighting each other. Louis died in 840, and even after a final partition was agreed upon in 843 with the Treaty of Verdun, the three surviving brothers were happy to encroach on each others' territory if the opportunity presented itself. Only gradually was it accepted that Francia had become two states—France and Germany—with the two eventually gobbling up the middle brother's share,

LEFT *Ruler portrait of Charles the Bald, from the contemporary Metz Psalter.*

the territory known as Lotharingia (Lorraine), named after the eldest brother, Lothar, who held it. More than once, Carolingian rulers hired Vikings to fight against their fellow Christians.

Especially in the western part of the Kingdom of the Franks (which gradually came to be known as "France"), monarchy itself weakened under the combined onslaught of Vikings and Christian rivals. Kings who cannot protect their people earn little respect, and weak acts, as in 886 when Charles the Fat paid the Vikings to raise their siege of Paris, garnered contempt. The emphasis was on local defense, and increasingly people rallied to a local lord—anyone with a fortified castle—who could keep them safe. It was in this period that most free peasants lost their rights, signing away their personal liberty in return for protection. The result was the gradual creation of a class of serfs, women and men with personal freedom but legally bound to the land, as the free peasantry's status was depressed and that of the large, enslaved populace actually improved somewhat as the two formerly distinct classes merged. The legally unfree status of serfs over time became the norm in other regions as well. Local strongmen maintained a force of professional fighters, increasingly turning to armored cavalrymen who could respond quickly to raids, and were often laws unto themselves.

The Viking attacks could also serve as the rallying point for centralization. Nowhere was this true to such a high degree as in the kingdoms of what is now England. The initial confusion of the Germanic invasions had led gradually to

the consolidation of five to seven independent kingdoms, frequently weakened by conflict with each other and succession disputes. And then came the Great Heathen Army, as contemporary chroniclers named it. A force of several thousand Vikings, led by at least three petty kings, arrived on the island in 865 and set out on a path not just of devastation but conquest and rule. In 866–7,

RIGHT *Winchester was the heart of the kingdom of Wessex; this 1901 bronze statue by Sir W. Hamo Thornycroft commemorates Alfred the Great's achievements.*

the Great Army conquered the kingdom of Northumbria, moving on in 869 to East Anglia. Mercia soon followed, and attacks began against the strongest of the states, Wessex.

Wessex nearly fell to the relentless Viking attacks, but the West Saxons were soon rallied by an extraordinary king, Alfred (871–99). He fought the Scandinavians to a stalemate in the Battle of Edington (878); unable to force the Great Army from the other English kingdoms they had seized, at least Alfred opened the door to future better relations when the remaining Viking king, Guthrum, agreed to baptism. For the rest of his reign, Alfred fought off recurrent Viking attacks, his people accepting extraordinary burdens in the cause, most notably building and garrisoning a series of fortified places of refuge, the *burhs*, throughout Wessex. The West Saxon king sponsored a small renaissance of learning in which, unusually, he encouraged the translation of Latin works into Old English so that semi-literate clergy could learn to read them more easily. And Alfred began the process, completed by his grandson, of refashioning the tattered English kingdoms into a single country, England, presenting himself as the spokesman for all Englishmen and women, including those under Scandinavian rule.

Trade and Raid in the Mediterranean

As the Scandinavians made the North Sea and Baltic a more vibrant—and dangerous—region for commerce, a similar process was taking place in the Mediterranean. A number of small Muslim emirates came to specialize in piracy, their lightning raids against Italy and southern France every bit as audacious as those of the Vikings further north; the Leonine Walls around the Vatican City were constructed in 848–52 to protect St. Peter's Basilica from these "Saracen" incursions, since the Vatican Hill lay outside Rome's ancient walls. Like the Vikings, Muslims also engaged in trade, and a number of port cities of Italy began their rise as commercial centers in this period. Chief among them was Venice.

Venetian merchants were trading in Egypt by the 820s. We know this because of one of history's more audacious thefts, when Venetians stole the relics of the evangelist St. Mark in 829. The sailors went to pray at Mark's tomb during their stay in Alexandria, and decided the prestigious saint's relics belonged in a Christian land rather than languishing under Muslim rule. So, they broke into the church one night and stole Mark's bones. The church's clergy naturally complained, but the Venetians successfully smuggled the relics out of the city by hiding them in a barrel of pork, which the Muslims were naturally unwilling to examine closely. St. Mark arrived in Venice in triumph, where he remains the patron saint of the "City of St. Mark."

A Venetian bronze winged lion, symbol of the evangelist St. Mark.

BULGHARS AND SLAVS

In some of the vast territory inhabited by Slavic-speakers, larger states formed, sometimes under the rule of newcomers to the region, as Slavs tried to protect themselves from the depredations of more powerful neighbors. Two important examples of this phenomenon from the 9th century are the state of Kyivan Rus' and the first Bulgar Empire. The Scandinavian Rus' people, as they pushed into the territory of modern Ukraine, never constituted more than a small minority of the population, although for generations Scandinavian adventurers reinforced their military. The Rus' princes ruled over a largely Slavic populace and soon began to adopt the Slavic language and culture for themselves. Similarly, the Bulghars began as a nomadic Turkic people. As they moved south into Europe, they gradually became known as "Bulgars" and the territory they settled is today known as Bulgaria. Ruling over a much larger Slavic population, however, they soon became cultural and linguistic Slavs.

BELOW *Monument to Kyi, Shchek, Khoryv, and their sister Lybid, legendary founders of Kyiv, by Vasiliy Boroday and Nicolay Feshenko.*

ABOVE *A 14th-century painting of Khan Krum banqueting after his victory over the Byzantines.*

By the early 9th century, the Bulgars were strong enough to cause concern to their Byzantine neighbors. The dynamic khan Krum (d. 814) incorporated part of the Avar realm into his own growing empire. By 811, the Byzantine emperor, Nicephorus I, planned a great campaign against the Bulgars, rejecting Krum's efforts to make peace. Krum then proved his mettle, trapping Nicephorus's army in a major ambush. Much of the Byzantine army died, including Nicephorus himself; the emperor's skull was made into a drinking bowl for the khan. The new emperor also refused Krum's peace overtures, so Krum stormed the Byzantine fort of Debeltos and in 813 plundered the suburbs of Constantinople itself before sacking Adrianople. Relations between the two states only became rather more peaceful when Khan Boris I of Bulgaria was forced to submit and accept baptism and allow Byzantine clergy into his country after a campaign in 864. Although after that point the Bulgarian elite picked up many elements of Byzantine culture— Tsar Symeon (d. 927) had even studied in Constantinople for a decade before coming to the throne—the Bulgars remained a frequent threat until Byzantium succeeded in conquering them at the dawn of the 11th century.

Byzantine diplomacy was more successful with other Slavic groups. Most notably, Moravia had probably coalesced as a major state of eastern Europe because of the Frankish threat to their west, and the Moravian princes were content to negotiate with the Byzantines as a counterweight to the Carolingians. The

Moravians began converting to Christianity in the 830s, but the process was pushed forward when their prince, Rostislav, requested missionaries be sent from Constantinople to avoid the domination of the nearby Latin Christians. The brothers Cyril (Constantine) and Methodius were dispatched. Although the German bishops of the frontier protested their activities, even capturing Methodius in 870 to keep him away from the disputed territory, the mission was unique in receiving the blessing of both the pope and the patriarch of Constantinople. With the patriarch's encouragement, the brothers created Glagolitic script to write Slavic, introduced a Slavonic liturgy, and began the translation of the Bible into Old Slavonic; Cyril and Methodius are regarded as the founders of Christianity among the Slavic peoples.

THE DECLINE OF THE ABBASID CALIPHATE

As we have seen, the Islamic world had a voracious appetite for slaves, employing those enslaved in a wide variety of contexts. It was this reliance on slaves—especially on Turkish enslaved soldiers—that over the course of the 9th century stripped the caliphs of much of their power. The decline was abrupt. Harun al-Rashid (d. 809) was immensely powerful and wealthy; he reportedly possessed more than 2,000 female enslaved people—concubines, servants, and musicians—in his harem. All was not well in the caliphate, though, which maintained a military and court establishment out of all proportion to the state's real wealth. Economic tensions were clear in the "revolt of the naked" in Baghdad shortly after Harun's death, so called because the poorest of the poor rose in rebellion against the government they thought should be providing them with some relief. But it was Harun's misguided plans for the succession that precipitated a real political decline. Harun favored not one but two sons, declaring one to be his immediate heir but designating the younger as his brother's successor, assigning him a large, effectively autonomous province to hold during his brother's reign. The elder brother, al-Amin, then tried to undermine Ma'mun, preferring that his own son rather than a brother succeed him. The two drifted into war by 810, only a year after their father's death. Al-Amin was killed in 813 but the civil war continued, with key courtiers jockeying for power in Baghdad and rebels proclaiming yet another brother as caliph.

Ma'mun eventually triumphed, but was forced to rely on still another brother (the dangers of unrestrained polygamy were particularly clear after Harun's death), who in 833 took the throne as Caliph al-Mu'tasim. He had begun to build up a corps of military slaves in 814/15, buying Turkic

BELOW *An early 9th-century wood panel from Iraq, featuring the six-pointed star common to Islamic art of the period.*

ABOVE *Now an empty shell, the Great Mosque and minaret of Samarra, Iraq, was for a time the largest in the world. It was destroyed by the Mongols in 1278.*

adolescents who were trained and disciplined into a highly effective fighting force of 3–4,000 men. While technically enslaved men, the members of this corps were privileged and wealthy. Their sense of privilege caused tensions to escalate in Baghdad so far that Mu'tasim began construction of a new capital, Samarra, to house his Turks and the rest of his administration; the court only returned to Baghdad in 892.

Once created, this Turkish military elite proved to be unstoppable. Caliph al-Mutawakkil tried to end his reliance on them, arranging the

assassination of their most powerful Turkish officer. It is hardly surprising that the Turks felt their position threatened; they rose in a desperate coup and murdered the caliph in 861. From then on, a clique of Turkish generals controlled the government, a series of coups placing their preferred caliphs on the throne. If a caliph proved obdurate, he was replaced, as in 869 when the troops abused Caliph Mu'tazz, forced him to abdicate, and then starved him to death. By the late 9th century, demands from the military along with the caliphs' ambitious

building projects had drained the Abbasid treasury. The provincial administration left unpaid by the central government, local warlords or former governors took control of Islam's provinces. The process began as early as the civil war at the start of the century, when the rebel Babik succeeded in establishing an independent state in Azerbaijan that endured for about 20 years. Sometimes, breakaway provinces even increased the lands under Muslim rule, most notably when Arab pirates took Crete in 828, and in the slow conquest of Sicily by the emirs of Ifriqiya (828–902).

Despite political chaos, the 9th century remained a golden age for Islamic learning. In 830, Caliph al-Ma'mun established the House of Wisdom in Baghdad, a research center and library to translate and develop the works of Greek medicine, philosophy, and mathematics. Two of the greatest intellectuals of the age were Ibn Musa al-Khwarizmi (c. 780–c. 850), and Abu Ma'shar (787–886). Al-Khwarizmi was a Persian mathematician who was appointed head of the House of Wisdom's library in 820, famed for his development of algebra—he even coined the

LEFT *Modern statue of the Iranian revolutionary Babik, who died in 838, in Khorramdin, Azerbaijan.*

words algebra and algorithm. Abu Ma'shar was a major astronomer and philosopher of Baghdad who had a deep influence on both Islamic and Christian intellectual history. It was also an important age for historiography. The major historian Muhammad ibn Jarir al-Tabari, who flourished in the second half of the 9th century, also took advantage of Baghdad's intellectual atmosphere to write his *History of the Prophets and Kings*, as well as an enormous commentary on the Qur'an.

The Revolt of the Zanj (869–883)

While Turks supplied the core of later Abbasid armies, the preferred agricultural enslaved people were brought from East Africa; slave raids into the African interior provided one of the important early exports of the Swahili states. Large numbers of these East African enslaved people, known as the Zanj, were employed to reclaim the marshland of southern Iraq, the only part of the Islamic world with large-scale agricultural enslavement. Living and dying under brutal conditions, the Zanj were ripe for rebellion when a Shi'ite Arab, 'Ali bin Muhammad, began preaching among them, proclaiming that the enslaved would be free and rich and their masters punished. The Zanj rose in revolt, soon joined by many Arab and Persian malcontents. Their rebellion was the most successful slave rising in history before the Haitian revolution, creating an independent Shi'ite state and proclaiming their inspirational leader as the *mahdi*, the messianic leader expected to come at the end of time to cleanse the world of evil. It took a four-year war (879–83) to bring down the would-be state.

A 13th-century slave market in Yemen.

ANOTHER BLOW TO CENTRAL GOVERNMENT: TANG CHINA

The Tang Dynasty's ability to govern practically dissolved by the end of the 9th century. On the face of it, it is hard to see why. In particular, China's two greatest external threats, the Uighur and Tibetan Empires, had both collapsed by mid-century. The Uighurs had extorted a great deal from the Tang government in the wake of An Lushan's rebellion, demanding vast quantities of silk in return for providing horses—often of very poor quality—for the Chinese military. But the Uighurs had gradually become more interested in commerce than military endeavor; their adoption of Manichaeism is a symptom of that refocused interest. They had come to dominate the money-lending profession in China, where their arrogance and contempt for the law made them hated. There was probably widespread relief in China when bloody power struggles broke out in the Uighur court in 832, followed by a major revolt of their Kirghiz subjects. When the Kirghiz sacked the Uighur capital in 840, the Uighur peoples scattered in all directions; those who sought refuge in China were mostly slaughtered. Tibet's decline was not as spectacular but was nearly as thorough. Facing economic difficulties, provinces began to break away from the central government by the mid-9th century; the beginning of the end was when the Tibetan leader U'i Dum brtan was assassinated in 842 and the dynasty split between two rival factions.

The Tang government was weakened by factionalism, however, especially the growing power of the court eunuchs, several thousand castrated men who increasingly held key administrative positions in competition with the traditional scholar-elite. Early in the century Emperor Xianzong (805–20), known as "the Restorer," strove with some success to re-establish control over the provinces, only to be murdered by two eunuchs. No successor was strong enough to hold the system in balance. In 827, eunuchs murdered another emperor, Jingzong, and when his heir tried to curb the eunuchs' power his only recourse was to plot the assassination of their leaders. When the plot was uncovered, Emperor

BELOW *A demonic figure from the complex of rock-cut caves at Bezeklik, China, one of hundreds of Buddhist murals.*

LEFT *A Uighur king and his attendants, a mural from Mogao Caves.*

Wenzong was left powerless in the hands of his own household slaves. Successive emperors with little real power turned instead to luxuries and esoteric religious practices; a number of emperors were accidentally poisoned in their search for drugs that would extend their lifespans.

With central control faltering and massive exactions to support the court, a wave of rebellions and mutinies of unpaid soldiers began in 858. Large bandit armies destroyed whole cities. Most notable was the bandit army of Huang Chao, active from 878 to 884. Huang Chao, a salt merchant turned highway robber, appealed to his followers' xenophobia, targeting foreign merchants as his army sacked a series of cities. In 879, the bandit army took Guangzho, massacring a reputed 120,000 foreign merchants; Huang Chao also ordered the felling of mulberry trees in the hope of upsetting the lucrative silk trade. In 881, the bandits sacked the capital Chang'an itself in an orgy of mass slaughter and looting. Huang Chao's rebellion was finally suppressed in 884 with the help of the Shatuo Turks, but the Tang emperors never succeeded in regaining control of their country. By the time the dynasty officially ended in 907, a power vacuum had existed for 30 years.

Probably the only people who benefited from the Tang decline were the peoples of Southeast Asia. Vietnam had been a Chinese colony for a thousand years, rebelling repeatedly and resisting all efforts to force assimilation. Annan in the northern part of the peninsula was able to break free as an independent kingdom in the course of the 9th century. Also taking advantage when Chinese interventionism faltered, the kingdom of Angkor was established in Cambodia in 802, founded by Jayavarman II.

BELOW *Mural celebrating the Tang Dynasty's victory over the Tibetan Empire in 848, from the Mogao Caves.*

ABOVE *The great Mahayana Buddhist temple at Borobudur, Indonesia, constructed during the Sailendra Dynasty.*

The Great Persecution

East Asian religions have no notion of "exclusive truth," and Chinese rulers had mostly been happy to welcome new religions as long as they were not harmful to the state. The great exception to this general attitude of toleration occurred in 842–5, when Emperor Wuzong proscribed the foreign religions operating in China. The persecution practically destroyed the Western-influenced religions—Christianity, Mazdaism, and Manichaeism—in China, and crippled the much more omnipresent Buddhism. Unlike the Western religions, Buddhism had taken deep root in China, and the imperial edict led to the expropriation of more than 4,600 monasteries, temples, and estates. More than 260,000 Buddhist monks and nuns were laicized, rendered liable to pay taxes. Only one Buddhist temple was to be allowed per prefecture, with four in each of the main capitals; each could house at most 30 monks or nuns.

Several reasons lay behind the persecution. The Neo-Confucian reaction against Buddhism as fundamentally un-Chinese had developed strength after the turn of the century. Xenophobia in general was on the rise in China, as An Lushan's rebellion had inspired wariness of foreigners and Manichaean Uighur moneylenders were as popular as moneylenders always are. Most important, however, was the government's growing financial desperation. The Buddhist monasteries and temples were wealthy and monastic estates enjoyed privileged tax status. The suppression of Buddhism allowed for massive confiscations, allowing the empire to operate for a time in the black.

CHAPTER 5

Great States of the 10th Century: Ideal and Reality

Even in the modern world it is difficult to keep large states intact. Those difficulties were magnified in the medieval millennium, when news could travel only as quickly as a horse could gallop—and usually much slower than that. The 10th century, however, saw particularly rapid transformations as external threats served as a pressure-cooker for change. China faced the challenge of invasion by the semi-nomadic Khitan, the rising confidence of Kyivan Rus' threatened Byzantium, and the German state consolidated to face the threat of the Magyars, even as England centralized in the wake of the Viking Great Army. Other states simply failed to live up to the challenge of central power, as the caliphate continued to weaken and the caliphs fell under the "protection" of a Turkish dynasty or simply lost territory to rivals. A particularly interesting case study is also provided by Japan, as its early promise of a strongly centralized government under divinely descended emperors faltered in the 10th century.

RIGHT *Song Dynasty officials, a mural in Tiankuang Hall of the massive Dai Temple in Shandong Province.*

THE CURRENTS OF WORLD CLIMATE

The 10th century saw the beginning of a meteorological shift known as the Medieval Climate Anomaly. It was an era of lower global volcanic activity, which, combined with greater solar radiation, meant warmer temperatures in much of the world. The weather for the next three centuries was on the whole kind to most of Europe, as it was to the parts of Asia affected by the monsoons, whose regularity in this period allowed considerable agricultural growth. The same was true especially of Northern Europe, where the large-scale

BELOW *The Aksum Stelae, dating to the 4th century, continued to attest to Aksum's greatness during its long decline.*

clearance of woodland and marsh was underway by *c.* 950 and demographic and economic growth continued until the 14th century.

By contrast, the eastern Mediterranean, Middle East, and Central Asia suffered frequent droughts in this and succeeding centuries. Egypt in particular, for many centuries the breadbasket of a very large region, suffered catastrophic famines in the 960s and again in the 1020s and *c.* 1200. It is probably not a coincidence that the kingdom of Aksum (modern Ethiopia) collapsed in *c.* 960. The kingdom had flourished at the start of the medieval period, most notably in the 6th-century reign of King Kaleb, but a long decline had already begun in the 7th century. Above all, Aksum's rulers had lost control of the Red Sea, first to the Persians and then to the Islamic caliphate. Left with few resources, the ruling Dynasty could not stand out against the Jewish queen Judith (or Gudit) who invaded and devastated the region. Droughts also affected both northern and central Africa. These weather

patterns caused great hardship that should be remembered as the backdrop to political events in both Asia and Africa, as governments wrung more in taxes from subsistence farmers and the failure of grasslands often drove nomads to attack their sedentary neighbors.

Although not nomadic, climate-induced hardship was probably also an important factor in the Polynesian conquest of Oceania. The Polynesians reached Tahiti, the Marquesas, and the Northern Cook Islands in the 10th century. By *c.* 1000 they were settling the Hawaiian Islands and had discovered Easter Island by 1050. The last of the islands of Oceania to receive Polynesian colonists was New Zealand, in *c.* 1200.

Of all world regions, the Medieval Climate Anomaly had the most dire effect on the western coastal area of the Americas. Strong La Niña conditions prevailed, throwing much of the American West into almost perpetual drought for 400 years (900–1300). Especially hard-hit were the developed sedentary communities in what

BELOW *The Polynesian migrations.*

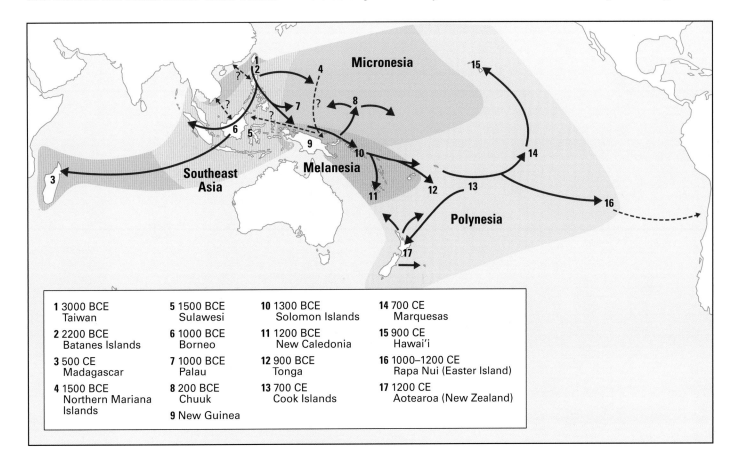

1 3000 BCE Taiwan	**5** 1500 BCE Sulawesi	**10** 1300 BCE Solomon Islands	**14** 700 CE Marquesas
2 2200 BCE Batanes Islands	**6** 1000 BCE Borneo	**11** 1200 BCE New Caledonia	**15** 900 CE Hawai'i
3 500 CE Madagascar	**7** 1000 BCE Palau	**12** 900 BCE Tonga	**16** 1000–1200 CE Rapa Nui (Easter Island)
4 1500 BCE Northern Mariana Islands	**8** 200 BCE Chuuk **9** New Guinea	**13** 700 CE Cook Islands	**17** 1200 CE Aotearoa (New Zealand)

is now the southwestern United States. Chaco (see Chapter 3) declined as it became ever more difficult to feed its population, until the site was finally abandoned in the early 12th century. At first the Ancestral Pueblo congregated for defense against predator neighbors at Mesa Verde, but then abandoned the plateau by *c.* 1300. Further south, the Maya did not disappear, but some cities failed in favor of others better able to buffer their populace from the challenges of the age. Most notably, in the 10th century the Itzá people rose to be the most powerful Maya state in alliance with coastal traders. Their capital, Chichén Itzá, was a major center that adopted much of the religious and political symbolism of the Toltec capital, Tula, which became a major confederation in its own right in the later 10th century. Further south, the Andean Chimú Empire developed in the same period. Its position as a major state probably owes much to the need to organize large-scale irrigation. Only a central authority could arrange public works like the 50-mile-long (80 km) La Cumbre canal.

BELOW *Mesa Verde, Colorado, one of the best-preserved settlements of the Ancestral Pueblo.*

ABOVE The Temple of Kukulcán, also known as El Castillo, dominates the ruins of the Maya city of Chichén Itzá on the Yucatán Peninsula in Mexico.

LEFT Chan Chan Peru, the largest mud-brick city of the world, capital of the Chimú Empire.

CHINA DIMINISHED

China was the greatest state of the medieval millennium. Its emperors ruled as much as a third of the earth's population (about 80 million people in the 10th century), maintaining a complex bureaucratic system of which rulers elsewhere could barely dream. China's widespread literacy, extremely productive agricultural systems, and bustling middle class all help justify the sometimes-smug condescension with which the medieval Chinese elites viewed the "barbarians" of the rest of the world. Yet, despite the vast reach of imperial government, it proved impossible to maintain a single, unified state.

As we have seen, the Tang Dynasty ended in 907. One of many rebels, Zhu Wen, seized the capital in 901, in 905 killing the emperor and most of his family and placing a puppet on the throne. In 907, however, he declared himself

first emperor of the new Liang Dynasty. The usurpation was ambitious but incomplete. By 907, the Chinese empire was divided among at least ten warlords, most of whom were peasants or robbers and at least one of whom was a former slave. The following period of confusion, which lasted 907–60, is known as the period of Five Dynasties and Ten Kingdoms, as the many faction leaders sought to reunite China under *their* personal control.

China's chaos provided an opportunity for a semi-nomadic people of the frontier, the Khitans, to rise to prominence. The Khitans united under a single khagan, Abaoji, in 907. By the time of his death in 926, Abaoji had conquered Mongolia and the East Asian kingdom of Parhae, and after his death his widow Yingtian executed the great Khitan plan to invade northern China, seizing control of 16 prefectures on China's

BELOW *Yingxian Wooden Pagoda, Fogong Temple, China, originally built in 1056.*

Khitan Women

Khitan society was patriarchal, but women could control wealth and elite women held civil and military commands as a matter of course, as was typical in the nomadic societies of Central Asia. The empresses of the Liao Dynasty should be regarded as co-rulers, especially Yingtian, who ruled with Abaoji and then controlled the state until her own death, displacing their unworthy eldest son in favor of his younger brother. Yingtian had to break gender norms even among the Khitan to seize such a prominent role as a widow. When Abaoji died, tradition dictated that his wife die and be buried with him. But Yingtian refused on the grounds that her children needed her, instead cutting off her own right hand to be entombed with her husband.

Khitan women during the Liao Dynasty, from a Khitan tomb on Mount Pao.

The freedom of Khitan women was a matter of scandal for the Chinese, and Confucian scholars condemned the nomads' supposed immorality for allowing their women so much freedom of movement. It is probably not a coincidence that it was in the 10th century, a period of active resentment and fear of nomads, that the foot-binding of girls became popular in China. Over the following centuries, millions of Chinese girls were purposely crippled by having the arches of their feet systematically broken so it would be difficult for them to walk and they could thus be regarded as virtuous.

side of the crumbling Great Wall. And there the Khitans remained for centuries, Abaoji's descendants creating a dual administration of their nomadic and sedentary subjects known as the Liao Dynasty. For centuries, the restored Chinese government to the south resented and resisted Liao control of the 16 prefectures, but was ultimately forced to pay the Khitans a large annual tribute of 100,000 ounces of silver and 200,000 bolts of silk (about 1,500 miles, or 2,400 km, of cloth when unwound) to ward off further conquest.

Both Korea and Vietnam also took advantage of Chinese weakness in the 10th century. In Korea, the Silla state had controlled the whole country since 668. But a new kingdom called

Goryeo (918–1392) rose to prominence in the 10th century, and its pressure forced the last king of Silla to abdicate in 935. Unlike Korea, Vietnam had been under direct Chinese control for several hundred years, but the Dai Viet leader Ngo Quyen seized the opportunity provided by the Tang Dynasty's collapse, triumphing over the regional Chinese forces in the Battle of the Bach Dang River in 938. Ngo Quyen established a capital at Co Loa (near modern Hanoi), keeping much of the political structure he inherited from the Chinese. The path of state genesis was not easy, however. When Ngo Quyen died in 944 a great power struggle ensued, known as the War of the Twelve Warlords. In 968, the head of the winning clan, Dinh Bo Linh, established a

RIGHT *Rafter finial shaped as a dragon's head, the hanger for a wind chime. Early Goryeo period, Korea.*

new dynasty, only to have the first king and his eldest son assassinated in 979. China's newly established Song Dynasty tried to reconquer the lost province, but the Great Viet State (Dai Co Viet) survived both that and a naval attack by the Southeast Asian Cham state in 979. In 982, the Viets destroyed Indrapura, the Cham capital, and future Chinese efforts to reannex Vietnam—by the Song, Yuan, and Ming dynasties—all failed.

It took 20 years of fighting for the Song Dynasty (960–1279) to reunify most of China. The founding emperor, Zhao Kuangyin, had been commander of the Zhou palace guard; his regnal name is Song Taizu. His resolve to regain China's northern territory from the Khitans won him the backing of key army leaders, although legend reports that once he was established on the throne the emperor forced those senior generals to retire and live in luxury in the capital, where they could be watched carefully. That action sums up the Song Dynasty very well: although the entire

BELOW *Tomb of Ngo Quyen, founding king of Vietnam's Ngo Dynasty (939–44).*

LEFT *Taizu, founding emperor of the Song Dynasty (d. 976).*

span of the dynasty was a time of unprecedented external threat, the Song emperors emphatically did not trust the military, perhaps having learned the lesson of An Lushan's rebellion too well. The Song built up a massive military establishment, by *c.* 1020 maintaining a million-man standing army; the military cost about three-quarters of the entire annual tax revenues of the state. The soldiers were recruited for life and served into their sixties. They were not kept under military discipline, however, and for the most part provided a pool of laborers for state projects. The Song never recovered the 16 prefectures that the Liao Dynasty ruled.

The Song also invested in a new and promising military technology—gunpowder. Daoist alchemists discovered the formula for exploding powder in their quest for an elixir of eternal life, but soon discovered that the "fire medicine" they compounded was a tool for death rather than life. In the 10th century the discovery began to be utilized for military purposes, first

with fire arrows, and by 969 ignited to propel arrows down tubes, the earliest form of gun. The first Song emperor fully recognized the potential of the invention, and in 975 the Song navy made devastatingly effective use of fire arrows and incendiary bombs to destroy an enemy fleet on the Yangzi, the final stage of the wars of unification. By the 11th century, the government maintained large factories to produce gunpowder and gunpowder weapons; an extant source from 1083 tells of 100,000 gunpowder arrows sent to a single garrison, with 250,000 dispatched to another. By the 13th century, the Chinese military was even using hard-shell explosives.

The Song maintained a highly advanced bureaucracy, providing greater central control than ever before with an entire nervous system of control and command. In a world otherwise heavily reliant on hereditary privilege, the Song civil service was a meritocracy. The first Song emperor institutionalized civil service exams. Candidates for government office were tested for their mastery of what was essentially a liberal arts curriculum, including poetry-writing and calligraphy, but above all on their understanding of the great classics of Confucianism. Qualifying exams were held in each prefecture; by the end of the 11th century, about 80,000 young men took the prefectural exams each year. A higher-level examination was then carried out by the Ministry of Rites, after which the emperor himself tested the very top candidates. The mass of the poor could not of course afford the education needed for the examinations, but study was surprisingly within the reach of perhaps as much as a fifth of the populace, thanks to village school teachers,

BELOW *Guanyin Pavilion at Dule Buddhist Temple (the Temple of Solitary Joy) in Tianjin, China.*

prefectural Confucian schools, and the fact that woodblock printing on paper had reduced the cost of books by about nine-tenths. The system, with its enormous emphasis on the ethics of government and social life, produced many generations of competent officials. Although the system did not encourage innovative thought, these highly-educated administrators did introduce some significant improvements, including the revolutionary introduction of paper money in 1024.

ABOVE *A Song-Dynasty inkstone.*

BELOW Literary Garden, *a masterpiece of China's Five Dynasties period, by Zhou Wenju.*

JAPAN'S SPECIAL WAY

Although eager to embrace many ideas and technologies from the mainland, the Japanese islands charted their own unique course through the medieval millennium. Despite cultural contacts with Korea and China, Japan was relatively isolated; the virulence of its Great Smallpox Epidemic (735–7) suggests a lack of earlier exposure, for instance. As we have seen, in the 7th century Japan's rulers imposed a central government modeled on that of China, buttressing an apparently strong and highly venerated monarchy, its members claiming descent from the sun goddess Amaterasu. Perhaps that central authority was always more illusion than reality, however. The emperors made no effort to undermine Japan's strong hereditary nobility. The long wars to conquer the Emishi populace of the northeast in the later 8th century—with repeated revolts for centuries thereafter—also put a high priority on military rule in the northeastern province, allowing regional authorities great autonomy. It is really in the 10th century, though, that we can see how Chinese political ideas, implemented by a very different culture, could lead to very different results.

The central power of the Japanese state showed great promise in the 8th and into the 9th century. The Chinese-style capital Nara was founded in 710, giving its name to a period of Japanese history that forcibly implemented Chinese-modeled rule. The Nara state began ambitious projects, such as minting coins for the first time in 708. The rulers, however, failed to impose a true money economy, continuing to collect taxes in kind. Emulating China, the throne also provided large-scale patronage and encouragement to Buddhism, as in 741 when Emperor Shomu ordered the establishment of a Buddhist temple and nunnery in each province, staffed by clerics from the capital. The Great

BELOW *The Eastern Great Temple (*Todai-ji*) Buddhist temple complex in Nara, Japan. Originally constructed in the 8th century, it has been rebuilt several times.*

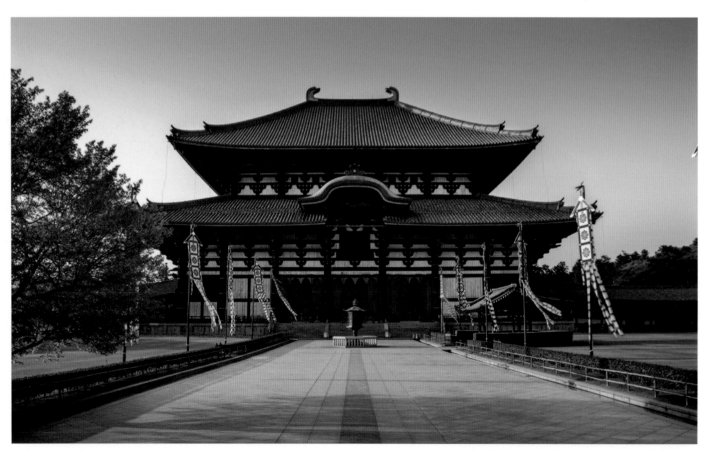

Eastern Temple in Nara (Todaiji), completed in 752, is still the largest wooden building in the world. But Japan's rulers were less successful than their Chinese counterparts (and those elsewhere in Asia) at controlling the Buddhist establishment they encouraged so strongly. Shomu and his daughter and successor Koken were criticized for their lavish support of Buddhism, Koken in particular giving excessive privileges to the monk Dokyo, a reputed magician who became *de facto* chancellor and ruthlessly destroyed his enemies. When Koken (known in her second reign, after a period of abdication, as Shotoku) died in 770, Dokyo actually tried to take the throne for himself.

LEFT *16th-century portrait of Emperor Kammu.*

BELOW *Tobatsu Bishamonten, Japan's Guardian King of the North, depicted in Chinese armor (Heian period).*

The move of the capital to Heian-kyo (later known as Kyoto) in 794 shows an even stronger drive toward centralization, Emperor Kammu building on a larger scale, revitalizing the Tang-based administrative system, and asserting the throne's absolute authority. But like the Nara state, the Heian period suffered from significant weaknesses. Kammu issued more than 30 decrees trying to correct the Buddhist clergy's abuses, including money-lending at exorbitant interest rates and practicing black magic. After Kammu's death in 806, the Buddhist clergy were soon as entrenched as ever. The great secular wealth and power of the monasteries—and their tax-exempt status—made them an increasingly autonomous force that the imperial government could not control. As the 10th century progressed, the monasteries increasingly used force when their interests were threatened, many of the monks themselves bearing arms. The first large-scale incident came in 940, when 56 monks got into a fight protesting the appointment of an official of whom they did not approve. More common than actual force, though, was intimidation, thousands of monks surrounding a building and refusing to leave until their demands were met.

A major reason for the limited government response was a significant failure of the imperial government itself. Already at the end of the 8th century, the government was spending considerably more than its revenues, ambitious building projects and the war

with the Emishi exacerbating tax declines as the Japanese population sank. Unable to pay officials what they thought they deserved, the state civil service—exam-based like that of China—was faltering by the start of the 10th century. More ominously, the authority of (although not the reverence for) the emperor was disrupted. It started in 842 with the Jowa Incident, when a major noble clan leader, Fujiwara no Yoshifusa, successfully deposed the crown prince, replacing him with the previous emperor's son by a Fujiwara woman. This inaugurated a long period of dominance by the Fujiwara clan, as for several generations they arranged for daughters of the family to marry emperors, then assured that it was a son carrying Fujiwara blood who succeeded, with the head of the clan doing the actual ruling. Child emperors became common; until the 1090s more than half of those that ascended to the throne were aged 12 or younger. The Fujiwara gradually excluded the other clans from the senior state offices so that, for example, in 1028 22 out of the 25 senior ministers were Fujiwaras, with the other three related by marriage. When emperors came of age, they had little choice but to leave rule in the hands of the deeply entrenched Fujiwara, rather like the relationship between the Frankish Merovingian Dynasty and their Carolingian mayors of the palace.

The state also failed to rein in the autonomy of large secular estates, the *shoen*. The *shoen* had their start with government incentives for landlords who cleared wasteland, providing tax exemptions and allowing the nobles who owned them to develop an independent military establishment, which they used to keep order on the estate and to resist encroachment, whether from other *shoen* or from provincial governors. These militarized states became a law unto themselves. By the 930s, they formed networks of leading regional warriors, a practice that at first the government opposed, but soon supported. Thus began the age of the *bushi*, military professionals (often misleadingly called "Samurai" in English-language accounts). The new professional military class replaced the

national army of the 8th century, an infantry force made up of peasant conscripts. Japan's "military revolution" of the 9th century saw the creation of bands of mounted, heavily-armored archers as the key military force. Some served the state's military and police structures, but they coexisted with their privately-employed fellows.

Lawlessness spread from the *shoen*-owners to officials and even to the imperial clan itself. Emblematic is the case of Fujiwara no Sumitomo, who had held office as a minor official but turned pirate starting in 936. In 939, he seized a vice-governor, mutilating him, killing his son, and

carrying off his wife. The government's response at first was to try to appease the pirate with offers of rank; he was only defeated militarily in 941. This burst of piracy coincided with what is known as the "Discord of the Johei and Tengyo Eras" (931–47), when a member of the imperial clan, Taira no Masakado, rebelled and tried to proclaim himself emperor. The rebellion was only suppressed when the central government enlisted the help of the *shoen*, confirming their wealth and military strength in the process. The warriors had clearly emerged as an independent political force by the mid-10th century.

A PARALLEL CASE: THE DECLINE OF THE CALIPHATE

Tenth-century Japan demonstrates that, even when stripped of the reality of political power, many states were unwilling to take the final step of actually deposing the person on the throne. In Japan, universal belief in the emperor's divine descent provided vital protection; individual emperors might be pressured to abdicate, but the dynasty itself continued, and endures to this day. In the Islamic world, caliphs could claim no divine descent, but the notion that the office of caliph was divinely ordained was strongly embedded in society. Even when the caliphs had little real power, they continued to assert influence and received respect. As the 10th century progressed, their longevity increased, as long as they did not set themselves against the men with true power. The only real challenge they faced was the specter of rival caliphs, the Umayyads still controlling Spain and a new, Shi'ite-led caliphate emerging in Egypt.

The Abbasid caliphate as it had existed proved to be unsustainable with the rule of Caliph al-Muqtadir (908–32). The first child caliph, he was purposely chosen for the throne because he was a weakling, and throughout his disastrous reign his advisors manipulated, exploited, and

deceived him. All of the advances of al-Muqtadir's predecessors unraveled, as Iraq's devastated agricultural lands could not support the state's ambitions. The region's elaborate system of irrigation canals required constant maintenance, which they did not receive; they never recovered.

BELOW *Caliph al-Muqtadir (d. 932) from the* Zubdet-ut Tevarih, *a genealogical work compiled in 1598.*

RIGHT *Gold ewer inscribed with the name of Buyid ruler Abu Mansur, an Iranian work of the later 10th century.*

Al-Muqtadir himself was murdered in a coup, and the Abbasid government could not recover from the ensuing anarchy, which included even the rebel Mardavij ibn Ziyar's effort to restore Sasanian rule and Zoroastrianism. Finally, in 946 the head of the Persian Buyid Dynasty, already established as the ruler of western Iran, occupied Baghdad. He retained the caliph as a puppet ruler, but from then until the end of the caliphate the caliph remained a mere figurehead. It was an odd compliment to the Abbasid clan that the Buyids made no attempt to replace them, even though the Buyids themselves were Shi'ites and the Abbasids had long been firmly on the Sunni side of the theological divide.

The Buyid "protectorate" was unable to prevent a Byzantine resurgence that pushed deep into Islamic territory, in the 960s regaining Tarsus and Antioch, which had been under Muslim rule for more than 300 years. Under a series of militant emperors, several of whom seized the throne in coups, Byzantium moved from strength to strength, alternating between wars with its Muslim neighbors and the Bulgars. Practically simultaneously with the capture of Antioch, Byzantium purposely restarted war with Bulgaria by refusing to pay tribute in 966. Nicephorus II sacked several border forts and bribed the Rus' to attack as well. When John I Tzimiskes (who had usurped Nicephorus's throne with the help of Nicephorus's wife, Empress Theophano) campaigned in 971 he captured the Bulgar tsar Boris and declared the extinction of the independent Bulgarian state. Although Byzantine rule was challenged, the victory allowed the emperor to turn his attention eastward, as in 975 when John invaded Syria, apparently aiming for the reconquest of Jerusalem.

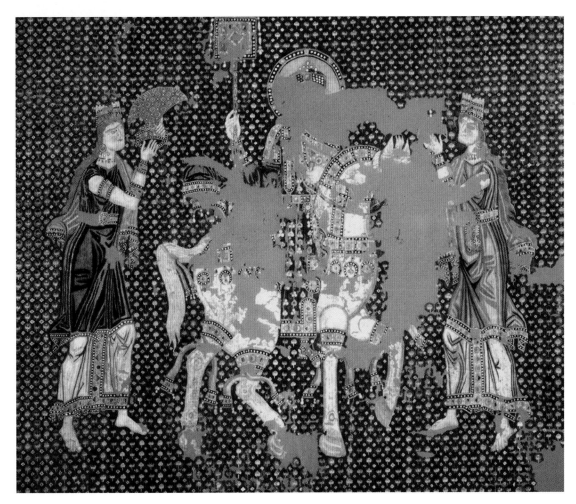

LEFT *Byzantine Emperor John I Tzimiskes celebrating victory over the Bulgars, an 11th-century silk tapestry known as the* Bamberger Gunthertuch.

RIGHT *Spanish Muslim carved box from the court of 'Abd al-Rahman III; it would have been used to store jewelry or cosmetics.*

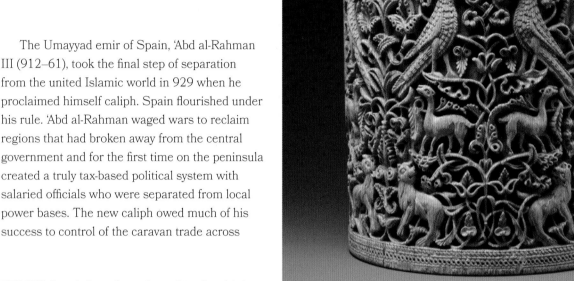

The Umayyad emir of Spain, 'Abd al-Rahman III (912–61), took the final step of separation from the united Islamic world in 929 when he proclaimed himself caliph. Spain flourished under his rule. 'Abd al-Rahman waged wars to reclaim regions that had broken away from the central government and for the first time on the peninsula created a truly tax-based political system with salaried officials who were separated from local power bases. The new caliph owed much of his success to control of the caravan trade across

BELOW *Cairo's first place of worship, the al-Azhar Mosque was dedicated in 972.*

the Sahara; the western route alone reportedly provided him an income of 500,000 gold dinars per year. The Umayyad palace city near Córdoba, Madinat al-Zahara, was suitably grand; its gardens contained exotic plants imported from as far away as India.

As the caliphate fragmented, some new rulers, like the Buyids, simply sought political control. More challenging to the whole concept of a united caliphate was the upsurge of religious dissidents, especially Shi'ite Muslims, who rejected the Abbasid caliph completely in favor of a ruler descended from the prophet Muhammad. Most serious was the rise of the Fatimid Dynasty in North Africa, descendants of the prophet's daughter Fatima. In 908, Berber religious rebels enthroned 'Ubayd Allah as caliph in the breakaway province of Ifriqiya (Tunisia). In their first decades these self-proclaimed Fatimid caliphs suffered repeated rebellions, mostly led by rival would-be messiahs. The Fatimids triumphed, however, protecting themselves by constructing the highly defensible fortress city of al-Mahdiyya. They also immediately sought to expand, attempting the conquest of Egypt in 913–15 and 919–21, before finally succeeding in 969. Control of wealthy Egypt, with its limited Arab population and large Christian majority, placed the Shi'ite Fatimids in direct conflict with the Abbasid caliphate. Immediately after their conquest, the Fatimids founded Cairo, just north of Fustat, the first Arab fortress city in Egypt. It was very carefully planned to house the Fatimid administration and its Berber army, thus avoiding clashes with the local populace. The new city became the center of a wealthy and flourishing court.

The Fatimids remained expansionist after the conquest of Egypt, soon launching campaigns in attempts to control the eastern seaboard of the Mediterranean. The caliphs also revived Red Sea trade, encouraging Indian Ocean shipping to operate via Aden rather than ports on the Persian Gulf; their efforts helped make Alexandria in Egypt a massive transshipment point.

For the most part, the Fatimids were content to let their subjects continue their religious traditions undisturbed. The great exception was the reign of Caliph al-Hakim (996–1021). Ascending the throne at age 11, al-Hakim attained personal control in 1000 (when the caliph and a servant murdered his tutor and guardian). He soon proved to be mentally unstable. In time, the caliph killed most of his senior officials, usually without trial or even explanation. Al-Hakim banned alcohol (not surprising for a pious Muslim ruler) but also watercress, chess, and the killing of dogs. He also began attacks on both Jews and Christians, in 1009 even destroying the Church of the Holy Sepulchre in Jerusalem. Starting in 1017, al-Hakim spread the doctrine that he himself was God. There was probably general relief when the caliph vanished in 1021 and was never seen again. Most likely he was killed by order of his sister Sitt al-Mulk, who became effective ruler of the Fatimid caliphate for the next five years. The Druze religious sect of the Near East still believes that al-Hakim is a messianic figure who will come again.

Ibn Fadlan's Journey to the North

Although the Abbasid caliphate was in serious decline by the 10th century, the ruler could still make his influence felt far beyond his borders. An interesting example of that influence occurred in the year 922, when the ruler of the Volga Bulgars wanted leverage against other steppe tribes. So he asked the caliph for builders to construct a fortress and a mosque. An embassy was dispatched. Fortunately for history, one of its members was a man named Ahmad ibn Fadlan, who wrote an account of the journey.

Ibn Fadlan was a keen observer, repelled but also interested in the strange customs he saw. Besides the Bulgars, his account is almost the only contemporary written evidence we have about Kyivan Rus'. Ibn Fadlan describes the worship of idols, notions of sanitation, and above all the elaborate ceremonial when a chief died. His body, along with those of sacrificial animals and an enslaved woman who was ritually raped before being killed, was placed in a ship and set afire. Ibn Fadlan's descriptions are often taken as evidence of "Viking" behavior, although it is impossible to sort out which traditions had come from Scandinavia and which were adopted from the larger Slavic populace.

THE HIGH VALUE OF TRADE

The Fatimids were so eager to control Indian Ocean trade because it produced so much wealth. The Song reunification led to an upsurge of prosperity in China, and also the start of direct Chinese trade into the Indian Ocean, as the Song tried to limit the role of foreign merchants. Everyone tried to profit, including merchants from southern India, who began to make the voyage to Indonesia in ever-greater numbers. Chinese mariners had to compete above all with Muslim networks, however. Arabs took the lead in improving shipping. An interesting example is a very simple navigational aid invented in the 10th century, the *kamal*. It is simply a wood card attached to a knotted string and aligned with the horizon to calculate latitude.

Southeast Asia profited from the shipping that passed through the Strait of Melaka. Srivijaya had dominated trade in the region, but faced increasing competition from the rulers of Java in the 10th century. Java suffered a major crisis in c. 925, when an explosive eruption of Mt. Merapi forced the royal court to relocate from the center of the island to the east—in 2010 an intact temple, buried by lava, was discovered at

BELOW *Carving of a Javan merchant ship, Borobudur Buddhist Temple.*

Yogyakarta. The Javanese began acquiring spices and sandalwood from eastern Indonesia to trade directly. This aroused the dudgeon of Srivijaya, which responded with a mixture of diplomacy (making trade deals with India and Sri Lanka), and aggression, initiating a series of wars with Java that began *c*. 925. The most devastating of these conflicts was in 1016, at which point the Srivijaya ruler began calling himself "king of the ocean lands."

The other great trade state that dominated the 10th century was Kyivan Rus'. The Islamic world in the 9th and early 10th centuries imported an estimated 500,000 furs per year, much of the trade passing along the river systems that the Rus' controlled. However, the growing economic crisis in the Abbasid caliphate as its silver mines failed made the Rus' look first to forcible seizure of all the Islamic market share they could get and then to other markets. The Kyiv state consolidated under the rule of Igor the Old (912–45), the Scandinavian ruler dominating a mostly Slavic populace; their wealth can be seen in the large burial mounds excavated at Gniozdovo. Prince Igor attacked the Byzantine Empire in 941, forcing both the Byzantines and the Bulgars to

ABOVE *Kimpulan Temple, Yogyakarta, Java. Buried by a volcanic eruption, the temple complex was only rediscovered in 2009.*

LEFT The Baptism of Prince Volodymyr of Kiev *by Viktor Vasnetsov (1890).*

pay him tribute. In 944, he campaigned against the semi-nomadic Turkic Pechenegs, then assaulted Byzantium again. Igor's successor, Sviatoslav, brought the Khazar kingdom to an end, sacking and destroying its capital Atil in 965. The Rus' did not have everything their own way; Pechenegs besieged Kyiv in 968 and in 972 ambushed and killed Sviatoslav. Nonetheless, the princes of Kyiv ruled a large state, one that covered almost as wide an area as the Carolingian Empire at its height, and their control of trade assured wealth and a steady flow of Scandinavian warriors eager to sign on as mercenaries.

While sometimes hostile toward Byzantium, increasingly the Rus' were happy to trade instead of raid. The door to a more permanent relationship between the two states opened in 987, when Emperor Basil II desperately needed

RIGHT *Monument to Mieszko I and Boleslaw Chrobry, the first Christian rulers of Poland (Golden Chapel, Poznan Cathedral).*

ΠΩΜΗΚΩΜ. Ηραιοδε και τοοσκλαςω πρωολοωιπυρι

ολεερωμαη πυρπολ τον τωνενλητφολον

ABOVE *Deployment of Greek fire against enemy ships, from a 12th-century manuscript of John Skylitzes'* Synopsis of Histories.

military assistance. Prince Volodymyr of Kyiv provided 6,000 warriors and in return was promised marriage with the Byzantine princess Anna—as long as he and his people converted to Christianity. Volodymyr was duly baptized in 988 and enthusiastically set about suppressing polytheism in his realm. Thus began a long and fruitful alliance between the Rus' and Constantinople, as Greek missionaries helped spread Orthodox Christianity and provided most of the higher clergy for centuries.

The Kyivan state was unable to sustain the level of centralization Volodymyr had enforced, breaking down into civil war among his successors and gradually creating a number of independent princely states. Other Slavic states fared better, however. Both Bohemia and Poland converted to Christianity in the course of the 10th century, Duke Mieszko of Poland in particular forging an alliance with the papacy to help maintain his country's ecclesiastical independence from Germany. Mieszko's son, Boleslaw I, was crowned Poland's first king in 1025. Bohemia was recognized as a fief of the German empire; its dukes did not claim the royal title until the later 12th century.

MAGYARS AND THE GREATER GERMAN EMPIRE

Viking and Muslim raids against Europe continued, and, starting in the late 9th century, the last of the great external threats to European stability also emerged—the Magyars. Like many peoples of the steppe, their early history is largely a mystery. They first appear in the 9th century as subjects of the Khazars. But, in one of the many chain reactions of the steppe, the Magyars were driven westward by the expansion of the Turkic Pechenegs—themselves displaced by Oghuz Turkish expansion in the Syr Darya region. The Magyars reached Pannonia in the 890s, settling in the nearly deserted Carpathian basin. There they formed a predatory state, largely autonomous warlords launching large-scale raids of thousands of horsemen that pillaged wide swathes of land before returning to their bases. Their raids caused devastation in Bulgaria and the Byzantine Empire, and in the west reached as far as France, Italy, and even Lérida in Spain. It was Germany, immediately to the west, that bore the brunt of their attacks, however.

Germany, as we can now call the eastern Kingdom of the Franks, had not suffered as much as France in Viking raids. The king was weak for a different reason: German territory consisted of several large duchies, such as Saxony, Thuringia, and Bavaria, that had been independent kingdoms and whose dukes still maintained a great deal of autonomy. However, no single duke could muster the necessary forces to defeat one of the Magyar great raids, as was obvious in 907 when the Magyars destroyed a Bavarian army at Bratislava. The late Carolingians were unable to rally the German elites to fight in a common cause. But the last eastern Carolingian died in 911 and, instead of reuniting with the western Franks, the nobles instead elected one of their own as king. The first non-Carolingian was not very successful, but the tide turned quickly when the duke of Saxony was elected king in 919. Henry I, first ruler of the Ottonian Dynasty (919–1024) worked with the dukes. He paid tribute to the Magyars for a number of years, using the peace he bought to build up a contingent of heavy cavalry that could meet the highly mobile raiders on more equal terms. When he was ready, in 933 Henry inflicted a significant defeat on the Magyars at Riade.

Henry arranged for his son Otto to be elected and crowned in his lifetime, a means of assuring continuity. Otto I, the Great (936–73) built on his father's successes, with successful campaigns

BELOW Legends tells that the pope sent the Holy Crown of Hungary for Stephen's coronation in 1000; however, it is actually Byzantine work of the later 11th century.

ABOVE *Legend tells that seven chieftains led the seven Magyar tribes into the Carpathian Basin in 895. They are commemorated in Heroes' Square, Budapest, Hungary.*

LEFT *St. Wiborada, a recluse at St. Gall (Switzerland) was killed by Magyar raiders in 926.*

against Lotharingia, the western Slavs, and the Lombard kingdom of northern Italy. In 955 came the greatest victory of his reign, when with a force drawn from all the duchies Otto crushed a large Magyar army in the Battle of Lechfeld. Following that defeat and Byzantine victories over them in 961 and 970, the Magyars soon settled down, their first great king, Stephen (1000–38), converting to Christianity and consolidating a new Hungarian state.

Otto I literally crowned his success in 962 when the pope invested him as emperor, an office extinct since 925. This was the true beginning

The German imperial crown, perhaps crafted for the coronation of Otto I as emperor in 962.

The German Imperial Crown

One of the 10th century's greatest artifacts is the German imperial crown, created either in 962 for Otto I's coronation or 967 for that of his son Otto II (who was crowned in his father's lifetime). Probably made in Germany, the crown is rife with symbolism. It is crafted of eight hinged gold plates, its octagonal form invoking the heavenly Jerusalem. The crown is decorated with 144 precious stones, alternating with panels depicting the godly kings of ancient Israel. The cross at the front of the crown was detachable, so the bearer could carry it in his hand, meditating on the image of the crucified Christ etched on the reverse. Several generations later, Emperor Conrad II had the arch added at the top, a "closed" crown marking imperial, rather than simply royal, dignity. The crown is now displayed in the Imperial Treasury of the Hofburg in Vienna.

of the first German empire (later named the Holy Roman Empire). Otto and his successors successfully built a greater Germany (including northern Italy and protectorship over Rome) into Europe's strongest state, Otto I even gaining Byzantine recognition of his title and a Byzantine princess, Theophanu, as his son's bride. The Ottonians, aided by the discovery of a very rich silver mine on their family territory in Saxony, had the resources to make themselves obeyed. Their influence extended deep into the Slavic lands. Although Otto I's extensive conquests in that region were mostly lost to a great rebellion in Otto II's reign, the Germans exerted a hegemony over the rising states of Bohemia and Poland, which both converted to Christianity in this period.

It was not just Germany that saw a consolidation of central power in the 10th century. Central and Eastern Europe were

RIGHT *Christ crowning of Otto II and Theophanu. A masterpiece of southern Italian Byzantine art, the ivory plague commemorated their marriage in 972.*

rapidly coalescing into states. In England, Alfred the Great's successors gradually conquered territories held by Scandinavian kings, welding them together into a single "England." Scandinavia itself saw a number of efforts to unite into larger kingdoms, such as Harald Finehair's (d. *c*. 932) attempt to unite Norway. Most successful was Harald Bluetooth (958–*c*. 987), who boasted that he was king of all Denmark, and who also helped consolidate his rule by adopting Christianity in *c*. 965. Even Ireland, a land of many small kings, coalesced into larger territorial blocks until, after a series of wars, Brian Boru (976–1014) was able to proclaim himself first "king of Ireland." It would be an overstatement to say that Europe was catching up with the great states of Asia, but it was showing promise of things to come.

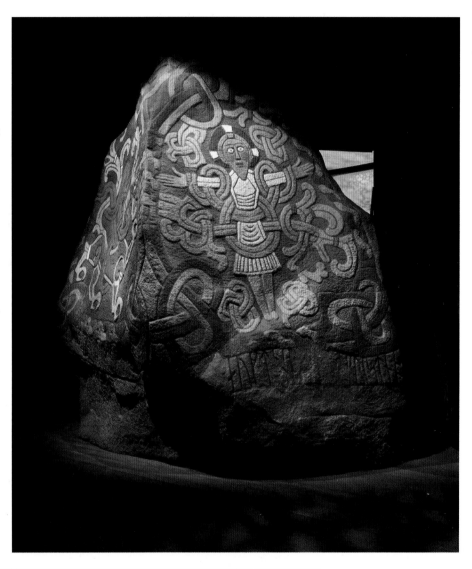

RIGHT *The Greater Jelling Stone, a colorized copy to show the carving more clearly. The two Jelling Stones celebrate Harald Bluetooth of Denmark's family and conversion to Christianity.*

A Medieval Democracy

Most regions during the medieval millennium were monarchies, the only significant exception being mercantile oligarchies in places like Venice or the Swahili city-states—and Iceland. Scandinavians settled Iceland beginning in 870. Much later sagas tell that many of the early colonists were independent-minded men and women, unwilling to accept Harald Finehair's violent unification of Norway. Whether that was true or not, for its first several centuries Iceland maintained its independence from Norway and never came under the rule of a single individual. Instead, the islanders governed themselves with assemblies, probably reflecting Scandinavian norms before kings began to consolidate their power. A hierarchy of legal assemblies had at its apex the annual meeting of the Althing, an all-Iceland assembly. Of course, not everyone had a say; it was a meeting of property-owning men, an oligarchy. But leadership was largely based on individual charisma, rather than hereditary right. The Althing settled legal controversies and could enact new law, as in the year 1000 when the assembly voted that the island would convert to Christianity.

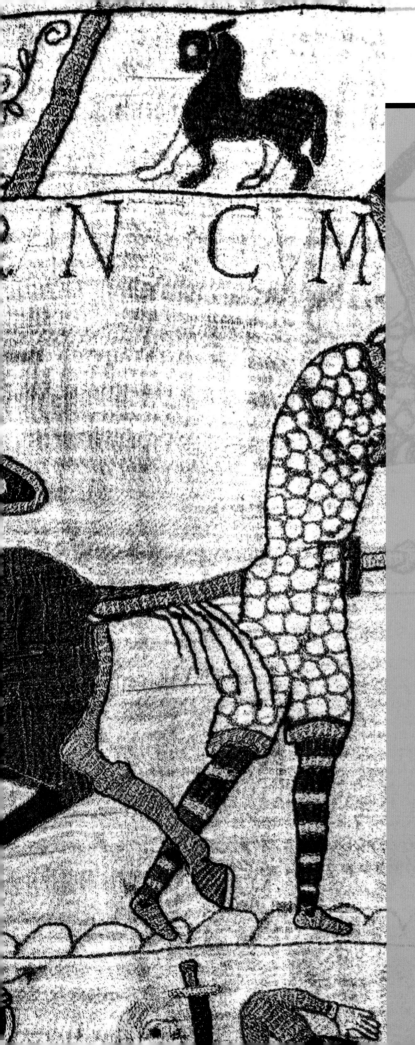

CHAPTER 6

War & Holy War

Warfare was nothing new in the 11th century. "Holy war," however, became a much larger issue than ever before. It was normal on campaigns to invoke divine blessings on the endeavor, and smart leaders tried to instill in their followers a sense that their cause was just and virtuous. War waged with a specific ideological program had been rare, though, such as when Charlemagne forced the conversion of the Saxons or Heraclius destroyed Zoroastrian fire temples. Religion can be a great motivator of behavior, however, and any religion that claims a unique truth is bound to attract zealous defenders. The Abrahamic monotheisms—Judaism, Christianity, and Islam—have been especially prone to fight for their faith, against both the followers of other religions and heretics. The 11th century saw the growing virulence of holy war in both Christianity and Islam, as Muslims and Christians fought, not to convert others forcibly to their religion, but to claim rule over lands that historically had been ruled by coreligionists. The concept of holy war extended beyond a Muslim–Christian struggle especially in Europe, as Scandinavian rulers rigorously brought their subjects into religious conformity and the rising authority of the papacy led to massive consequences for the future of both European and Near Eastern history.

LEFT *Scene from the Bayeux Tapestry, a 230 ft (70 m) long embroidered cloth commemorating the Norman Conquest of England.*

THE ARRIVAL OF HOLY WAR IN INDIA

India, a geophysical region naturally separate from the rest of Eurasia thanks to the barrier of the Himalayas and Tibetan plateau, had to a large extent followed its own course. Buddhist pilgrims were frequent visitors, as were merchants at the Indian Ocean ports, but these groups had little impact on the political life of the subcontinent. For the first half of the medieval millennium, India was not united into a single empire. In the south, a number of significant states operated, most notably the Chola kingdom, which under Rajaraja the Great (985–1014) began a century of expansionist glory that included the conquest of Sri Lanka.

BELOW *Constructed by order of Rajaraja I from 1003 to 1010, the Hindu temple at Brihadisvara was dedicated to the worship of the god Shiva.*

After moving into the Ganges valley, in 1025 Rajendra Chola even sent a fleet to impose his suzerainty over the southeastern Asian maritime state of Vijayara. Northern India too saw the development of a would-be superpower with the Pratihara state. Bhoja (836–85) and his son Mahendrapala I (885–910) won hegemony over most of the north, but dynastic feuds and regional wars remained common.

Into this world of squabbling Hindu states burst a wave of Muslim attacks beginning in the late 10th century. Ghazni, based in what is now Afghanistan, became an independent state in 963 when its Turkish governor, Alptigin, rejected

the overlordship of the Samanid Dynasty of Iran. Alptigin's son-in-law and eventual successor, Sabuktigin (d. 997), expanded the Ghaznid state and launched attacks against the Hindu Shahi kingdom of the Punjab. Mahmud of Ghazni (998–1030) continued the expansion into India after Sabuktigin's death.

Mahmud's onslaught was something new for India. Arabs had conquered the state of Sind in 712, after shipwrecked Muslim pilgrims had been ill-treated. But Arab rule over Sind had little to do with ideology, despite Hindu polytheism and the use of religious imagery in their worship, both of which are theoretically anathema to Muslims; the two religions coexisted peacefully. The same was not true of Mahmud of Ghazni's expeditions into the Punjab, which began in 1000. From the beginning, Mahmud presented his aggressive, expansionist war as *jihad*, a religious struggle. Thus, for the first time in Islamic history, *jihad* became an important justification for conquest. *Jihad*, which means "struggle," appears in the Qur'an, but normally to describe the interior

struggle of each Muslim for righteousness. While the early Islamic expansion had certainly included an ideological component, invasions had never been understood as attacks on followers of other religions, but rather as an effort to establish Muslim rule so that Muslims in a region could practice their faith freely. Recognizing the threat, Jayapala, ruler of the Shahi kingdom, organized a confederacy of Hindu rulers, but they failed to repel the invaders, suffering serious defeat in 1001. Jayapala could not bear the shame and burned himself to death; the conqueror sold many of the Hindu king's relatives into slavery.

The Ghaznavid attacks, 17 of them between 1000 and 1026, were extremely violent, marked by wanton destruction and large-scale enslavement. Most notorious was Mahmud's attack on the marvelously wealthy temple of Somnath on the shore of the Arabian Sea, deep in hostile territory. In a great raid in 1026, the Ghaznavid army ransacked the great shrine to Shiva, looting it and destroying its holy images. Legend tells that 50,000 devotees of Shiva

ABOVE *Mahmud of Ghazni receiving a robe of honor from Caliph al-Qadir, a miniature painted in 1314.*

died trying to protect the holy place. The destruction of Somnath teaches an important lesson about holy war: ideology is very rarely the sole motivation for warfare, although it can play a vital role in inspiring troops. Did Mahmud attack Somnath from loathing for false "idols," or because he desired the temple's wealth? Most likely he was motivated by both, as well as honor and reputation and any number of other reasons. Certainly he needed money, because the Ghaznavids relied heavily on enslaved soldiers, as had become the norm in the Islamic world. A standing professional army of that sort was extremely expensive to maintain, which helps explain the predatory nature of the Ghaznavid attacks. While Mahmud devastated northern India, he certainly was not completely hostile to Hinduism, employing Hindu administrators and accepting the allegiance of Hindu client kings.

LEFT *Chola-Dynasty bronze statue of Shiva Nataraja ("Lord of the Dance").*

The Romani Begin Their Wanderings

One of the most unexpected side effects of Mahmud of Ghazni's attacks is the likelihood that they precipitated the westward migration of an Indian group known in modern times as the Romani, or Roma. Known for centuries as "Gypsies" in Europe because of their supposed origin in Egypt, the Roma actually originated in the region of Rajasthan, India. Their original name, *doma*, marks them out as members of the Dalit caste of traveling musicians and dancers. Their waves of migration began around the turn of the millennium, making the disruptions of Mahmud's invasions a likely cause. The Roma gradually worked their way from the Ghaznavid Empire toward Europe, reaching the Byzantine Empire in the 12th century and Europe in the 14th. The Roma in many regions have preserved their original Indo-Aryan language. It was only the international Human Genome Project (1990–2003), though, that conclusively proved that the wandering population had its start in northwestern India.

DAWN OF THE RECONQUISTA

The rising shadow of ideology as a motivation for war was not exclusive to Islam. In the small Christian kingdoms of northern Spain, the elite classes continued to pride themselves on their Visigothic heritage and longed to regain the land that had been "stolen" from them in the Muslim conquest of most of the peninsula. While the caliphate of Córdoba remained strong, though, the best those Christian rulers could hope for was to beat off regular raids from Muslim-ruled territory. The situation altered dramatically in the late 12th century, however. The Umayyad caliphate was weakened by the inheritance of the 15-year-old al-Hisham II in 976. A military leader seized power, giving himself the title al-Mansur and relegating the caliph to figurehead status. For a time, the central state remained strong; the capital, Córdoba, was a major center of trade and culture, with a population of at least 400,000 in the early 11th century, far eclipsing any other city in Europe. But when al-Mansur's son died in 1009, the caliphate rapidly descended into civil war. The scramble for power included members of the Umayyad clan, palace eunuchs, Berber mercenaries, and even Slavic slaves; by 1031 Muslim Spain had broken into more than 30 independent states, known as *taifas*.

Although the Christian kings of the north could not hope to take on the might of the caliphate, attacks on individual *taifas* were well within their grasp, especially as the *taifas* constantly fought each other for hegemony. And the Christian kings soon received help from their coreligionists beyond the Pyrenees. Sancho Ramirez, king of Aragón and Navarre, in 1063

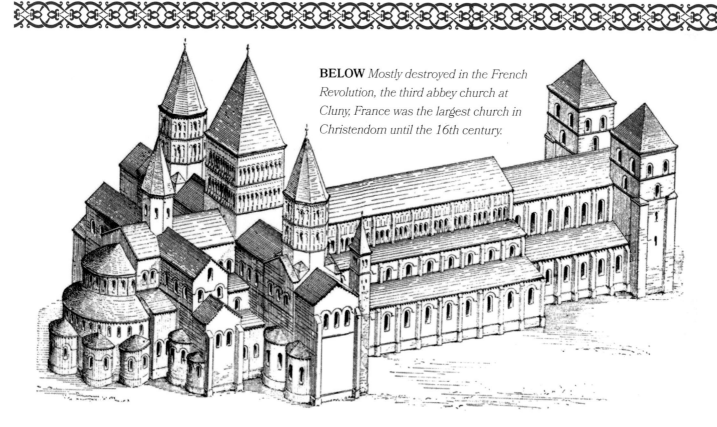

BELOW *Mostly destroyed in the French Revolution, the third abbey church at Cluny, France was the largest church in Christendom until the 16th century.*

achieved a major propaganda victory: Pope Alexander publicly urged the warriors of Europe to assist the king in what was characterized as a Christian emergency, encouraging assistance to reconquer lands that rightfully belonged to the Christians. Thus, the Spanish reconquest, the *reconquista*, was born. In 1064, a large force—Spanish, French, Norman, and Italian—attacked the city of Barbastro in the *taifa* of Lérida. In return for serving, the fighters were promised a great spiritual reward. By this time, the pope was recognized throughout Western Europe as the spiritual heir of St. Peter, and Christ had entrusted the keys of heaven to Peter. The pope offered participants full absolution for any sins they had confessed and repented, essentially promising a free pass to heaven—what is known as an indulgence.

The most successful of the northern kings in these wars of both ideology and territorial expansion was Alfonso VI of León-Castile (1065–1109). After reuniting the lands his father had divided among his sons, Alfonso set out on the path of conquest, constructing careful alliances to win a moral underpinning for his wars. His collaboration with the great Burgundian monastery of Cluny above all won him not only many preachers for his cause but clergy for areas he conquered, while he was assured of ongoing papal support by aligning himself with the Roman reform program of his time, including replacing the native Mozarab religious liturgy with Roman practices. Alfonso's crowning achievement was the conquest of the *taifa* of Toledo in 1085.

Alfonso's successes provoked a Muslim reaction, upping the ideological stakes of warfare on the Iberian Peninsula. The remaining *taifa* rulers begged for help from a new Muslim power that had risen in northern Africa, the Almoravids. This was a Berber dynasty that came to power in 1061 at the head of a religious orthodoxy movement. Under their great leader Yusuf ibn Tashifin (1061–1106), they united much of North Africa and even invaded West Africa, in *c.* 1076, taking Koumbi Saleh, the capital of Ancient Ghana. They appear to have

ABOVE *13th-century miniature of Alfonso VI from the Tumbo A codex.*

been motivated by both poverty and religion. The imam of the puritanical movement was concerned to convert the West Africans and sent missionaries. But the Berber forces also made a point of capturing trading centers through which African gold passed. Invited urgently to Spain after the fall of Toledo, Yusuf ibn Tashufin arrived with an army in the summer of 1086. What ensued was a 20-year fight between the Almoravids and Alfonso. Contemptuous of the laxness of the *taifas*, the Almoravids soon started annexing them, complicating the situation as some *taifa* rulers preferred the overlordship of a Christian to that of a Muslim rigorist. It is a useful reminder that the wars of the *reconquista*, although they had a strong religious component, were never exclusively about religion. Indeed, as the Almoravid hold on Spain weakened and Christian kings again pressed south, they proved just as happy to tolerate their Muslim and Jewish subjects as the Muslims had been to accept Christians.

Christian Spain's expansion is a good example of Europe's growing means for aggression. The Medieval Climate Anomaly was kind to much of Europe, especially as two centuries of high solar irradiance began in the later 11th century. Crop yields were up,

BELOW *Probably used for ritual washing before prayer, the Qubba in Marrakesh, Morocco, displays well the grace and detail of Almoravid architecture.*

and grasping landlords forced agricultural innovations, including labor-saving devices like mills, upon their peasants. Europe's rising productivity supported an increasingly self-confident military class of heavy cavalry—knights. However, recognizing that dividing estates among multiple sons would soon make it impossible to cover the high costs of knighthood, much of Europe began to impose primogeniture, with the eldest son inheriting the lion's share of a father's estate and younger sons left to fend for themselves. This practice created an ever-larger class of young men with privilege but few prospects, who flocked to the schools and rapidly transformed bureaucracies with their new expertise, or served as freelance knights, eager to prove themselves and win lands of their own. Nor was Europe's economic rise restricted to the agricultural world. It was in the 11th century that Europe's Mediterranean trade really took off, as the mercantile cities of Italy built fleets and went to war with large Muslim pirate enclaves in Sicily and northern Africa. Most strikingly, in 1087 a joint expedition of Pisa, Genoa, and Amalfi captured the major pirate emirate of Mahdia, freeing up much of the Mediterranean for Christian shipping. Europe's commercial revolution had begun.

BELOW *Pisa Cathedral, with the famous leaning bell tower to the right. Completed in less than 30 years (1063–92) it attests to the wealth of the mercantile city.*

THE RISE OF THE PAPACY

Europe in the 11th century was undergoing a religious reform current comparable to that of the Almoravids. It began at a grassroots level, a monastic movement arguing that the clergy should live purer lives, not engaging in sexual activities (it was normal in the early Middle Ages for priests to be married; celibacy was only imposed on bishops), and above all not buying their ecclesiastical posts or selling them to others, the sin of simony. The reform moved to a much higher level in 1046 when the papacy was forcibly brought on board. The instigator was a German king, Henry III, who wanted to be crowned emperor, which only the pope could perform. But three men were simultaneously claiming the throne of St. Peter. So Henry marched to Rome with an army at his back and convened two church councils that deposed all three rival pontiffs. Henry then imposed his own choice as pope, a German

Constantinople, 1054

As the Roman popes tried to assert their position as leaders of Christendom, their aspirations inevitably led to conflict with the patriarch of Constantinople, leader of the Church in the Byzantine Empire. In early Christianity, the principle was established of five patriarchates—Antioch, Alexandria, Jerusalem, Constantinople, and Rome—the bishop of each holding special authority because their city's Christian community had been established by an apostle. The Roman pope received special reverence as the spiritual heir of St. Peter, but that position was not held to include authority over the other patriarchs. There had been occasional clashes over issues of doctrine in the preceding centuries, with popes occasionally claiming preeminence as Peter's vicars. The situation escalated sharply in 1054, however. The Eastern and Western churches had diverged on a number of issues over the centuries, but two points in particular were problematic to the reformed papacy. First, the Eastern Orthodox Church expected its clergy to be married, while the Western reformers insisted on clerical celibacy. The second issue was that the Western church had changed the text of the Nicene Creed, the key statement of belief hammered out by ecumenical councils in the 4th century.

At issue was that the patriarch of Constantinople argued vehemently that nobody has the right to change a text approved by an ecumenical council, and Pope Leo IX responded just as strongly that the pope, as the heir of St. Peter, could in fact do so. Leo sent inflammatory advisors from the inner reform circle to "reason" with the patriarch, and the upshot was that they stormed out of Constantinople after excommunicating the patriarch, with the patriarch returning the favor. The events of 1054 did not mark the final breach between the Latin and Greek Churches, but they are an important marker that is often regarded as the beginning of the great East-West Schism that is still not completely healed today.

The Cathedral of Holy Wisdom, Kyiv, is the best surviving example of middle Byzantine architecture.

bishop strongly aligned with the reform movement. The emperor installed five reforming German popes in a row, and the papacy was transformed as they installed like-minded staff and organized their key assistants into the college of cardinals. The papal reform had enormous consequences because the popes had always enjoyed theoretical rights over the Christian world as the successors of Peter, prince of the apostles; now they sought to transform that ideal into reality, and the papacy for almost the first time became a major player in the political affairs of Europe. Although at first the reform popes were eager to work with the German emperor, Henry III died young in 1056, leaving his throne to a child. Pope Nicholas II in 1059 then issued a decree mandating the conduct of future papal elections—election by the college of cardinals, with the emperor playing no role but to be informed after the fact. It was a papal declaration of independence.

It did not take long for two rival views of Christian authority—was it the pope or the emperor who was the vicar of Christ on earth?—to clash. Henry III's successor, Henry IV (1056–1106), deeply resented the undermining of the crown's authority during his tumultuous minority. Pope Gregory VII (1073–85) for his part was a key member of the Roman reforming circle for decades before his election, an unbending personality with a profound sense of the righteousness of his cause. The two clashed over the selection of an archbishop of Milan, Henry wanting to appoint the archbishop as rulers had always done and Gregory insisting on election by the city's key clerics. Henry angrily demanded the pope's abdication, but without being in Rome with an army to enforce his will. Gregory responded by excommunicating the German and claiming it was within his power to release Henry's vassals from their oaths of loyalty to him.

The great conflict between German ruler and papacy is known as the Investiture Contest, because a key issue was whether the ruler had the right to symbolically "invest" a newly chosen bishop with the symbols of his authority. The conflict escalated after Gregory VII excommunicated Henry IV in 1076 and Henry's vassals proclaimed they would choose a new king unless Henry was reconciled to the pope, but then guarded the pass through the Alps to keep Henry from reaching the pope in Italy. Despite that,

LEFT *Bishop Bernward of Hildesheim commissioned this bronze column in c.1020. A masterpiece of Ottonian art, it displays scenes from the life of Christ.*

Henry won through, reaching the pope at Canossa, where Gregory had no choice but to raise the excommunication—after keeping Henry waiting as a penitent in the snow for three days. Many German nobles refused to accept the settlement, and warfare swept through Germany and Italy for nearly 50 years, as royal vassals, who did not care for strong central authority, used the papal stance as an excuse to abandon their king. They chose several rival kings in succession, and Henry angrily selected several anti-popes, one of whom crowned the German as emperor after Henry captured Rome in 1084, forcing Gregory to flee. Two of Henry's own sons eventually joined the rebels, and the emperor suffered the ultimate humiliation of being forced to abdicate in favor of his younger son Henry V. The new emperor had a long, hard fight to pacify has lands, finally reaching a compromise with the papacy on investiture, the Concordat of Worms (1122), which failed to resolve the key issue of ultimate authority. In the course of the wars of the Investiture Contest, Germany, which in the late 10th century had been Europe's strongest state, had its central authority repeatedly compromised, and the German emperors completely lost control of their territories in northern Italy. The wars began a spiral of decentralization that by the end of the Middle Ages had divided the German-speaking lands into hundreds of independent statelets.

BELOW *A 19th-century engraving of Henry IV's "walk to Canossa," presenting himself as a penitent to Pope Gregory VII.*

EUROPEAN EMPIRES

Of course, not all wars of the 11th century had an ideological component. Europeans' growing ability to engage in protracted, large-scale military enterprises can be seen in the creation of two significant empires, both based around the North Atlantic and the North Sea, and both ruled by the descendants of Vikings. The first was a Scandinavian empire, called into being by Svein Forkbeard of Denmark and his son Cnut; the second was created by the Norman conquest of England in 1066.

By the early 11th century, much of the populace of Denmark and Norway had converted to Christianity, many forcibly brought into the fold by rulers who employed religion as a tool of centralization. Denmark's kings in particular proved to be strong rulers, as Harald Bluetooth and his son Svein suppressed dissent. Like their forebears, however, Denmark's kings recognized that the ability to reward their men was a key component of success. They needed loot, and England's weakness in the late 10th century provided an opportunity. Aethelred II "the Unready" came to England's throne in 978 as a boy, his reign already under a shadow because his older half-brother was murdered and

Aethelred's mother was implicated. Scandinavian raids against his kingdom began in 980, soon increasing in size and scope. The king of the Danes himself began to lead the onslaught, and by 1013 Svein was aiming for the outright conquest of England. Svein himself died in 1014 after ruling England for only six weeks (Aethelred had fled to Normandy); his son Cnut completed the conquest in 1016.

Cnut held together a great North Sea empire until his death in 1035. Norway was added to his possessions when he attacked and killed the Norwegian king St. Olaf in 1030. Cnut's two sons were able to inherit in turn, and the empire would likely have survived had his line not died out. Instead, a native prince, Edward the Confessor, was able to return as King of England in 1042, and in 1046 St. Olaf's brother Harald Hardrada gained control of Norway.

It was the childless Edward the Confessor's death in 1066 that opened the door for the second great Western European empire. Vikings had settled in northwestern France by treaty with the French king in 911. These Northmen—or "Normans"—assimilated quickly, Christianizing and intermarrying with the native population.

RIGHT *Cnut battling Edmund Ironside for control of England, scene from an illustrated manuscript of Matthew Paris'* Chronica Majora.

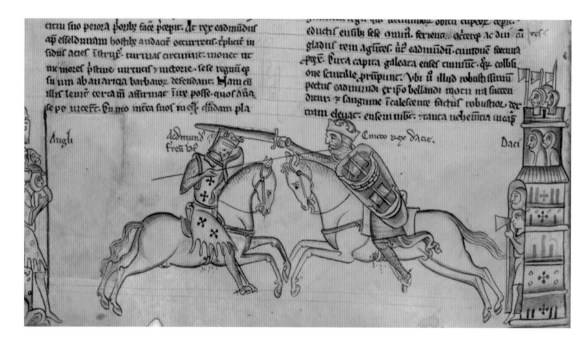

LEFT *Pope Nicholas II investing Robert Guiscard as duke of Apulia in 1059 at the Synod of Melfi.*

The highly forceful successors of Rollo, the first leader of the settlers, enlarged their territory and welded it into a strong duchy. The descendants of the Vikings took to the new heavy cavalry fighting style and soon won an international reputation as disciplined and ruthless fighters.

Normans were actually responsible for the conquest of two regions. Small groups of Norman knights, for the most part younger sons with few prospects at home, began enlisting as mercenaries in the frequent wars of southern Italy by the 1020s. Within a decade, they had turned against their paymasters and began to carve out an independent principality in the region. Pope Leo IX assembled a coalition to fight them; it was the first time a pope offered remission of sins for waging war against "ungodly" enemies. But after Leo's defeat in 1053, the popes soon learned that these southern Normans were useful allies, the Normans providing a vital counterweight to the German emperor, the pope in turn providing these upstarts with legitimacy. Under Robert Guiscard and his successors, the Hauteville family became first dukes and in time kings as papal vassals. They soon pushed into Muslim-ruled Sicily, taking the great city of Palermo in 1072. The Italian Normans even thrust into Byzantine territory in the Balkans, attempting to take advantage of Byzantine weakness, although a new ruler, Alexius Comnenus, defeated the Norman force in 1083.

Meanwhile, back in Normandy, Duke William proved to be a ruthless centralizer. He was also on friendly terms with his cousin King Edward of England, who had spent decades in Normandy. Apparently, at some point Edward had promised William the succession to the English crown (although the king had no actual right to bequeath the throne). When Edward died, the assembly of English nobles (the *witan*) elected one of their own, Harold Godwinson, as king. But William of Normandy immediately staked his claim as well, his cause buttressed by the fact that Harold had been forced to swear to accept William as the next king. William declared Harold an oath-breaker and won papal approval for the invasion of England he immediately planned. Simultaneously, Harald Hardrada of Norway, allied with Harold Godwinson's malcontent younger brother, also asserted his right to rule England.

Roger II of Sicily

One of the most brilliant courts of medieval Europe was that of King Roger II of Sicily (d. 1154). A Norman of the Hauteville dynasty, Roger inherited Sicily in 1105, which his mother Adelaide del Vasto ruled until he came of age. In 1127, he also claimed the rule of southern Italy. The Normans of Italy finally won a royal crown in 1130, when Roger supported one of the rivals for the papacy during a schism and was named king as reward.

Roger ruled a multi-ethnic kingdom, Greeks and Lombards predominating on the peninsula and Greeks and Arabs on Sicily, with a Norman military class ruling all. It was Roger's task to weld it all into a cohesive political unit, which he did by respecting the religious traditions of his predecessors and by making full use of the Arabic administrative expertise he found in place in Sicily. Roger made Arabic his administrative language, adopting in particular Fatimid governmental methods. A true appreciator of Arabic culture, Roger patronized some of the leading scholars and artists of his age.

Mosaic of Roger II of Sicily being crowned by Christ, Church of Santa Maria dell' Ammiraglio, Palermo.

RIGHT *In this scene from the Bayeux Tapestry, Duke William's presumed death has caused panic. He reassures his men by raising his helm so they recognize him.*

The result was that England suffered a double invasion in 1066. Harald Hardrada attacked in the north, winning a first battle but then losing a second at Stamford Bridge to a force that King Harold had hastily marched to Yorkshire. Harold was still in the north when a large Norman army—probably 6–7,000 men—landed in the south. Harold force-marched his army to deal with the new threat, only to be defeated and killed in a battle near Hastings. King William the Conqueror (1066–87) was soon crowned. Although he had to suppress a number of rebellions, his greater Anglo-Norman state endured. His territories, briefly divided among his two eldest sons, were soon reunited under a single ruler.

THE RISE OF THE SELJUKS

As mentioned above, Byzantium had moved from a position of great strength to one of extreme weakness by the year 1080. At the dawn of the century, Emperor Basil II (976–1025) spearheaded a major expansion of his empire, including the brutal conquest of Bulgaria. By the time of his death, Basil ruled over about 12 million people. But Basil had never married, and his heirs after the brief reign of his brother Constantine were two elderly nieces who had never married either. For the next 30 years, the empire was ruled in fractious and contested fashion as court and army factions struggled to assert their power.

Byzantium particularly needed a strong hand at this time, because a new threat was looming on the horizon. The steppe of Central Asia,

LEFT *Empress Zoe Porphyrogenita, mosaic from Hagia Sophia, Istanbul.*

BELOW *Arp Arslan's triumph at Manzikert, 1071.*

The Long Reach of Arabic Medicine

Although the Abbasids had little political power by the 11th century, they still controlled considerable wealth and could patronize learning. Indeed, scholarship flourished in the Arabic world more generally in this period, as regional courts maintained schools and sponsored scientific endeavors in rivalry with each other. Especially impressive were advances in medicine, as Muslim physicians mastered ancient Greek learning on the subject and pushed beyond to ever greater achievements.

Two of the most important figures in the history of medicine were near contemporaries, and illustrate how learning could be transmitted throughout the Islamic world and beyond. Abu al-Qasim (939–1013), known in Western Europe as Albucasis, was a court physician at the Umayyad court in Córdoba. He was a famous surgeon, and his treatise on surgery remained influential in both Muslim and Christian lands for half a millennium. His contribution, however, is overshadowed by that of Abu Ali ibn Sina, or Avicenna to westerners (980–1037). Avicenna was a Persian, a native of Bukhara, who served at a number of courts in Iran during his career. Although frequently challenged because of his religious unorthodoxy (he was a proponent of Aristotelian philosophy), this polymath enjoyed a highly successful career, above all as a physician. He is most famous for his *Canon of Medicine* and *The Book of Healing*. Within a century of Avicenna's death, his works were known on the far-away Iberian Peninsula, and soon crossed the Pyrenees to become central texts for Christian physicians that were not superseded until the 17th century.

Avicenna treating a patient. Cover of a deluxe copy of the *Canon of Medicine* (1632).

inherently unstable, saw the migration of the Oghuz Turks in the late 10th century; their most important exodus into Muslim lands was led by a dynasty called the Seljuks after their first major war chief, who created a confederation of Turks and converted to Islam. These Seljuk Turks, as they are usually called, decisively defeated a large Ghaznavid army in 1040, gaining effective control of Khurasan. Almost immediately, the Seljuk rulers began minting coins, a statement that they wished to be regarded as traditional Muslim rulers. In 1055, the Abbasid caliph al-Qa'im, eager to free himself from Shi'ite Buyid control, actually invited the Seljuks to attack and establish their own protectorate over Iraq. The Seljuks, given the title "sultan" ("power"), by that point were pressing against the Byzantine Empire.

Turks had been migrating into the Byzantine-held Anatolian plateau for some time. The Seljuk sultan Alp Arslan (1063–72) drew them together under his rule, posing a direct threat to Byzantine rule. In response, in 1071 Emperor Romanus IV Diogenes decided that he needed a major victory, both to intimidate the Turks and to suppress Byzantine opposition to his rule. He mobilized a very large army, perhaps as many as 100,000 men, and marched deep into Anatolia to confront the intruders. The result was a devastating Byzantine defeat at the Battle of Manzikert, a battle that became a rout because a traitor caused panic by spreading word the emperor had fled the battlefield. Much of the Byzantine army was destroyed, and Romanus himself was captured. The battle itself was not a catastrophic blow to Byzantium; Alp Arslan offered generous peace terms. The collapse of Byzantine rule in Anatolia soon followed, though, as a vicious civil war broke out between rivals for the throne. The Seljuks permanently occupied considerable Byzantine territory, and also moved into Syria and Palestine, where Fatimid rule had been weakened by their own civil war. The Turks captured Jerusalem in 1087.

MAKING THE FIRST CRUSADE

Byzantium recovered under the strong rule of Alexius Comnenus (1081–1118) and began to regain territory that the Seljuks had overrun. With the loss of the Anatolian plateau, though, Alexius had lost a prime recruiting ground for soldiers, besides which his experiences fighting the Normans in the Balkans had impressed him with the prowess of Western knights. So, in addition to the thousands of Scandinavians who already formed the imperial (Varangian) guard, Alexius set out to recruit fighting men from Europe, in early 1095 sending an embassy to Pope Urban II, asking for his assistance.

Pope Urban—and Western Europe more generally—had his own agenda. Urban certainly wished to help fellow Christians free themselves from Turkish dominion. He also wanted to win European support for the papal cause in the ongoing wars of the Investiture Contest. And he

LEFT *Miniature of Christ blessing Alexius I Comnenus.*

BELOW *Monastery of St. John on Patmos. Alexius Comnenus donated the land for the religious community in 1088.*

ABOVE *Pope Urban II journeying to France and proclaiming the First Crusade at the Council of Clermont (14th-century miniature).*

desired control of the holy places of Christianity in the Near East. The preceding century had seen a sea change in Western European spirituality, focusing much more on the life and sufferings of Jesus. Pilgrimage to Jerusalem, the site of Christ's death and resurrection, had become a massive business in the 11th century, and many Europeans were dismayed to suffer ill treatment at the hands of the "infidels" who controlled the holy places. And so, rather than simply sending letters to help the Byzantines recruit mercenaries, Urban, at the Council of Clermont in November 1095, preached holy war. He called on the Christian warriors of Europe to stop fighting each other and instead join in the holy cause of rescuing their fellow Christians—and above all regain Jerusalem for Christianity. Participants were promised a plenary indulgence—that the suffering and expense of the expedition would take the place of all penance for sins they had

confessed, wiping their spiritual slates clean so they could enter heaven directly upon death.

Thus was born the phenomenon that later historians named "Crusades," a long series of campaigns to take and hold the eastern littoral of the Mediterranean. Urban's message struck a deep chord among Europeans, as piety, hope for land and advancement, and longing for adventure coalesced. A reasonable modern estimate is that perhaps 100,000 fighting men set out for Jerusalem in five great armies at intervals between 1096 and 1097, along with many more noncombatants. Great lords commanded some of the armies, such as the duke of Normandy (who mortgaged his duchy to his brother the king of England to pay expenses) and the count of Toulouse; several other contingents were inspired by charismatic preachers like Peter the Hermit and, ill-disciplined, charted a course of destruction that included the first pogroms

against the Jewish communities of the Rhineland. A number of these badly-organized "people's" Crusade armies were destroyed, including Peter the Hermit's large army, annihilated by the Turks after insisting that the Byzantine emperor allow them to proceed into Turkish territory without waiting for the princely armies. After great hardships and near destruction during their long siege of Antioch, a remnant of the original crusading force took Jerusalem on July 15, 1099, in a bloody assault and massacre of the populace. After a final battle against a Fatimid relief force that had been sent from Jerusalem, most of the survivors returned to their lives in Europe, leaving a small, not-yet-viable collection of "crusader states" in their wake.

The Crusade phenomenon had a massive impact on Western Europe and far beyond. The first expedition would never have succeeded without the support of the maritime cities of Italy, and the incomplete nature of the conquest—and the fact that hordes of Europeans now wanted to make the pilgrimage to Jerusalem—assured their rapid growth. The Crusade had also precipitated a shift in the relationship between Western Europe and the Byzantine Empire. Emperor Alexius at first supported the crusaders' efforts, but his failure to assist them when the Westerners were nearly destroyed at Antioch gave the crusade leaders a pretext to permanently occupy former Byzantine land as well as a permanent grudge against the "untrustworthy" Greeks. And of course the First Crusade and the many expeditions that followed threw Western Europe into a long-term antagonistic relationship with the Islamic lands, making them the ultimate "other" for many centuries.

BELOW *An artist's imaginative depiction of the Christian forces defeating the Turkish Kerbogha at Antioch during the First Crusade.*

EAST ASIA'S WARS

Of course, not all wars in the 11th century were ideological. Nonetheless, the period as a whole was marked by militarization. In Japan, the rural elite was ever more defined in military terms, committed to defending their *shoen* (great estates) against all enemies, including the central government. The emperors made a concerted attempt to regain real control from the Fujiwara clan that had dominated the government for over a century, with Emperor Go-Sanjo taking the throne in 1068 as the first emperor in 170 years whose mother was not a Fujiwara. Go-Sanjo began a unique Japanese experiment in indirect rule, the era of cloister government. Emperors would rule until they had begotten a son, then abdicate and control the government behind the scenes for the new child ruler. A prime example of the phenomenon is Shirakawa, who became emperor in 1073 (at age 19), abdicated in 1087, and continued to control the government in retirement until his death in 1129. Neither emperors nor retired emperors could stem the rising tide of warfare, however. The Earlier Nine Years' War (1051–62) and Later Three Years' War (1083–7) against the Emishi of the far northeast starkly demonstrated

BELOW *Scroll depicting a military clash in Japan's Later Three Years War.*

the government's dependence on warlords, who increasingly fortified their homes as central government weakened.

Southeast Asia also saw a rise in warfare. The kingdom of Angkor (Cambodia) expanded under Suryavarman I (1002–50), who waged repeated war with his neighbors. Vietnam too was united under the Ly Dynasty (1009–1225), especially thanks to Ly Phat Ma (1028–54), a great king who consolidated royal power and led a major naval expedition against the Chams to the south. It was another naval attack, from Chola in northeastern India, that shattered Srivijaya control of trade through the Straits of Melaka in 1025. After that, no one power was able to gain control of Southeast Asian shipping lanes for a number of generations.

ABOVE *Originally dedicated to the Hindu God Vishnu, the great temple of Angkor Wat (Cambodia) was converted to Buddhist use in the 12th century; it was built by Suryavarman II.*

DEVELOPMENTS IN THE WESTERN HEMISPHERE

Least understood, for want of written sources, were efforts to create stronger states in the Americas in this period. In Mesoamerica, Toltecs and Maya continued their tradition of city-state rule, with Tula and Cholula especially important as ceremonial and governmental centers. To their north, the greatest pueblos of Chaco Canyon were constructed in the 11th century; by 1100 this culture had more than seventy communities spread over much of the American southwest. The most impressive new development in this period, however, was the flourishing of Mississippian Culture, especially its major center of Cahokia.

By the 10th century, the Mississippians were constructing elaborate towns in river valleys, especially characterized by great platform mounds, grouped into chiefdoms of all sizes. By about 1050, Cahokia rose to prominence among these chiefdoms, developing a great

BELOW *Monk's Mound, the largest structure at Cahokia (Illinois).*

center for elaborate ceremonies. Cahokia is by far the largest pre-European site north of central Mexico, with more than a hundred monumental mounds and thousands of homesteads; the site at its height had a population of about 15,000. The Mississippian culture flourished for about 600 years, although the large ritual centers were already feeling the effects of drought in the 11th century. Azatlan, the northernmost Mississippian town, was highly defensible with a strong palisade; Cahokia itself constructed palisades four times, coinciding with periods of serious drought. The competition for scarce resources was ultimately unsuccessful and by 1350 Cahokia was largely abandoned, although many of the centers survived until European contact. A great number of the sites were destroyed in the 19th century, as railroad workers found the Mississippian great mounds convenient sources of earth for railbed fill.

LEFT *The Keller Figurine, found at Cahokia. The female figure is processing maize and may have been a fertility symbol.*

The Dresden Codex

Although the Maya created a full written language, a trail of purposeful destruction has left us with only four of the many books the Mesoamerican culture produced. Christian missionaries purposefully burned these invaluable records of the Maya past. One of the very few surviving Maya books is known as the *Dresden Codex*, a 78-page work that folds accordion-style. The pages are made of *amate*, a bark paper. The text is mostly scientific, with astronomical tables and information about the conjunction of planets and the moon. It also contains medical teaching, suggesting that the Maya regarded heavenly motions and human health to be interlinked. The *Codex* was most likely produced in Chichén Itzá in the 11th or 12th century. It probably first made its way to Europe as a gift to the Holy Roman Emperor, Charles V. The manuscript was vital in the 20th-century decipherment of Maya writing. Its complexity hints at the vast extent of Maya knowledge that has been lost.

The Dresden Codex.

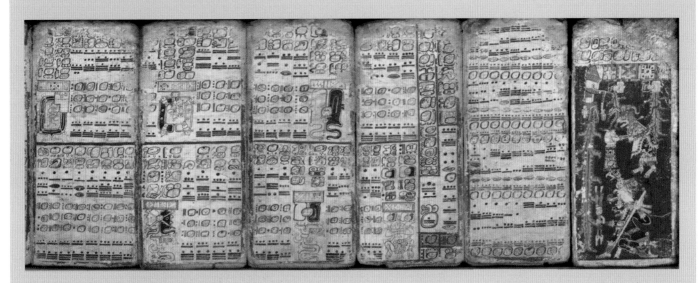

CHAPTER 7

The Colliding Cultures of the 12th Century

At the dawn of the 12th century, much of Eurasia was on the verge of change. China might have appeared stable to the casual observer, but both the Liao Dynasty and the Song Dynasty in the divided lands suffered systemic weaknesses, while yet another people of the steppe, the Jurchen, grew ever stronger. Further west, the Seljuk Turkish Dynasty, which had swept all before it for much of the 11th century, was weakened by dynastic strife and the inherent difficulties of ruling a large empire, a problem that also faced their Fatimid rivals in Egypt. Division within the Islamic world, which had enabled the First Crusade to succeed, allowed the new rulers of the crusader states to consolidate their gains, thanks to repeated waves of fighting men and gifts from Europe that supported their efforts. At mid-century, it appeared unlikely that the rising tide of Europe could be stemmed. History is full of surprises, however, and one of its greatest was the rise of a Kurdish captain, Saladin, to rule over a large Islamic state that included Egypt and that soon conquered almost all of the European enclave in the Near East, including the recapture of Jerusalem.

RIGHT *Knights departing on crusade, Church of St-Jacques-des-Guérets, France (12th-century fresco).*

HVGO·DE·

THE JURCHEN CONQUESTS

China under the rule of the Song Dynasty enjoyed a brilliant culture. It was a great age of poetry and historiography, of painting, calligraphy, and ceramics, financed by an economic revolution that included propagation of new rice strains and more intensive settlement of the south. Even poor peasants had access to iron tools, thanks to massive mining and smelting operations. The government invested massively in the means for war—but was very unwilling to fight, instead repeatedly emphasizing the need for civilian control. The Song government's general policy was to coexist with the "barbarians" on the frontiers, making a number of humiliating treaties and relegating the desire to regain the prefectures lost to the Liao Dynasty in the northeast to a distant dream.

Troubles began, not against the Song-ruled part of China, but against the rival Liao emperors. The Liao, Khitans who had invaded northern China from the steppe, continued to rule an empire that included both pastoral and agricultural lands. Among their vassal peoples were the Jurchen, many of whom still lived as steppe nomads. For reasons that are unclear, the Jurchens' Liao overlords systematically humiliated their vassals, demanding an annual tribute that included virgins for their brothels and even sexually abusing married elite Jurchen women. In 1112, the Liao emperor went too far, ordering the Jurchen leaders to a feast to pay homage and then demanding that they dance for his amusement. One of the tribe's most important chiefs, Aguda, refused. His refusal sparked a resistance

movement, and Aguda had soon created a Jurchen confederation that in 1114 inflicted a devastating defeat on the Liao army.

Almost the entire Jurchen population migrated into the conquered Liao territory, Aguda and then his brother Waqimai declaring themselves emperors of a new Jin dynasty. And they did not stop there, soon sweeping into Song territory. Emperor Huizong was more concerned to construct incredibly elaborate gardens than to defend his empire, and the ruthlessness of his agents (the infamous Flower and Rock Network) sparked a massive rebellion that made the Jurchens' task easy. Waqimai defeated the Song armies in battle in 1125 and, although the next year the Chinese emperor accepted humiliating terms, including the superiority of the Jin emperor to himself, fighting soon continued. After a short siege, the Jurchen took and looted

the Song northern capital, Kaifeng, probably the largest city in the world with a population of about one million. Victory was consolidated by capturing Emperor Qinzong and his father Huizong, who had abdicated in the panic that the invasion had caused. The period known as the Northern Song had ended, but despite repeated attempts the Jurchen were unable to conquer China south of the Yangzi River, which continued under the rule of Qinzong's younger brother and is known as the Southern Song. One of the most tragic stories in the invasion is that of the heroic Song general Yue Fei (1103–42). A brilliant leader, he rose to high rank despite his low birth. He engineered a number of daring successes against the invaders, and pressed the emperor to go on the offensive rather than following the preferred Song policy of accommodation. Yue Fei was relieved of his command and imprisoned.

BELOW *A section of* A Thousand Li of Rivers and Mountains *by Wang Ximeng, a famed painter of the Northern Song period.*

No legal case could be made against the hero, so he was poisoned in his cell; his admiring jailers stole the body and buried it secretly. Although Yue Fei's memory was soon rehabilitated, the Southern Song never made a real effort to regain the north. The Jin emperors, ruling a populace that was at least 90 percent ethnic Chinese, rapidly sinicized, in 1138 even reinstating the civil service exams in their territory.

The vicissitudes of the Song Dynasty of course had wider ripple effects in Asia, which can be seen especially in international trade. The fall of Kaifeng closed the caravan routes that ran over the Central Asian steppe, leading enterprising Chinese merchants to develop sea trade more than ever

BELOW One of the thousands of "relic stones" collected at great expense for Emperor Huizong's garden at Genyue.

ABOVE One of China's greatest inventions, the compass was used for navigation by the 12th century.

before. As Chinese ships moved into the Indian Ocean, they proved highly competitive. Chinese junks were better than Arab lateen-rigged ships, larger and able to tack in a headwind more easily. Their division into watertight compartments also made them less likely to sink if they struck rocks. Chinese mariners also increased their edge by employing one of China's great inventions, the compass, as a navigational aid. The compass had been invented in China a millennium earlier, but as a tool for divination; the first recorded use of one in a ship was in 1119. The idea quickly spread to the Arabs and from there to Europe.

A number of Southeast Asian states took advantage of the wealth generated by trade. By the 12th century, the port cities of Java had won hegemony over the Straits of Melaka, replacing Srivijaya's dominance. The merchant elites, for the most part Muslims, assured that Islam became the basis for sovereignty in the region. Elsewhere, Buddhism remained strong. For example, in Cambodia Jayavarman VII (1181–1218), a devout Buddhist who

was already 60 years old when he came to the throne, expended enormous resources on building Buddhist temples, although his modeling of religious compassion also led him to found hospitals and improve roads.

The kingdom of Pagan (Burma), which reached its height under Narapatisithu (1173–1210), was also a Buddhist state, the Buddhist temples enjoying enormous royal patronage. Indeed, the rulers periodically had to reestablish balance when Buddhist institutions had gained control of too much state wealth by "purifying" the Buddhist religious establishment, denouncing them as corrupt and worldly and forcing monks to give up worldly possessions in return for reordination.

LEFT *A legend of Yue Fei tells that the hero's mother tattooed "serve the country with the utmost loyalty" on his back, as depicted in this modern statue in Hangzhou.*

BELOW *Some of the many temples of Pagan (Myanmar).*

REORGANIZING THE MIDDLE EAST

The Jurchen conquests caused a chain reaction that was felt far into the Middle East. When the Jurchen smashed the Liao Dynasty, a Khitan prince and his followers escaped the destruction, moving westward into Seljuk territory and creating a new empire, known as the Kara-Khitay. In 1141 they inflicted a heavy defeat on Sanjar, the Seljuk sultan of Iran, in the Battle of the Qatwan Steppe near Samarkand.

By the time the Kara-Khitay defeated the eastern Seljuk sultan, the Seljuks had long fallen on hard times; indeed, their decline started with the death of Sultan Malikshah in 1092, when the end of the conquest period meant the Turkish rulers had fewer resources to secure the loyalty of their followers. The ruling family had divided into eastern and western branches, both frequently riven by succession disputes. Increasingly, the eastern sultan, leader of the region known as the Great Seljuk Empire, was ruler in little more than name, the governors of various provinces (*atabegs*) holding the real power. Since of course there was still an Abbasid caliph, the result was a unique "triarchy" with not one but two figurehead rulers—with the various levels frequently at odds with each other.

BELOW *The tomb of Sanjar, constructed in Merv (Turkmenistan) after the sultan's death in 1157.*

After the Kara-Khitay defeated them, things rapidly went from bad to worse for the eastern Seljuks. Especially destabilizing was that the governor of the eastern province of Khwarazm repeatedly rebelled, given the opportunity to break free of Seljuk control by a major Turkman rebellion in 1152, during which Sultan Sanjar himself was captured and held for three years. The resentment the caliphs felt at being figureheads for the Seljuks is clear at this point; Caliph al-Muqtafi tried to assert his own right to rule, capturing several contenders for the Seljuk throne after Sanjar's death. The new sultan, Muhammad, responded by besieging Baghdad in 1157, but proved too weak to succeed. By the late 12th century, the revived caliphal state was a significant power. When the Khwarazmians killed last eastern Seljuk sultan, Tughril III, in battle in 1194, the triumphant Khwarazmian shah sent the sultan's head to the caliph as a present.

The Legend of Prester John

The Kara-Khitay leader Yelü Dashi's major defeat of the Seljuks in 1141 was the inspiration behind one of medieval Europe's strangest legends: that of a Christian priest-king far in the east who would save Christendom from the Muslims. This mythical figure, who came to be known as Prester John, first appears in the chronicle of the great 12th-century German historian Bishop Otto of Freising. A confused rumor about a great defeat the Muslims had suffered reached Otto's ears, and his imagination turned the Buddhist Yelü Dashi into a Christian hero.

Although a product of Christian wishful thinking, the legend of Prester John had a long life. At first he was believed to be a Nestorian Christian king in India, perhaps a descendant of one of the Three Wise Men. Soon it was assumed that the great patriarch-king lived somewhere in Central Asia, and many Europeans regarded the rise of the Mongols to world dominance in the 13th century as a sign that Prester John was in fact coming from the east to crush the Muslims. In its final version, the Portuguese of the 16th and 17th centuries situated Prester John in Ethiopia.

Prester John as emperor of Ethiopia in a Portuguese map of the 1550s.

CRUSADING AND THE CRUSADER STATES

As we have seen, the warriors of the First Crusade had carved out several small enclaves in the Near East, focused on Antioch, Jerusalem, Edessa, and soon Tripoli. They soon stopped massacring every Muslim (or person they mistook for a Muslim) and settled down to rule a largely non-Christian population. The early crusader states were, however, fragile entities, without sufficient manpower or territory to exist as viable polities. Two circumstances in particular saved them and indeed allowed them to flourish. First, for several generations the enemies of the Kingdom of Jerusalem and the principality of Antioch were local Turkish governors; the Christians did not face the full power of either the Seljuk sultanate or the Fatimid caliphate of Egypt. When the Seljuks waged war in the Near East they were much more concerned to combat the radical Muslim Ismaili sect than the Christian interlopers, while the Egyptians soon retreated to their own borders. The other feature that allowed the crusader states to thrive was the ongoing massive outpouring of support the new Christian rulers received from Western Europe.

The numbering of crusades, the work of modern historians, disguises the repeated, wavelike nature of the crusading phenomenon, suggesting that crusades only occurred every 40 years or so. The reality was far more complex and profound. In the 12th century, besides the First (1096–99), Second (1147–9), and Third (1189–92) Crusades, large armies headed eastward a number of times to aid the crusader states, including the massive ill-fated Crusade of 1101, the Crusade of King Sigurd of Norway (which took the port of Sidon), and the Venetian expedition of 1122–4, which worked with the king of Jerusalem to destroy the Fatimid fleet and

BELOW The Order of Knights Hospitallers constructed the great fortress of Krak des Chevaliers (Syria) from the 1140s to 1170, with further additions in the 13th century.

conquer the major port of Tyre. Besides larger expeditions, hardly a year passed when hundreds of western fighters did not come to support the cause with their swords. Those who could not fight themselves financed the establishment of several religious orders of knights who vowed to defend pilgrims and the holy places, donating a massive network of estates and other resources in Europe, the proceeds of which paid not just for the upkeep of a substantial fighting force but enabled the construction of massive fortresses like Krak des Chevaliers.

The weakest and most isolated of the crusader states, the county of Edessa, fell to Muslim attack in 1144, provoking a panicked reaction in Europe. Once again major armies set out, this time with the kings of France (Louis VII) and Germany (Conrad III) in command, in a major event known as the Second Crusade (1147–9). The expedition to the Holy Land proved to be an embarrassing failure. As they passed through Constantinople, the Byzantines regarded them with suspicion; not only was Emperor Manuel Comnenus at war with the Normans of Sicily at the time but the princes of Antioch had done their considerable best to sow suspicion of Byzantium in the West. The crusade's problems went deeper, however. Since Christians already ruled Jerusalem, the crusaders did not have an obvious goal as they had in the 1090s. Some argued the need to reinforce the principality of Antioch in the north, which would have helped secure the land route from the Byzantine Empire to Jerusalem. The pro-Antioch party included the queen of France, Eleanor of Aquitaine, whose support for her uncle Raymond of Antioch led to a rupture with her husband that ended in divorce. Eleanor lost, however, and the crusade force, badly weakened by Seljuk attacks, marched southward. The leaders finally decided to attack Damascus. They had not made any real preparations for a siege, though, and simply gave up within a few days. Far from strengthening the remaining crusader states, the crusaders had only succeeded in emboldening their enemies. The surviving crusaders had barely slunk back to Europe when the Seljuk governor of Aleppo, Nur

al-Din, attacked the principality of Antioch with assistance from Damascus. He soundly defeated the Antiochenes in the Battle of Inab in 1149, killing Prince Raymond and then symbolically bathing in the Mediterranean as a symbol of the Muslim resolve to win back the land under Christian rule.

Although a complete failure in the Near East, the Second Crusade had a much more universal agenda. German nobles, eager to push their dominion eastward into the western Slavic lands, received the same plenary indulgence granted to Holy Land crusaders. They enjoyed only temporary success, but the influx of crusaders gave new force to the German "drive to the east" (*drang nach osten*) as the nobles who controlled the German frontier, especially Albert the Bear of Brandenburg (d. 1170) and Henry the Lion of Saxony (d. 1195), pushed into the territory between the Elbe and Oder Rivers, offering generous incentives to attract Western European colonists to their new lands. By 1168, west

BELOW *Henry the Lion, Brunswick, Germany (1874). Duke Henry founded both Brunswick and Munich.*

ABOVE *Frederick Barbarossa's charter granting the new city of Lübeck the right of self-government..*

Slavic polytheism officially ended with the Danish destruction of the temple at Arkona, as the Danes also claimed a share of the land grab.

The Northern Crusades are but one example of a major trend toward private enterprise that coexisted in Europe with the rising power of the state in many regions. The closest parallel is a Norman noble known as "Strongbow" who led an army to Ireland to try to gain himself a crown; Henry II of England became so concerned about Strongbow's power that he intervened in Ireland himself and claimed the island for England. German nobles, besides subjugating the western Slavs, proved to be astute businessmen, founding towns (such as Lübeck in 1143 and Munich in 1158) and offering generous terms to encourage merchants to settle in them. Noble-founded cities prospered in this environment, those on the North Sea and Baltic forming a league, the Hanse, in 1160 to protect trade routes. Another important civic league of the 12th century was the Lombard League in northern Italy, formed to resist German Emperor Frederick I's demand for the return of imperial lands that had been lost in the Investiture Contest. Trade was flourishing and merchants did not want rulers' interference in their business.

Fighters in Spain's *reconquista* were offered the same plenary indulgence as other crusaders. A contingent of English crusaders on their way to the Holy Land was diverted to help King Afonso I of Portugal besiege the Muslim-held city of Lisbon. Their conquest of that major city was the only significant victory of the many-fronted Second Crusade. Nonetheless, the massive scope of the expeditions of 1147–9 show how self-confident Europe's core lands had become, what resources Europe's rulers and nobles could muster, and the unique and inextricable combination of religious fervor (by the mass of crusaders) and opportunism (by local leaders who pursued their own ends) that

marked the crusades. The determination of the Christian kings of northern Spain to take back the Muslim-ruled lands that "belonged" to Christianity continued unabated. Almoravid rule proved to be only a temporary check, as both Muslim and Christian subjects resented the northern African rigorists.

By 1144 a peninsula-wide rebellion against the Almoravids raged, while their heartland in Africa fell under attack by the Almohads, a new Islamic puritanical movement. The Almohads, whose name means "unitarian" in affirmation of the oneness of God, coalesced under Muhammad ibn Tumart (1077–1130), who proclaimed himself the Mahdi. Ibn Tumart's successor 'Abd al-Mu'min went further, taking the title caliph and conquering the Almoravid capital Marrakesh in 1146. The Almohads soon expanded onto the Iberian Peninsula, in 1148 conquering Córdoba and by c.1170 replacing the Almoravids as rulers of the south. The result was 30 years of intensive war between the Almohads and the Christian states

RIGHT *Almohad silk banner, captured at the battle of Las Navas de Tolosa (1212).*

ABOVE *Tinmal Mosque, Morocco, constructed on the site where Almohad founder Ibn Tumart was buried.*

RIGHT *Choir of the monastic church of St-Denis, France, where Gothic architecture was born in the 1140s.*

of Spain, Almohad control of the south only weakening after a Christian coalition inflicted a major defeat in the Battle of Las Navas de Tolosa (1212).

Strangely, despite their failure, the fact that they had made the sacrifice to go on crusade enhanced the prestige of both Louis VII of France and Conrad III of Germany. France's monarchy was growing stronger all the time. Louis VII's father had wrested effective control of the royal domain around Paris from independent-minded barons, enhancing royal income (since of the European rulers only kings of England could impose taxes) and honor. The highlight of Louis VI's reign was arranging the marriage of his heir to the greatest heiress of Europe, Eleanor, whose large and wealthy duchy in southwest France more than doubled the area under effective royal control. Although the marriage

ended in divorce after producing two daughters and Eleanor soon arranged a second marriage to Louis' chief rival (the future Henry II of England), as a whole the 12th century was a time of centralization for France.

The same could not be said of the German empire. Henry IV and Henry V bartered away many royal rights for support in the wars of the Investiture Contest, and northern Italy simply followed its own course without any real royal control for 50 years. Moreover, the hereditary succession to the throne broke down. Always a matter of election by the great nobles (as it was in other European countries), whenever possible the nobles had voted for the "natural" heir—the previous ruler's eldest son. During the Investiture Contest, however, the nobles had elected a sequence of their own as king, ignoring heredity in favor of other factors. When Henry V died childless in 1125, Conrad III and Lothar III had fought over the throne, dividing Germany effectively between two rival families.

The German state saw some recovery when, on his deathbed, Conrad III designated his nephew Frederick I (Barbarossa) as successor in preference to his own son, since the blood of both rival families flowed in Frederick's veins. Frederick (1152–90) proved to be a dynamic ruler but faced an uphill battle against the centrifugal forces that had gained such strength under his predecessors. Barbarossa soon obtained papal coronation as emperor, but almost immediately tensions with the papacy escalated, as both emperor and pope claimed a sweeping universal authority. It was in the context of his propaganda war with the papacy that Frederick's court intellectuals first articulated the German emperor's special authority as "holy" and "Roman." The war was not just one of words, however, with popes several times excommunicating Frederick for his assertion of control over the German and northern Italian Church, Frederick supporting several anti-popes, and the papacy actively joining in a league of northern Italian cities that opposed Frederick's attempt to reassert his authority by force of arms.

Despite years of campaigning, Barbarossa won only very limited rights over the former kingdom of Lombardy, especially as the most important of his German vassals, Henry the Lion of Saxony, failed to support the emperor in the key Battle of Legnano in 1176. In the course of his Italian expeditions, Frederick gave up still more royal rights north of the Alps.

BELOW *The Cappenberg Head, a reliquary bust created in c. 1160 and believed to be a portrait of Frederick Barbarossa.*

The Eleanor Vase

Despite frequent conflict, trade and even alliances continued between Muslims and Christians. One of the most beautiful reminders of this cross-culture contact is a rock crystal vase, known as *The Eleanor Vase*. The Islamic world prized rock crystal, which was mined in eastern Africa, and thousands of goblets, vases, and so on would have decorated the homes of Muslim elites. Few have survived. But a Fatimid crystal vase, embellished with gold and jewels, made its way to Spain, probably as a diplomatic gift. In *c.* 1120, the emir of Zaragoza then presented it to Duke William IX of Aquitaine, who was his ally at the time. William's daughter, the heiress Eleanor, then gifted the vase to her husband Louis VII as a wedding present. Finally, Louis offered it to the great royal monastery of St-Denis, where it remained until the French Revolution. The unique and much-traveled vase is now in the Louvre.

The Eleanor Vase.

At first glance, the most surprising absence from the Second Crusade was the king of England, although as we have seen, some English crusaders conquered Lisbon. The reason was that the greater Norman state William the Conqueror had created had broken down into civil war after William's last son, Henry I, had died in 1135. Henry's only legitimate heir was a daughter, Matilda, who had returned to her father after her husband Henry V of Germany had died. Despite the Norman Henry's efforts to secure the succession, demanding oaths from his nobles to accept Matilda as reigning queen, her cousin Stephen of Blois snatched the crown. The result was soon civil war, as Matilda and her second husband Geoffrey of Anjou succeeded in gaining control of Normandy but ultimately failed in their bid to capture the English throne for the putative queen. Exhausted by decades of conflict, Stephen finally accepted Matilda's son—yet another Henry—as his heir, and Henry II (1154–89) was able to inherit, although it took him several years to reestablish royal control.

THE CRUCIBLE OF THE CRUSADER STATES

After the humiliation of the Second Crusade, enthusiasm for large-scale expeditions to the Holy Land faded and was indeed less necessary, as the remaining crusader states were now viable entities. The rulers of Jerusalem were wealthy and the military might they could command by hire or as vassals was greatly supplemented by the military religious orders, especially the Knights Templar and Knights Hospitaller. By the 1160s, King Amalric of Jerusalem could plausibly invade Egypt, taking advantage of chaos within the Fatimid government. Unfortunately, this new level of Christian aggression provoked a hostile response from Nur al-Din, who by this time had created a greater Syrian state. Much of the Turkman's success came from invoking an emotional response among his supporters, a drive to wage war against the Christian intruders that was inspired by ideology rather than just pragmatism. It was Nur al-Din who harnessed the Qur'anic language of *jihad*—struggle—specifically for

military confrontation with nonbelievers. Calling for what was in effect a counter-crusade, Nur al-Din was able to accomplish what was probably his primary goal, the conquest of Muslim Syria. The Kingdom of Jerusalem's assault on Egypt gave him the opportunity to combine ideology and opportunism. Nur al-Din sent his general Shirkuh to Egypt, who helped coordinate the Fatimid resistance to the attack. The Fatimid caliph was soon pressured to appoint Shirkuh as *wazir*. Although Shirkuh soon died, Syrian engagement with Egypt continued, as the commander's nephew Salah al-Din Yusuf ibn Ayyub, known in English as Saladin, took charge.

Saladin (d. 1193) rapidly consolidated his control of Egypt, seizing revenues to maintain his Syrian forces. This provoked a revolt of the Fatimids' Black troops, who were bloodily suppressed in 1169. Then, when the Fatimid caliph al-'Adid died in September 1171, Saladin simply ordered prayers for the Sunni Abbasid caliph at Friday worship, thus ending the Fatimid

RIGHT *The triumphant Saladin at the Battle of Hattin, sculpted by Abdallah al-Sayed to commemorate the 800th anniversary of the sultan's death (Damascus, Syria).*

caliphate. Saladin maintained tenuous loyalty to Nur al-Din, but when the latter died in 1174 Saladin seized control of Muslim Syria, creating a large if artificial Muslim state known as the Ayyubid Empire. The peoples of Egypt and Syria had little in common, but Saladin was able to win them, along with volunteers from other Muslim regions, to the common cause of *jihad* against the crusader states.

Of the crusader states, the Kingdom of Jerusalem in particular was very heavily armed, protected by impressive castles and endlessly supplemented with manpower and money from Europe, especially sent in support of the military religious orders. Jerusalem's downfall came about not because Saladin attacked with overwhelming strength but due to internal dissension. One of the greatest tragedies of the 12th century is that when a brilliant young king, Baldwin IV, ascended the throne of Jerusalem at the age of 13 in 1174 he was already suffering from leprosy. Baldwin proved well able to inspire his fighting men and several times beat off major Muslim invasions. But as the disease ate away at the king, crippling and in time blinding him, the issue of leadership became paramount. Baldwin's disease made it impossible for him to father a child, so his natural heir was his older sister Sibyl. Her first marriage had produced a son, but her husband, who it had been assumed would command Jerusalem's military forces, died very soon thereafter. Fearing the independence of his greatest nobles, Baldwin rapidly arranged a new marriage for Sibyl to a man of good blood but few prospects, Guy of Lusignan. Soon, however, Baldwin turned against Guy, stripping him of the regency that had been conferred on him as the king's sickness deepened.

The result was tragedy for the Christian kingdom. Baldwin decreed that his young nephew should inherit, bypassing Sybil and Guy, but when the boy died Sybil became queen and assured Guy's recognition as king. By this point, Jerusalem's nobles had divided into factions, some of the most important refusing to recognize Guy's rule. Then, in 1187, Saladin invaded yet again. Guy, desperate to prove himself, drained the Holy Land's fortresses of manpower and marched against Saladin. The Muslim leader cunningly trapped the Christian force away from access to water, then won a complete victory over Guy in the Battle of Hattin on July 4, 1187. Few escaped the rout and the king himself was captured. Members of the military orders who were captured were summarily executed. Saladin was then able to take nearly every fortified place of the Kingdom of Jerusalem, including Jerusalem itself in October.

News of the defeat at Hattin and the fall of Jerusalem caused shock and consternation in Europe. It also evoked an enormous *need* to win the holy city back that led wave after wave of fighting men to throw themselves against the Ayyubid Empire for the next 70 years. When news reached Europe tens of thousands of men took the crusaders' vow, including King Henry II of England, King Philip II of France, and Emperor Frederick I Barbarossa, who became the leaders of what is known as the Third Crusade. Henry died before setting out, but his much more enthusiastic son Richard I (Lionheart) took up the torch. As they completed preparations, contingent

BELOW *Coronation of Baldwin IV of Jerusalem, from a 13th-century manuscript.*

ABOVE *The arrival of Philip II Augustus at the Siege of Acre during the Third Crusade.*

after contingent set out for the east. Their goal was the vital port city of Acre, which Saladin had captured but which Guy and Sibyl began to besiege as soon as Guy had been ransomed.

The hope of regaining Jerusalem was blighted early, when Frederick Barbarossa, leading an enormous army via the overland route, drowned in a river in Anatolia. The German army disintegrated, although some made their way to Acre despite the emperor's death. More important, the loss of a senior, respected figure who could mediate between the rival kings Philip and Richard meant that tensions between the

two escalated until Philip simply packed up and went home as soon as he decently could after the conquest of Acre. With Philip's return to France, Richard became the undoubted leader of the crusaders and the surviving settlers. Despite a number of victories over Saladin, whose troops dogged the Christians at every step, Richard failed to win the decisive engagement that would allow him to regain Jerusalem, and finally had to return to his own kingdom.

Saladin's death in 1193 presented an opportunity to the Europeans, as the Ayyubid Empire's territories were divided among members of Saladin's family, although his brother al-'Adil soon won ascendancy. Frederick Barbarossa's son Henry VI planned a new major campaign, known as the Crusade of 1197. Henry himself died before the expedition could set out, however, and rivalry for the German throne made many of the empire's greatest nobles unwilling to depart for the east. Although the remaining crusaders did regain a number of important ports of the Kingdom of Jerusalem, they did not satisfy the Christians' desperate longing for Jerusalem itself.

THE FOURTH CRUSADE

When Innocent III (1198–1216) became pope he devoted enormous effort to mustering Europe for another onslaught against the Ayyubid Empire. The result was the Fourth Crusade (1202–4). No kings enlisted in the new effort—England and France were at war and Germany was torn by a succession struggle, while the Christian kings of Spain had their own fight against the Muslims. Nonetheless, the call for a crusade inspired large numbers of French nobles and their followers. The council of crusade leaders realized that a major weakness of the Third Crusade was that participants arrived at different times, often leaving before new contingents arrived. Instead, they resolved to take advantage of the growing naval strength of Italy to have all the crusaders

transported at a single time, contracting with the city of Venice to supply transports, supplies, and a fleet of warships.

The venture was in dire straits, however, when only about one-third of the crusaders appeared at the rendezvous, many participants making their own travel arrangements or delaying departure. The crusade's leaders could not pay the Venetians for the fleet that had been meticulously prepared, which would have been a crippling blow to the city's economy. So they made a deal. The doge of Venice agreed to delay collection on the rest of the money owed if the crusaders would conquer the city of Zara. The crusaders did so, despite the fact that Zara was a Christian city subject to the king of Hungary. And then a golden opportunity presented itself, in the form of a Byzantine prince whose father had been deposed and imprisoned. In return for a show of force at Constantinople, Prince Alexius promised to pay the balance owed to Venice and take the cross himself with a large army, making the reconquest of Jerusalem probable.

The Byzantine Empire had fallen on hard times. After the misunderstandings of the Second Crusade, Emperor Manuel Comnenus (1143–80) had proven willing to work with Western Europeans, and indeed trained to fight as a Western-style knight. By the latter part of his reign, though, tensions had risen especially with the mercantile city-states of Italy. Manuel had attempted an invasion of Norman Italy in 1155–6, granting massive trade privileges to Genoa in return for assistance. Although the expedition was a complete failure, the Genoese retained their privileged trade status, joining Venice in completely dominating Byzantine commerce. In 1171,

Manuel imprisoned thousands of Venetians after they destroyed their rival Genoa's new quarter in Constantinople. Relations were eventually patched up, but resentment lingered. Then in 1176 Manuel suffered a serious defeat at the hands of the Seljuk Kilij Arslan in the Battle of Myriokephalon, ending any Byzantine hope of regaining Anatolia.

Manuel left his throne to an adolescent son who survived only three years before being deposed and assassinated by a cousin, who whipped his supporters into a frenzy to hunt down and murder all of the hated Western Europeans they could find. The new emperor Andronicus did not last long, a new usurper seizing the throne and leaving his rival to be dismembered by a mob. Then, in 1195, the latest emperor, Isaac II Angelos, was deposed and blinded by yet another rival.

When the crusaders—French soldiers and Venetian mariners—arrived at Constantinople

BELOW *The Latin conquest of Constantinople, an unexpected end to the Fourth Crusade.*

in 1203, they were shocked that the Byzantines did not welcome them as liberators and eagerly restore their deposed emperor. The show of force turned rapidly into reality, with Venetian warships breaking through the chain that barred entrance to the Golden Horn and the French crusaders attacking the land wall. As the Westerners gained the upper hand, the emperor fled and the city authorities did indeed restore the former emperor to the throne. All was not well, however. Prince Alexius had lured the crusaders with golden promises, but the weakened Byzantine state simply did not have the means to pay the crusaders' debt and equip the promised expeditionary force. After a tense stand-off, in 1204 the crusaders proceeded to force their way into Constantinople, looting the city and then establishing one of their own, Count Baldwin of Flanders, as emperor of a new Latin empire.

Baldwin and his successors were able to extend their conquest to much of Greece, but always had to face opposition not just from Turks but from their own resentful subjects and territories that remained in Byzantine hands. Finally, in 1261 one of the rival emperors, Michael VIII Palaiologos, was able to retake the empire's capital city with little opposition. But although the native dynasty regained the great city in 1261, the Byzantine Empire never recovered, and existed essentially as a city-state until Constantinople's fall to the Ottoman Turks in 1453. East–West relations also never recovered, especially as the Western rulers of Constantinople persecuted the Orthodox Christian clergy in the period of their occupation.

BELOW *The Bronze Horses of San Marco, Venice, looted from Constantinople's hippodrome during the crusader sack of the city.*

The 12th-Century Renaissance

The 12th century was a time of great intellectual ferment through much of Europe. Already in the 11th century schools had risen in importance, as centralizing rulers sought trained administrators and younger sons jockeyed for honorable careers. Soon, scholars clustered at certain centers, such as Paris, Bologna, or Oxford, creating what in time became Europe's first universities. While most of the students sought the skills needed to get ahead in the world, the intellectually curious made great advances in legal studies and theology.

What occurred was one of Europe's many "rebirths" of learning. Ancient Greek works, above all those of Aristotle, Euclid, and Ptolemy, were translated into Latin, often by way of Arabic translations. A key center for the transmission of Muslim and Jewish learning was the cathedral of Toledo, where Gerard of Cremona made over eighty translations to satisfy the eagerness of European students. Other scholars, such as Adelard of Bath, acquired mathematical and astronomical treatises in the libraries of Antioch and Damascus, translating them for the European market. The intellectual elite of Europe absorbed a large dose of Greek philosophy, especially Aristotelian logic, applying it to theology in the methodology known as "scholasticism," which simply means the method used in the schools. These schools soon developed into the first universities.

In the mind of educated Europeans, Aristotle became *the* Philosopher, and contact with the Arabic world soon provided translations into Latin of Aristotle's other treatises, including his noxious views on the natural inferiority of women. Aristotle did not enjoy universal esteem, however. In 1229, the University of Paris banned teaching Aristotle and commentators on his work, seeing the Greek's work as a threat to Christianity. More entertainingly, the 13th century also saw the creation of a popular tale mocking Aristotle and his pretensions. The story tells that the elderly philosopher became besotted with a beautiful woman named Phyllis, who hated him for his many slights to women. To strike a blow for all women, Phyllis pretended to return Aristotle's feelings, but said she wouldn't believe him, in light of his many misogynistic statements, unless he would consent to let her ride him as if he were a horse. Of course, Phyllis then arranged for all Aristotle's friends and rivals to spy on the debasing scene, having a good laugh at him in the process.

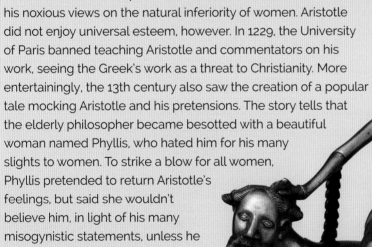

Decorative water ewer (*aquamanile*), illustrating the Phyllis and Aristotle legend.

CHAPTER 8

The Mongol Century

In the 13th century, few regions of Eurasia were left untouched by the creation of the Mongol Empire, the greatest empire the world has ever seen. The peoples of the Central Asian steppe, united under Chinggis Khan and his successors, carved a path of destruction through the states of Asia and the Middle East. The Mongols were not only destructive, however. Their unification of many lands under a "Mongolian Peace" (*pax Mongolica*) enabled trade to flourish. The very disruption of the conquest period also presented great opportunities to many who were not in the Mongols' path, as the Christians of Europe hoped an alliance with the Mongols would allow them to crush the Islamic states, and a new Muslim power, the Mamluks of Egypt, rose to prominence in large part by successfully fighting them. Although the Mongols cast an enormous shadow over the 13th century, it should not blind us to important advances in other parts of the world.

RIGHT *Mongols in combat, from* Jami' al-tawarikh *(Universal History), c. 1430*

STATE-BUILDING IN THE GLOBAL SOUTH

One of the most enigmatic processes of the medieval millennium was the settlement of the Pacific islands. DNA studies, occasional archaeological finds, and oral traditions allow scholars to understand the broad outlines of a process that took several hundred years to complete. Polynesians living in an environment of scarce resources, in many cases led by younger sons of chiefs who had few prospects at home, took to the sea in their large outrigger canoes, methodically colonizing uninhabited islands. The last links in the chain were the Hawaiian Islands and Rapa Nui (Easter Island), discovered in the 11th century, and New Zealand, initially settled within a generation of 1250. The modern Maori trace their heritage back to clans that arrived in a fleet of named canoes. The settlers carried an already-complex society with them, ruled by chieftains who could control labor and resources. Thus, soon after settlement the colonists on New Zealand's North Island were constructing monumental hillforts, centers not only for habitation but for storage, ritual, and sometimes defense. On Rapa Nui the settlers carved the great stone heads that still impress and mystify visitors.

More complex than the political structures of Oceania's small communities were those of sub-Saharan Africa, where regular contact with an international trade world encouraged the formation of larger states. Several significant central African states formed in a region that previously had

BELOW *Group of moai, human figures carved on Rapa Nui between 1250 and 1500. Hundreds were placed on stone platforms around the perimeter of the island.*

LEFT *Ruins of Nan Madol (Micronesia), which was constructed with huge stones starting in about 1200.*

consisted of hierarchical village alliances and small states that traded both westward and eastward. By the 11th century, however, the kingdom of Kanem had formed in the area of Lake Chad, its rulers benefiting from trade with Muslim-ruled northern Africa; their control of trade routes extended as far as southern Tunisia. The kings of Kanem converted to Islam and several made the pilgrimage to Mecca. Kanem reached its height in the reign of Dunama Dibalami (1210–48), reputed to have commanded a cavalry force of 40,000; his exchanges with the north included barbary horses, weapons, and armor, all of which made Kanem a major power. The area of modern Uganda also produced a large kingdom, that of Kitara, probably in the 13th century.

Along the Indian Ocean seaboard, African states reached new heights in the 13th century. It was a great age for the cities of the Swahili Coast, as can be seen from imported Arabic and Chinese pottery, textiles, beads, and many other goods. In turn, the Swahili merchants exported timber, ivory, grain, and iron. As trade connections ripened and significant Muslim communities flourished in the mercantile cities, for the first time in the 13th

century the native populace began to convert to Islam in large numbers. There is also evidence of a growing wealth divide, and in the 13th century some Swahili towns, such as Mombasa and Lamu, invested in major fortifications, protection against both trade rivals and internal rebellion.

An important element of Swahili trade was the gold mined to the south. The kingdom of Zimbabwe in the interior plateau began to coalesce in the 12th century in a good agricultural area that did not produce gold but was well-positioned to control the gold trade. Zimbabwe had a growth spurt toward mid-century, with the city of Great Zimbabwe founded in *c.* 1250, the first true city of southern Africa. The city demonstrated the greater pretensions of its rulers, showing improved stone-building techniques and featuring a royal enclosure surrounded by a 30-ft (10-m) wall. Elites dined on imported Chinese porcelain and Persian ware and enjoyed considerable luxury. At its height, Great Zimbabwe had a population of 15–18,000 and served as capital to a much wider state.

The region north of the Swahili coast also saw significant developments, the area recovering after

ABOVE *The Great Enclosure of Great Zimbabwe. The site was abandoned for unknown reasons in the 15th century.*

several centuries of economic decline and political fragmentation. The Christian kingdom of Maqurra in Nubia flourished for a brief period, gaining a share of Red Sea trade. Soon, however, trade led to the downfall of the native dynasty. When the Egyptians began to bypass Maqurra in favor of the Swahili town of 'Alwa and Ethiopia, the Maqurran king David raided Egyptian territory. The rulers of Egypt responded vigorously, defeating David and

installing a vassal ruler, finally imposing a Muslim king in 1316.

More successful was Ethiopia, successor to the ancient and early medieval state of Aksum. By the mid-12th century, the Zagwe kings had consolidated power in the north, establishing their capital at Roha. But in about 1270 a southern lord, Yekunno-Amlak, rebelled against the last Zagwe ruler, forcing him to abdicate. The new king founded a regime that dominated the region for the next 250 years, known as the "Solomonic" Dynasty, because the rulers claimed legitimacy by tracing their ancestry not just back to the pre-Zagwe kings of Aksum but to the queen of Sheba's liaison with King Solomon of Israel.

RIGHT *Church of St. George, Lalibela, Ethiopia, one of several churches carved from the living rock. They are traditionally dated to the reign of Gebre Mesqel Lalibela (1181–1221).*

In western Africa, Mali also benefited from international trade. After the Almoravids destroyed the Ancient Ghana Empire, several small states vied for control of the region; the eventual winner was the small Mandinka state of Kangaba, the core of what became the Mali Empire. Its first great ruler, Sundiata, began amassing victories in *c.* 1240 and over the course of two decades built a new empire that included all of Ancient Ghana and more, stretching to the Atlantic and asserting control over a number of tributary states, with Mandinka placed in key positions. Sundiata established a capital at Niani, an enormous royal complex with a host of surrounding villages for the trading class that served as the foundation for Mali's wealth. Trade reached deep into the interior of the continent and across the Sahara. Muslim merchants played an important, although not the only, role in trade, and Sundiata and his successors adopted Islam.

LEFT *Low-fired terracotta figurine of an archer, crafted in the Mali Empire.*

Indo-Arabic Numerals

Muslim commerce was greatly aided by the use of the Indian place-value system of numbers, which greatly simplified mathematical functions. While a few Europeans by *c.* 1000 had picked up on what came to be known as "Arab" numerals, the decimal system was only popularized in the years after 1200. The credit goes to an Italian merchant of Pisa, Leonardo Bonacci, most commonly known as Fibonacci (*c.* 1170–*c.* 1250). Fibonacci as a boy lived with his father at a Pisan trading post in what is now Algeria, where he studied arithmetic and discovered how much easier calculation was with Arabic numbers than with Roman numerals. He eventually produced *The Book of the Abacus*, which popularized Europeans' use of the simpler number system, including the zero and positional notation. Fibonacci was honored, both by Emperor Frederick II and by his own native city, for his services to mathematics.

Page from the *Book of the Abacus* by Fibonacci.

CHINGGIS KHAN

The end of Khitan rule had created a power vacuum on the Central Asian steppe. The people who moved to take advantage were the Mongols, fully nomadic pastoralists (unlike the semi-sedentary Khitans and Jurchen). The Mongols were not a large ethnic and linguistic group, numbering perhaps 700,000 people in total, divided into many independent kinship groups and loosely organized under a number of khans. They had a strong incentive to raid the settled lands on their borders, especially as Central Asia was particularly arid in the 1190s and early 1200s, leading the nomads to cull their herds and at times suffer famine. Like other peoples of the steppe, they were formidable fighters. There was no notion of "civilians" in their society and every man up to age 60 took part in wars. Also, like other nomads, they were very hard to fight, highly mobile (each man going into battle with a string of three to five horses) and fought with bows. The only thing that limited their threat was their own internal disunity. Recognizing that weakness, in the course of the 12th century they had begun a process of unification, especially to fight their traditional enemies, the Tatars.

Into this unstable environment came a young man named Temüjin, probably born in 1162. The son of a chief, after his father was poisoned Temüjin and his family barely survived, but when he reached adulthood he soon showed his mettle. The young man won allies, demonstrating extraordinary leadership ability and winning so many victories that in 1206 a pan-Mongol assembly acclaimed Temüjin as paramount leader, giving him the title Chinggis Khan—"universal ruler." Until his death in 1227, Chinggis Khan led his people to triumph after triumph, creating a massive empire.

A highly charismatic man, Chinggis Khan was able to impose rigorous discipline on the fighters he commanded. His first and most important innovation was to reform the Mongols' military

BELOW *The stainless steel statue of Chinggis Khan near Ulaanbaatar, Mongolia, is 130 ft (39.5 m) tall, the world's tallest equestrian statue. Created by sculptor D. Erdenebileg, it was erected in 2008.*

organization, dividing the fighters into units of 10, 100, and 1,000 in a way that offset the traditional tribal command system. As the Mongols conquered other peoples of the steppe, the great khan insisted on more than loose overlordship over a confederation, instead forcing defeated peoples to adopt Mongol language and culture so they lost their old tribal identities. He learned a great deal from earlier Khitan and Uighur rule, creating governmental structures that had taken generations to produce the first time around. Chinggis also built on even earlier traditions, centering his empire on the old holy grounds of the Turks to emphasize his own continuity.

Mostly, however, Chinggis Khan held his people's loyalty because he was enormously successful; he sometimes lost battles, but never a war. He made his people rich. Geography dictated that China would bear the brunt of attacks from the steppe, and Mongol raiders under the future great khan pushed into the Xi Xia state of the north in 1205. The Xia ruler asked for help from the neighboring Jin Dynasty but was refused. When a new Xia emperor came to the throne in 1211 he was so angry he made peace with the Mongols and they attacked the Jin state together.

Thus, from an early stage, the Mongol army included large numbers of cultural Chinese, employed as infantry and for garrison work; they also provided expertise in siegecraft, a practice hitherto unknown among the steppe peoples.

The Mongols' methodical raids against the Jin state were diverted, however, much to the dismay of the Islamic world of the Middle East. The fault lay with the overconfidence of 'Ala al-Din Muhammad II, ruler of Khwarazm (modern Turkmenistan and Uzbekistan). The shah had enjoyed his own military triumphs, seizing Transoxiana from the Kara-Khitai and conquering much of Afghanistan. He grievously offended Chinggis Khan, and Mongols were not inclined to forgive slights. In 1218 a Khwarazmian border governor massacred a caravan of 450 merchants from Mongol territory, claiming they were spies but probably simply to seize their goods. When word reached the khan he demanded reparation. But 'Ala al-Din, probably thinking the Mongols fully committed to war in East Asia, killed one of the envoys and shamed the other two by shaving their beards.

Chinggis Khan responded by halting his campaign in China and launching a massive

ABOVE *Mongol capture of the Khwarazmian queen Terken Khatun, from a Persian universal history, c. 1430.*

A Mongol Ambassador

Europeans traveling to the Mongol court have left us several accounts, but only one document survives describing the Mongol perspective. In the 1260s the Nestorian priest Rabban bar Sauma, who lived in the area of Beijing, decided to make a pilgrimage to Jerusalem. He failed to reach Jerusalem on his first attempt because of Mongol warfare, instead settling in Baghdad. In 1287, however, his ruler sent the elderly priest on a mission to the West. Rabban bar Sauma visited Constantinople and Rome, trying to arrange an alliance between the Western powers and the Mongols. His mission failed and bar Sauma retired to Baghdad, writing an account of his travels that gives a unique perspective on 13th-century Europe.

three-pronged attack into Khwarazm. The shah, unpopular with his own people, was soon forced to flee ever westward as the Mongols hunted him; he finally died on an island in the Caspian in 1221. The initial revenge campaign of 1219 included the total destruction of cities that refused to surrender, only sparing certain types of artisans useful to the Mongols. The cities that submitted were allowed to govern themselves in return for tribute, but woe betide any that then reneged on their agreement. The most extreme example is Nishapur. When the city rebelled in 1221, Chinggis Khan threw everything he had at it, including all the expertise of his Chinese subjects with stone-throwers, giant crossbows, and 700 tubes through which incendiaries could be hurled at the defenders. Once the city had been taken, the khan ordered the complete massacre of every living thing, including even the cats and dogs.

BELOW *The path of the Mongol invasions.*

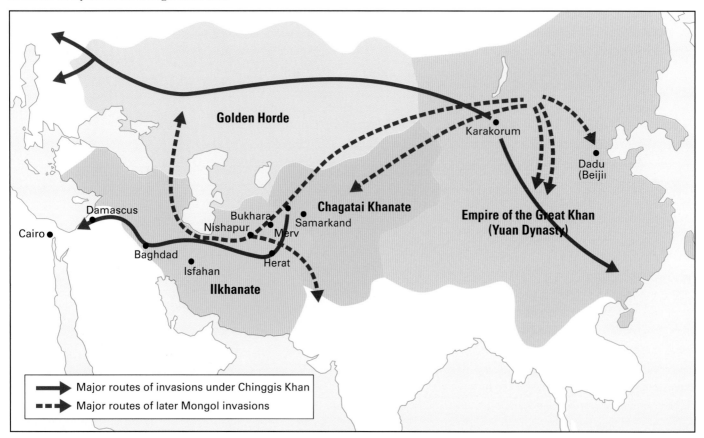

ONGOING MONGOL ADVANCES

Before his death in 1227, Chinggis Khan named his third son, Ögödei, his successor as great khan, although each of his brothers also received a state. And the conquests continued. The Jin Dynasty, despite stubborn resistance, fell to the Mongols in 1234. Their last emperor, known as Aizong, "the Forlorn Ancestor," tried desperately to get assistance from the Southern Song but was refused; he finally took his own life in order to avoid capture. Under Ögödei's generals, the Mongols also swept westward, at first on a more northern route from the steppe to defeat the disunited Russian principalities. In the course of 1237–40, they took every Rus' center except Novgorod, which was saved by a spring thaw; Kyivan Rus' ended on December 7, 1240, with the Mongol conquest of Kyiv itself. The steppe army then moved into Central Europe, where they inflicted an overwhelming defeat on a Hungarian army at Muhi in April, 1241, in an action intended to punish King Béla IV for giving sanctuary to the nomadic Cumans when they fled before the Mongols. Europe would have suffered much more, but the death of the great khan led the Mongol army to return to Central Asia to elect a new leader.

Ögödei Khan had taken important steps to centralize control of his massive empire, constructing a capital at Karakorum and establishing a massive network for couriers, the *yam* system, that could move urgent messages as much as 300 miles (483 km) per day. The *yam*'s 10,000 post stations played an important role in stimulating trade, as did the existence of a single great state. Favorable trade conditions between the lands under Mongol rule continued for some time, but the unity of the Mongols soon broke down, the empire falling into four increasingly independent khanates.

The last great westward thrust of the Mongols began in 1256, when Möngke Khan sent his brother Hülegü to attack the Muslim sect of Assassins, radicals who formed an independent Isma'ili state in Iran in 1090 and had engaged in frequent political terrorism, sending agents to

BELOW *The enthronement of Ögödei Khan after his elections in 1229.*

perpetrate hundreds of "assassinations" as they gave their name to politically-motivated murder. A contemporary account says the Mongol attack was provoked when the Assassins' leader, known as the Old Man of the Mountain, sent 400 disguised Assassins to Karakorum to kill the khan. Hülegü succeeded where a number of Turkish rulers had failed, capturing a number of Assassin fortresses in Iran, including the inaccessible stronghold of Alamut.

Rather than stopping once his immediate target had been neutralized, however, Hülegü proceeded with his army into Iraq. The Abbasid caliph failed to organize a sufficient defense, and factionalism and treason weakened resistance to the invaders. This internal division proved to be

the undoing of the Abbasid caliphate. In 1258, the Mongols took Baghdad itself after a short siege. The last caliph, al-Musta'sim, was killed on February 20, 1258, along with this family. The caliph enjoyed the dubious honor of dying by being rolled in a carpet and then trampled by horses—since for the peoples of the steppe shedding blood was shameful, they were in effect giving the caliph an honorable death. In a letter Hülegü sent to King Louis IX of France in 1262 he boasted that more than 20,000 people had been killed in the brutal sack of the city.

When Möngke Khan died in 1259, Hülegü established himself as the independent ruler of Iran and Iraq, the breakaway Mongol region known as the Ilkhanate. Soon, the Ilkhanate

RIGHT *Hülegü Khan surrounded by his courtiers, from Rashid al-Din's* History of the World, *c.1310.*

began what proved to be a long series of wars with the Golden Horde, the independent Mongol state to its north. The first decades of Mongol rule were very harsh, with taxes so extortionate that many peasants fled from the land. The agricultural disruption had a dire long-term effect on the region. Iran was especially dependent on underground water channels for irrigation, a complex system that needed constant maintenance. When these channels were allowed to fall into disrepair, the region soon became impoverished. Perhaps the last straw in the economic decline of the Ilkhanate was when Geikhatu Khan (1291–5) tried to fix state finances by issuing paper money, paying employees in paper but insisting that taxes be paid in gold. The experiment devastated commerce in the region. It took several generations for the Mongols to assimilate to some extent to the Muslim culture in which they found themselves. When Hülegü

Khan died in 1265, his funeral included human sacrifices; his successors were Buddhist. It was only in 1295 that Ghazan Khan converted to Islam, expelling the Buddhist lamas and razing Buddhist temples.

Although the Mongols controlled much of the Anatolian Peninsula until 1335, they never established themselves on the eastern seaboard of the Mediterranean. Christians still ruled several territories that were limited geographically but heavily fortified; they even briefly regained Jerusalem by treaty in 1229. But as the Mongols pressed westward, the Christian government based in Acre did its best to remain neutral, while in Antioch Prince Bohemond VI found it expedient to submit to Hülegü. The challenge to the Mongols came from further south, where in Egypt the Ayyubids had been replaced by new, ambitious rulers—the Mamluks (1250–1517).

ABOVE *Mongol siege of Baghdad, from Rashid al-Din's* History of the World, *c. 1310.*

The Powerful Women of the Mongol Empire

A striking feature of steppe societies in the medieval centuries was the prominent position accorded to women. This was especially pronounced among the Mongols. Chinggis Khan seems to have regarded his four daughters as more suitable to govern than his sons, investing them with strategically important sub-kingdoms. Similarly, Hülegü Khan's daughter-in-law Absh Khatun ruled Persia on his behalf for more than two decades (1263–87). Unlike much of the rest of the world, ruling women's competence seems to have been assumed with little question. Nowhere can this be seen more clearly than in the case of Töregene Khatun. The wife of Ögödei Khan, she filled the power vacuum when her husband died in 1241, ruling for five years as the Mongol forces pulled back from their conquests, gathering in their homeland to elect a new great khan. Once they assembled, Töregene engineered the election of her own eldest son.

Silver dirham of Töregene Khatun.

Chinggis Khan's daughter-in-law Sorghaghtani Beki, with her husband Tolui. She was one of the most powerful political leaders of the Mongol Empire.

COUNTERING THE MONGOL THREAT: THE MAMLUKS

Mamluks were the enslaved soldiers of the Ayyubid sultans. As with other enslaved troops in the Islamic world, they were purchased in the slave markets as boys, subjected to harsh discipline, and trained to be highly effective troops. Their generals claimed an ever-larger share of real power. In 1250, when the last Ayyubid sultan died (in the midst of Louis IX's crusade against Egypt), the Mamluks actually named his widow Shajar al-Durr sultan for a short time, although she soon married the leading Mamluk general and in a confused power struggle was herself killed. A succession of Mamluk sultans followed, the Mamluk corps strongly resisting each sultan's attempt to bequeath the throne to his own son. Soon, the Mamluks were pushing against the remaining crusader states, hoping to regain land that Saladin had once conquered and to end forever the threat of further crusades from Western Europe to support the troubled colonies in the Christian holy places.

This policy placed the new Mamluk sultan, Qutuz, on a collision course with the Mongols, who were pushing into Syria at the same time. Hülegü himself had to withdraw to Iran, probably because Syria did not provide adequate pasturage for the vast horse herds required for Mongol fighting. However, he left a holding force of 10–20,000. The Mamluks

LEFT *The Mamluk sultan Baybars, frontispiece of al-Hariri's* Maqamat, *1334.*

met them in battle at Ayn Jalut in September 1260 and inflicted a heavy defeat on the steppe invaders. Hülegü was unable to follow up because of the disturbed fighting among the Mongols after Möngke Khan's death, allowing the Mamluks to bask in the glory of having defeated such a formidable foe.

In the wake of Ayn Jalut, the Mamluks gained validity by installing an escaped Abbasid prince as caliph in Cairo in 1261 as well as welcoming many teachers and scholars who had fled the sack of Baghdad. Above all, the Mamluks' self-proclaimed role as protectors of Islam was seen in the nearly annual campaigns against the Christian settlers in the Near East. Sultan al-Zahir Baybars (1260–77) established the policy of demolishing Christian-held port towns when they were captured, making it ever more difficult for European crusaders to intervene. Antioch fell in 1268 and Tripoli in 1289, despite small support expeditions from the west. The final reconquest of the Holy Land came in 1291, when the Mamluks captured the great port city of Acre after a short siege.

RIGHT *The Mamluk Siege of Tripoli in 1289, which ended in a massacre of the Christian population and foreshadowed the final fall of the crusader states.*

EUROPEAN ACTIONS AND REACTIONS

Russia and Hungary suffered the full brunt of Mongol invasions. Poland too, fragmented at the time into five independent duchies, was also devastated in the Mongol invasion of 1240, losing so much population that the Polish dukes encouraged German settlement and welcomed Western European Jews fleeing persecution. Western Europe, however, was spared from direct Mongol attacks and a number of rulers, including several popes and Louis IX of France, saw the Mongols as a gift rather than a scourge sent by God. After all, the steppe conquerors were devastating the Muslim Middle East—if only the Mongols could be converted to Christianity, between them Europeans and Central Asians could wipe Islam from the face of the earth. Therefore, in 1238, when Muslim princes sent an appeal for aid to the rulers of Germany, France, and England, they received little sympathy. Instead, Pope Innocent IV sent four embassies to the Mongol khan between 1243 and 1253 and Louis IX sent an ambassador as well; the emissaries were members of a new, mission-oriented religious order, the

Franciscans. The khans were not, however, much interested. They responded by demanding the submission of Western rulers and, in one case, requested a hundred missionaries, which the pope was unable to provide. Even if the Mongols had eagerly embraced an alliance, the states of Europe were not in a position to take advantage of the opportunity. They could not even muster the manpower and resolve to safeguard the Kingdom

RIGHT St. Francis of Assisi Receiving the Stigmata, *a fresco attributed to Giotto.*

ABOVE *Aigues Mortes, France. Louis IX transformed the small fishing village into a city that could serve as a staging point for his first crusade.*

of Jerusalem, a goal much nearer to Western hearts.

Europe did see a number of crusades in the 13th century, including the conquest (and almost immediate loss) of Damietta in Egypt (1218–19) and the bizarre expedition of Emperor Frederick II (1228–9). Frederick, after an unsympathetic pope excommunicated him for delaying departure on crusade for too long, set out with only a token force and actually negotiated the return of Jerusalem to Christian hands, thanks to his own understanding of Islamic culture and internal dissension within the Ayyubid clan. When Jerusalem was lost again in 1244, Louis IX of France undertook a large crusade against Egypt, the heartland of Ayyubid power, only to be defeated and captured. Louis' second crusade, at

the end of his life in 1270, was diverted to attack Tunis in North Africa. At least a score of other expeditions set out in the 13th century, mostly to buttress the beleaguered remains of the Kingdom of Jerusalem against Mamluk attacks, but they only delayed the inevitable fall of the last crusader strongholds.

An important reason for diminishing crusade fervor in the 13th century was internal dissension in many areas of Europe. The later 12th century had seen a great strengthening of royal authority in many regions, and independent-minded nobles, townspeople, and even peasants fought back. As we have seen, England under Richard the Lionheart had participated massively in the Third Crusade—but after that took a back seat in the crusading enterprise, except for the small

"Crusade of the Lord Edward" (1271–2). The reason why was not hard to discern. The Angevin rulers of England, Ireland, and the western half of France had pushed too hard, financing increasingly ambitious projects by extorting every penny they could from traditional feudal obligations, since, like the rest of Europe, they lacked a regular tax system. When King John (1199–1216) lost control of Normandy he fought a series of cripplingly expensive wars to regain the duchy, and when he was forced to acknowledge failure in 1214 the nobles of England had had enough. Threatened with massive rebellion, John agreed in 1215 to limitations on royal power, Magna Carta (the "great charter") outlining what the king could demand from his vassals, the Church, and merchants. The agreement soon broke down into civil war, and noble rebellion also plagued the reign of John's son, Henry III.

Other regions also fought against royal overreach. King Andrew II of Hungary (1205–35) provoked a similar revolt, focused on complaints about granting land to favorites and his land policies. He was forced to agree, in the Golden Bull of 1222, to protect the rights of nobles. His successor, Béla IV, tried to overturn the Golden Bull, assuring that Hungary was in turmoil when the Mongols overran it. In many regions, kings did succeed in establishing a right to tax, but only at the expense of winning the consent of nobles and town oligarchies. Aragón had already instituted parliamentary gatherings, the *Cortes*, to approve taxes in the 1210s, and parliaments at which the king would promise to redress wrongs in return for consent to taxation were regular in England by the 1290s.

In the realm that Frederick Barbarossa had dubbed the "Holy Roman Empire," Barbarossa's death on crusade, followed only a few years later by the death of his son and successor, gave an

BELOW *Magna Carta, one of the four extant copies made in 1215 after King John was forced to agree to it.*

LEFT *Augustalis of Frederick II Hohenstaufen, consciously modeled on Roman coinage.*

opportunity to those opposed to a strong central power. Chief among these was the papacy. By 1215, with the Fourth Lateran Council the popes had claimed spiritual authority over the Christian world, an authority grounded in the popes' independence from the control of a secular ruler and rule of their own small state in central Italy. In the 12th century, the popes had fought vigorously against Barbarossa's effort to re-establish German power over northern Italy. Opposition to imperial power became hysteria when Barbarossa's grandson Frederick II became king of southern Italy and Sicily (inherited from his mother) and then emperor (by election), with the papal state wedged between Frederick's lands. After his crusade, the remainder of Frederick's reign was spent struggling with a series of popes, whose unedifying behavior (including declaring the emperor to be the Antichrist at the Council of Lyon in 1245) can be explained by very real fear, exacerbated by Frederick's own very effective propaganda war against the papacy. After Frederick died in 1250, the pope offered the throne of southern Italy to Charles of Anjou, Louis IX's brother. Charles hunted the last of Frederick's dynasty to extinction. In this environment, neither the emperors nor the popes had energy to spare for ventures in the east. There was no emperor at all between 1250 and 1273, although many competed to be king of Germany. Almost all proved willing to sign away crown rights in return for support.

Government exactions could drive even peasants to rebellion. A case in point is the second Bulgarian Empire, which gained independence from Byzantium in the wake of the Fourth Crusade. The rebel leader, Ioannitsa, assured his state's survival with a major victory over one of the rival Byzantine emperors in exile in 1230. But he and his successors soon lost ground again, as the Byzantines regained territory, Mongols frequently raided, and insistence on ever-greater taxes inflicted massive hardship. The dynasty was actually toppled by a peasant rebellion in 1278 and the peasants' leader, a minor noble so poor that he was nicknamed Ivailo "the Swineherd" was declared tsar of Bulgaria.

Mediterranean conflicts also left little energy for crusading. The mercantile city-states of Italy happily traded with Muslims, despite papal fulminations. While they had trade interests in the crusader states, as the Mamluk conquests increasingly cut that trade off both Genoa and Venice established colonies on the northern coast of the Black Sea in Crimea. By 1300, each city had a population of about 100,000, enormous by

BELOW *The Florentine florin was a gold coin of remarkably stable value, minted from 1252 to 1533. This 13th-century example has the city's patron saint, John the Baptist, on the reverse.*

Marco Polo

Wherever there was trade in the later Middle Ages Italian merchants were eager to exploit it. A famous example is that of the Polo family of Venice. The brothers Niccolò and Maffeo Polo journeyed all the way to Khubilai Khan's court at Beijing, taking advantage of how the Mongol conquests had eased travel across Asia. The Polos returned home, only to set out again with Niccolò's 17-year-old son Marco in 1271. Marco Polo ended up spending 24 years at the court of Khubilai Khan. When he finally returned home, the adventurer was imprisoned in Genoa as an enemy Venetian. Marco used his time to dictate the story of his travels to a fellow prisoner, the first detailed account of a European in China and other parts of the Far East. Although his work has often been dismissed as exaggerated or even made up, modern scholars have verified the truth of much of Marco Polo's account, such as Chinese paper money and the production of porcelain.

A caravan on the Silk Road from the Catalan Atlas (1375).

medieval European standards. Trade flourished, as can be seen by Genoa, Florence, and Venice all beginning to mint higher-value gold coins in the 13th century and by the establishment of great international banks, which became indispensable to royal finance throughout Europe. The Italian cities' aspirations can also be seen in their frequent warfare with each other, most notably in the 1284 great sea battle off the mouth of the Arno where the Genoese destroyed Pisa's fleet. Nor was southern Italy spared warfare. Charles of Anjou, imposed by the pope as king of Sicily, was hated and his people rose in rebellion in 1282 in what became known as the War of the Sicilian Vespers, since the signal for the rising was the church bells ringing for evening prayer. King Pere III of Aragón supported the rebels and the result was a Mediterranean-wide conflict that raged for 20 years.

THE LIMITS OF MONGOL EXPANSION

After Möngke Khan died in 1259, war broke out among Chinggis Khan's descendants for ascendancy. The eventual victor was Khubilai Khan (1260–94), although the Golden Horde and Ilkhanate remained largely independent of his authority. Khubilai, whose power base was in the east, focused his energies on the conquest of China's Southern Song Dynasty. Unlike earlier Mongol conquests, Khubilai's conquest of southern China was not very destructive, and the conqueror respected most landowners' property rights. Still, the south waged a stubborn fight that lasted into the 1270s. The final Mongol victory was a naval battle in March 1279 in which the last Song emperor was killed and surviving Song officials and their families committed mass suicide. Khubilai was soon proclaimed emperor of a new Chinese dynasty, the Yuan, and gradually established a Chinese-style administration with Chinese advisors. He and his successors adopted the symbolism of traditional Chinese rule, taking regnal titles and performing sacrifices to the imperial ancestors—although Khubilai planted a patch of steppe grass in the palace garden at Beijing to remind him of his origins. Khubilai himself became a tantric Buddhist, the branch of Buddhism unique to Tibet. It was a personal faith; other religions received state support and there was no real effort to convert the Mongol invaders.

Mongol armies had invaded Korea in 1231, but resistance remained as stubborn as it had been against Chinese aggression. It took seven major campaigns and 39 years of fighting before the Koryo Dynasty accepted Mongol overlordship, giving the Mongols an ascendancy that was more apparent than real. Khubilai and his successors remained convinced that Mongols should rule the whole world, but the geography of East and Southeast Asia did not favor their style of fighting, although they took readily enough to the sea. Khubilai Khan's armies had some

success against Vietnam between 1281 and 1285 (including the destruction of Hanoi), but a joint Vietnamese-Cham naval force ultimately defeated his aspirations there. Similarly, a Mongol force attacked the kingdom of Pagan (Burma) in 1287 but soon had to withdraw. Even more ambitiously, Khubilai sent a navy to attack the kingdom of Java in 1292–3, claiming the traditional Chinese right to supervise commerce in Southeast Asia. The campaign ended in humiliation, however. The

BELOW *Khubilai Khan hunting, painting on silk attributed to his contemporary Liu Guandao.*

successor of a deposed ruler used the Mongol fleet's arrival to eliminate the usurper who had seized the throne, then ambushed the Mongol force and drove them out.

The Mongols had no particular reason to attack Japan. The state at the time was impoverished and politically divided. The islands had suffered severe famines in the 12th century and debt slavery had increased massively. Japan's society was rife with violence, the *bushi* (private, professional warriors, often misleadingly called *samurai*) attached to each major estate not sparing women, children, the elderly, or noncombatants in the frequent wars between estates and between estates and the government. In the 12th century, great nobles had attempted several times to seize effective control of the government, for example in the Hogen Insurrection of 1156 when the Fujiwara family struggled for power with the retired emperor Go-Shirakawa. The Fujiwara failed, but an empire-wide civil war broke out in 1180–5, the Gempei War. It began with the rebellion of Prince Mochihito when he was passed over as emperor in favor of an infant, but at heart the warrior class wanted better income and recognition of their elite status. A struggle between the rival Taira and Minamoto clans

ensued. The victor was Minamoto no Yoritomo, who in 1192 declared himself shogun, essentially a military dictator who did not replace the emperor but nevertheless held effective power. Since Yoritomo ruled from the eastern city of Kamakura, the period is known as the Kamakura Shogunate (1185–1333). Japan was still not calm, however. Not only did the shoguns fail to prevent the warrior class's increasing usurpation of income and resources, but the emperors did not passively accept their role as figureheads. Most notably, in 1221 the Jokyu War broke out when retired emperor Go-Toba tried to overthrow the shogunate. The shogun's triumph, which included occupation of Kyoto and Go-Toba's exile, served to strengthen the shogunate temporarily.

ABOVE *The Mongols eagerly adopted Chinese military technology, as can be seen with this cannon from the Yuan Dynasty.*

BELOW *Scene from Japan's Gempei War, painted on a six-leaved screen.*

ABOVE *Battle of Bunei, 1274, during the first Mongol invasion of Japan.*

By 1280, however, internal fighting and large-scale outlawry had seriously weakened the Kamakura shogunate. The threat of foreign invasion, however, the first in Japan's history, placed a premium on central leadership. The first Mongol invasion came in 1274. Khubilai Khan sent a small army, which did enjoy some success against the Japanese *bushi*. A major storm, however, destroyed part of the Mongol fleet and forced their commander to withdraw. On the return voyage, another storm struck, the "divine wind" (*kamikaze*) sinking most of the fleet and drowning more than 10,000 Mongol soldiers. Mongols did not like losing, though, so a second, larger expedition was planned. The Japanese feverishly prepared, erecting a great line of walls, several miles long, along the coast of northern

Kyushu to defend against a hostile landing. When the second invasion came in 1281 it was 140,000 men strong. Fighting continued for about two months, before Japan was again saved by the "divine wind."

The other notable Mongol failure was in India, which endured invasions in 1296, 1297, 1303, and 1307–8, all of which ended in Mongol defeat. In India, the Mongols confronted the most warlike and united of 13th-century Muslim states, the Delhi Sultanate. The sultanate had its start at the end of the 12th century, when Muhammad of Ghur invaded northwestern India from Afghanistan. Muhammad left his slave Qutb-uddin Aibek to rule the conquered land, and when Muhammad was assassinated in 1206 Aibek became an independent ruler; when he died

RIGHT *Mongol grenades, discovered by underwater archaeologists in a wrecked ship from the Mongol invasion of Japan.*

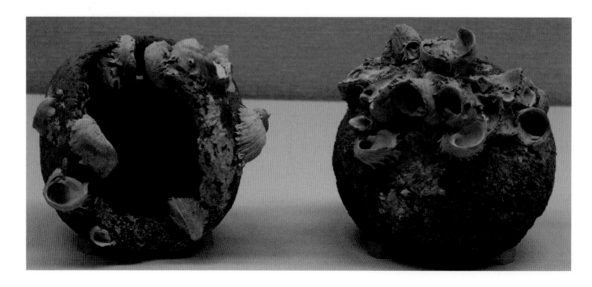

LEFT *Qutb Minar, Delhi, India, is a minaret constructed 1199–1220 to celebrate the Ghurid conquest of the region and perhaps promote conversion to Islam.*

in 1210, his son-in-law Iltutmish seized power (1210–36). The Delhi Sultanate proved to be a stable entity, despite Iltumish's unprecedented move of leaving the throne to his daughter Raziya (1236–9) in preference to her brothers. She was killed in a rebellion, but the dynasty continued and soon became the leading power of northern India, noted for trained cavalry and good horses from Afghanistan as well as a policy of toleration toward the majority Hindu populace. It was the Mongols' misfortune that their intervention in India coincided with the reign of another great warrior sultan, Ala-uddin Khalji (1296–1316), who conquered most of the subcontinent. And by that time, the Mongols had largely run out of steam. They had lost some of their traditional military strength by adopting the ways of the peoples they conquered and incorporating them into the military. Above all, as Mongol rule reached its third and fourth generations, the khans lost much of their drive for world domination, doubtless much to the relief of the peoples of Eurasia.

BELOW *Tomb of Sultan Iltumish, Delhi, within the Qutb Minar complex.*

CHAPTER 9

The Disasters of the 14th Century

I n 1978, Barbara Tuchman published *A Distant Mirror: The Calamitous Fourteenth Century*, a book whose evocative title prepares readers for a tale of catastrophic collapse. As Tuchman intended, the title is singularly appropriate for the *European* 14th century, as changing climate patterns brought on major famines and almost certainly precipitated the mutation of the plague bacillus, which then swept through the Islamic lands and Europe, killing perhaps one-third of the population. Still in Europe, warfare on a scale not seen since the Romans helped sow destruction, as England and France (and their allies) became locked in the Hundred Years War. Europe was never the whole story, though, and for decades scholars have attempted to uncover the parameters of the Black Death and the effects of climate change on areas with a sparser written record than Europe. Instead of making the 14th century seem less harrowing to the human experience, studies have heightened the sense of catastrophe. Outside of western Africa and the Americas, it was indeed a calamitous century.

LEFT *The Battle of Crécy, from an illuminated manuscript of Froissart's* Chronicles*.*

THE WORLD IN 1300

As the century dawned, few would have anticipated the disasters to come. In 1300, China was still by far the world's most populous and sophisticated state, despite its rule by the Mongol Yuan Dynasty, with a population as high as 125 million. Although the Yuan Dynasty was weakening, the state still functioned well, civil service exams providing a constant stream of scholar-bureaucrats who benefited from books printed with woodblocks on inexpensive paper. The government had even successfully popularized paper money, simplifying life for the flourishing merchant class. The Islamic lands in Asia had suffered in the Mongol conquests, but by 1300 the conquerors were assimilating to the religion and culture of the conquered, becoming less rapacious in their demands and enabling trade to flourish again. Islamization was also proceeding apace in much of Africa, merchants spreading their faith as they encouraged trade. The Americas were emerging from centuries of mega-drought, allowing a number of Maya city-states to prosper and encouraging the rise of a new major state in central Mexico. Even Europe, for long a primitive, underpopulated backwater, had reached a new level of population and sophistication by 1300. Between 950 and 1300, Europe's population had increased threefold, reaching perhaps 70 million, as land was cleared and towns expanded. And, while Europe could not boast the population of a Beijing or Baghdad, it did have true cities, centers of trade, religion, and government; in 1300 Paris may have held as many as 228,000 people.

Appearances were, however, deceptive. Many regions were pushing the limit of how many people could be fed using the agricultural techniques available and counting on favorable weather. Conditions soon worsened, however, as the Medieval Climate Anomaly came to an end, giving way to the Little Ice Age. The shift is sometimes taken to have begun with a great volcanic eruption on the island of Lombok (Indonesia) in 1257, the most powerful explosive eruption in 700 years. Of longer-term significance is that the sun began one of its periods of lower irradiance, the Wolf Solar Minimum, which lasted c. 1282–1342. There were ominous signs, including shifts in Asia's monsoons and bitterly cold winters in much of Europe. India experienced its first monsoon failure in the 1280s, while exceptionally dry conditions in southern China for two decades devastated a population heavily dependent on rice cultivation. Throughout the 14th century, climate disruptions left clear

marks in the historical record, ranging from renewed drought in the Pacific regions of the Americas to the complete failure of the monsoons in the 1350s and 1360s known as the "Khmer drought," which led to the fall of major kingdoms in Southeast Asia. Much of Europe suffered in the Great Famine of 1315–22, when epidemic cattle disease combined with bitter winters and summers of torrential downpour to kill perhaps 20 percent of the populace. Famine tends to kill the weakest, though—the elderly and young children—and the population rebounded quickly. But then a crisis on a totally different scale appeared, the pandemic known to Europeans as the Black Death.

BELOW *Prasat Bayon, Cambodia, was the state temple of the Khmer kings; it was a victim of drought in the 14th century.*

The Mechanical Clock

Inventions to measure time such as water clocks and sundials had existed for many centuries. We owe the invention of the mechanical clock to Europeans in the years around 1300, however, demonstrating a desire to make the workers of Europe's burgeoning cities as productive as possible. By the 1270s, scientists were actively trying to figure out how to create an accurate mechanical clock; the key development was the invention of the verge and foliot escapement in *c.* 1275. This invention controls the turning of a gear, so it can only advance one tooth at a time.

Large mechanical clocks were mounted in towers, from which their bells could project over their town; the earliest known is the tower clock of Norwich Cathedral, built *c.* 1321–5. The idea caught on rapidly, both as a convenience to regulate work hours and as a marker of civic pride. In the 1370s, for example, public clocks were set up in over 70 European cities.

The Salisbury Cathedral clock, built in 1386.

THE BLACK DEATH

The plague bacillus, *Yersinia pestis*, is endemic in the steppe region of Central Asia. It lives in the rodent population, and can be spread either via oral transmission or by the bite of a flea that has ingested the bacillus. Sometime in the late 13th century *Yersinia pestis* mutated, becoming much more virulent; a dominant theory is that a mega-drought on the Tibetan-Qinghai Plateau in 1271 was the environmental shock that caused this "big bang" creation of the more violent form of the disease. What ensued was a domino effect. The more virulent bacillus began to kill more of its host

animals (e.g., marmots) at the same time that drought in the steppe grasslands drove plague-infested animals closer to humans as they sought food and water. Once the plague began to infect humans, the relative ease of trade through the Mongol-ruled lands meant it was only a matter of time before infected rodents would be carried on a ship, infected fleas in a saddlebag, or infected humans would spread the disease orally.

The nature of our extant sources makes it hard to say definitively which regions of Afro-Eurasia were stricken in the 14th-century pandemic. At the heart of the problem is

BELOW *Spread of the Black Death in Europe and the Near East.*

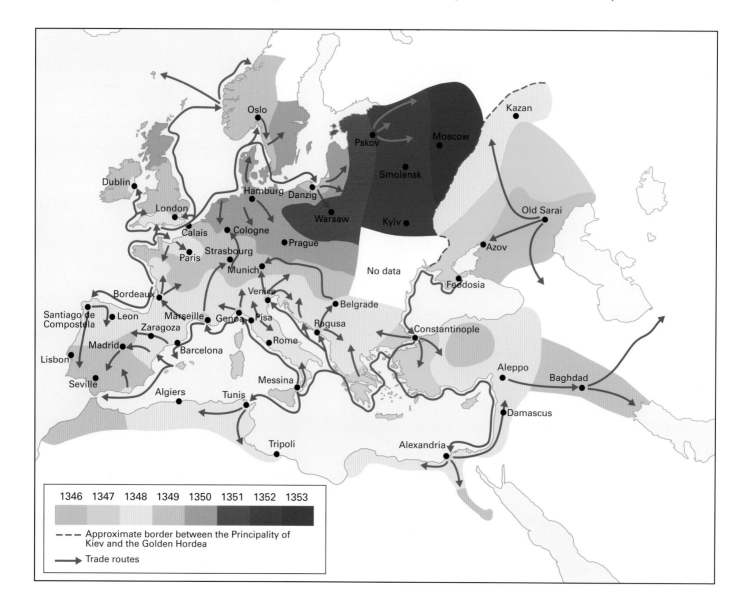

1346 1347 1348 1349 1350 1351 1352 1353

- - - Approximate border between the Principality of Kiev and the Golden Hordea

→ Trade routes

understanding which specific disease written sources are describing; for example, was a major epidemic in Kaifeng, China, in 1232 bubonic plague or another infectious disease? *Yersinia pestis* was only identified as the cause of plague in 1894, and the bacillus works so rapidly on the human body that it rarely leaves traces that can be uncovered archaeologically; only in 2016 did DNA studies conclusively prove that the plague bacillus devastated England in the 14th century, rather than a form of influenza as had been argued. Nonetheless, scholars have done a good job tracing the disease's path of destruction in the 14th century and beyond, often postulating its presence when written evidence is lacking.

China, whose thorough government performed regular censuses, suffered massive population decline in the 14th century, from about 125 million to 65 million people. There were some significant wars, especially as the Mongols were expelled and the new Ming Dynasty was established, and also famine induced by major floods. There are, however, also references to major epidemics, starting in Hopei province in 1331, antedating the first certain case of the second great plague pandemic, with the plague bacillus discovered in tombs in what is now Kyrgyzstan dating to 1338–9. Other regions of China also reported major epidemics beginning in 1345–6.

Rats—and their fleas—were a standard nuisance on ships, providing a means for the plague to spread in the Indian Ocean trade world. Again, scientists have been unable to prove the presence of bubonic plague in the region, but the available evidence is highly suggestive. Southern India suffered from an extremely virulent epidemic in 1344. There is good evidence that the plague reached Ethiopia, whether by sea or overland from Egypt we cannot know. And, although little genetic work has been carried out yet for sub-Saharan Africa, *something* seriously disrupted the Swahili trading centers of eastern Africa. Shanga and Tumbatu were completely abandoned, while Kilwa, which had dominated trade for centuries, was left mostly derelict.

Scholars have argued that the spread of disease inland to Great Zimbabwe may have led to the abandonment of that site.

Plague also spread westward along the caravan routes, killing perhaps a third of the population of the Muslim core lands of the Middle East and North Africa. By 1346, bubonic plague swept through the Mongol Golden Horde. Any epidemic is particularly dangerous when people are clustered tightly together, especially in unhygienic conditions, and the Mongols provided ideal conditions to incubate the disease while besieging the Genoese trade port of Kaffa on the Black Sea. Thousands of Mongols died before their commander abandoned the siege; according to one rather implausible report, before withdrawing, they catapulted the corpses of plague victims into the town. Whether by

BELOW *The Great Mosque of Kilwa. Ibn Battuta found its dome worthy of comment when he visited in 1331.*

ABOVE *Purchased from the Mongols in the late 13th century, Kaffa was a prosperous trade colony of Genoa, dominating Black Sea commerce.*

that means or another, the plague soon spread in the close, dirty confines of Kaffa. Then, perhaps while the disease still incubated, the mercantile Genoese gave *Yersinia pestis* a free ride to a number of ports. The plague reached Constantinople and Alexandria, and by October 1347 had appeared in Italy.

Even with modern medicines, bubonic plague can be deadly, and the populations the Black Death hit had neither built-up immunity nor drugs that could combat the bacillus, nor even any understanding of how the disease spread. In the

first outbreak of this second pandemic (the first being the Justinianic Plague of the 6th century), an estimated 50–60 percent of those infected died of the disease; probably many others died because nobody survived to provide basic care as they recovered. Urban centers were especially hard-hit, as the lack of waste-removal services created a rat- and flea-rich environment; in the first outbreak, for example, three-quarters of the population of Venice died. Despite the efforts soon made to quarantine, ports were especially vulnerable, since every ship was liable to bring more infected fleas, rats, and people. Villages too were stricken, although inland territories (for instance Serbia, Bulgaria, and among the Turks) were relatively less affected. One recent estimate is that between 40 percent and 60 percent of all the people of Europe, the Middle East, and North Africa died in the first onslaught of the disease.

The first outbreak of bubonic plague in 1347–1351 was a massive catastrophe, but by itself would not have had a long-term demographic effect. But then the plague came back. The horror of its return 11 years after the first outbreak must have been psychologically crippling, especially as those who died were above all children born since the first wave. Then the plague returned again and again, recurring in cycles up to the 18th century. The result was long-term population decline, accompanied by major upheavals as the people of stricken regions tried to pick up the pieces of their lives.

Local conditions determined whether the plague pandemic would work to the advantage or disadvantage of survivors. Two examples demonstrate this. In Egypt, which lost between a quarter and a third of its population in the mid-14th century and suffered 28 further outbreaks over the next 150 years, Mamluk estate-holders were ruthless in demanding their usual income, despite the loss of so much of the work force. Brutal suppression kept Egyptian peasants on the land, suffering a very real decline in their standard of living. By contrast, in Western Europe the plague in the long term stimulated economic development. Since land ownership was decentralized, peasant communities could bargain effectively for better wages, improving their standards of living and weakening the landlord class. By the end of the 14th century, the legal servitude of serfdom had practically died out in Western Europe.

BELOW *Plague victims, from the* Toggenburg Chronicle *(c. 1411).*

LEFT *Burning of Jews suspected of spreading the plague, from the* Antiquitates Flandriae.

The Erfurt Jewish Treasure

An extraordinary testimony to the pogroms against Jews during the Black Death was discovered in 1998 in Erfurt, Germany. Archaeologists digging into a cellar wall found a massive hoard of gold and silver, amounting to nearly 60 pounds (27 kg) of precious metal. The find included more than 3,000 silver coins, as well as ingots, gold and silver cups, and more than 700 pieces of jewelry. The finds included a gold wedding ring in the form of a Gothic tower with "*mazel tov*" inscribed on it, making the attribution to a Jewish family certain. The Erfurt house had been the home of a prosperous Jewish merchant and moneylender named Kalman von Wiehe. He probably hid his family's wealth before a mob attacked the Jews of the city on March 21, 1349—and did not survive to recover them.

The Erfurt Treasure.

Many theories were argued for the coming of the plague in both the Christian and the Muslim worlds, including divine chastisement for sin and unprecedented astronomical conjunctions. No explanation was more noxious in its effects than when Europeans, looking for scapegoats, blamed the Jews for purposely sowing the disease among Christians. The Jewish communities of much of Europe were already precarious before the plague's arrival. A Christian spiritual shift in the 11th century had focused attention more on the events of Jesus's life, causing many to condemn all Jews as "Christ-killers." The fact that a number of Jews engaged in international business were very prosperous helped focus resentment, as most people knew them only as money-lenders or administrators wringing money from the poor for various rulers. Resenting the Jews and increasingly imposing legal disabilities on them, it is unsurprising that Christians assumed the Jews of Europe also resented and hated Christians. In one of the most twisted conspiracy theories of history, the tale was spun in the 12th century that the international Jewish community sacrificed a Christian boy at Easter each year to demonstrate their contempt for Christ and the Christians. All these factors combined, causing several rulers, eager to seize Jewish assets and support their subjects' religious prejudices, to expel the Jews from their domains. Edward I of England (1272–1307) expelled the Jews from England, and they were driven from France for the first time early in the 14th century. When the plague arrived, many European Christians were primed to regard Jews with loathing. The story circulated that Jews had poisoned the wells, and mobs tore through Jewish communities. By 1351, Europe had seen more than 350 massacres of Jews. Surviving northern European Jews mostly moved eastward to Poland and Russia.

WHO'S IN CHARGE? A COMPARATIVE LOOK

Who should rule was fought out repeatedly during the medieval millennium, most rulers claiming a religious sanction for their sovereignty, even if it was reinforced by naked force. Sometimes, however, religious authorities claimed preeminence and came into open confrontation with secular rulers. This was particularly the

case in medieval Europe, where in the high Middle Ages the popes claimed sweeping rights over kings and emperors, demanding that their intervention be acknowledged in all matters involving human sin. Papal claims reached their apex at the dawn of the 14th century, only to suffer a precipitous decline when the popes came into open confrontation with rulers who also

LEFT *Pope Boniface VIII declaring a year of jubilee, painted by Giotto in the Basilica of St. John Lateran, Rome.*

ABOVE *14th-century miniature symbolizing the Great Western Schism, from the* Grand Chroniques de France *of Charles V.*

ABOVE *One of the greatest surviving examples of International Gothic architecture, the Palace of the Popes dominates the city of Avignon, France.*

claimed a "divine right." It is instructive to compare the European situation to that of Japan, where in the 14th century divinely authorized authority (in the person of the goddess-descended emperors) confronted the physical force of the shogun.

The highest claims ever made for papal authority were the work of Pope Boniface VIII (1294–1303), who declared that "outside of the Roman Church there is no salvation." The reality, however, was very different. The papal vendetta against the heirs of Emperor Frederick II, in which the popes employed spiritual weapons like excommunication and crusade indulgences for political ends, had diminished papal prestige. Then Boniface VIII became embroiled in a controversy with King Philip IV "the Fair" of France (1285–1314), who was attempting to centralize royal authority in his realm and demanded taxes from the clergy. The war of words between king and pope escalated, reaching its height in 1303 when Philip sent troops to arrest the pontiff and place him on trial for heresy. Although the attempt to arrest Boniface at Anagni failed, the shocked pope soon died. The threat to try Boniface posthumously for heresy soon brought his successors to heel, and the pope was soon induced to relocate the papal government to Avignon, a town bordering France that the papacy bought from Queen Giovanna of Naples. The papacy remained in Avignon from 1309 to 1376 and was widely regarded as the puppet of the French kings. Pope Gregory XI returned the papacy to Rome in January 1377, but on his death in 1378 the Italian cardinals elected a pope who remained in Rome, while the French cardinals elected a rival who immediately returned to Avignon. The result was the Great Western Schism of 1378–1417, during which two and then three rival popes further undercut the papacy's spiritual prestige, European monarchs supporting whichever pope offered the greatest advantage.

Japan's power struggles do not form an exact parallel, since Japan's emperors had always been, at least in theory, the rulers of the island state. The creation of the Kamakura shogunate relegated the emperors for the most part to a ritual and ceremonial role, however,

LEFT *Portrait of Emperor Go-Daigo, painted on silk by the Buddhist monk Monkanbo Koshin in 1339, on the 35th day after the emperor's death.*

although the emperors maintained some parallel administrative offices. Some emperors were restive under the control of the military rulers, however, and when Emperor Go-Daigo came to the throne in 1318 he immediately began to build a power base independent of the shogun, conspiring to overthrow the shogunate and re-establish the emperor's direct rule. Go-Daigo's plot was uncovered in 1324, although he himself was protected from repercussions by his quasi-religious status. In 1331, Go-Daigo tried again, personally leading military forces against the shogun. Defeated and captured, the emperor was forced to retire and exiled from the capital. Finally, in 1333, the supposedly retired emperor's efforts were crowned with success. Leading the ongoing rebellion against the Kamakura, Go-Daigo established his own direct rule, the Hojo family that controlled the military government committing mass suicide.

Ultimately, however, Go-Daigo's control of military might was not equal to his claims of authority, rather like the popes who had no dependable counter to the threat of force. Only three years into his independent rule, Go-Daigo faced a major rebellion by the military Ashikaga family. The Ashikaga established Japan's second warrior government, the Muromachi shogunate (1336–1573) and the imperial court lost the last vestiges of its government role. The ultimate result of Go-Daigo's restoration of imperial government was the devastation of Japan, as warfare to control the state raged from 1336 to 1394.

RIGHT *Armor of Ashikaga Takauji, founder of the Muromachi shogunate.*

THE IMPLICATIONS OF MONOGAMY

In most of the medieval world, rule was hereditary; even in the Holy Roman Empire, where the principle of election by the great nobles had been reinforced by the wars of the 11th and 12th centuries, the electors usually gravitated to an adult son of the previous emperor. The principle of hereditary succession was almost never a problem in Asia, Africa, and the Americas, where upper-class polygamy was the norm; indeed, the problem was typically too many potential heirs rather than too few. Even if a ruler failed to procreate, his forebears would have guaranteed the existence of a massive extended royal family, often a serious drain on state revenues, from which a new ruler could be selected. The great exception was Christian Europe, where not only had the principle of monogamy become firmly established but ecclesiastical law from the 9th century on had made divorce or the annulment of an unfruitful union very difficult. Add to the mix a strong European preference for rulers to take spouses of comparable rank—daughters of another king—and the stage was set for unique international entanglements at the highest levels of the state.

The 14th century as a result saw European countries ruled by foreigners in unheard-of numbers, besides additional claims that could

to be assured by the heiress's marriage, and contemporary theology loudly proclaimed that wives must be subject to their husbands.

The great exception in Europe to the throne passing to a woman in default of a male heir was France. Philip IV and his queen had secured the succession, producing three sons and a daughter. But after Philip's death in 1314 his sons each ruled only briefly before dying. One had a daughter, but she was widely regarded as illegitimate. So the lawyers, hunting for an excuse to deny her the crown, hit upon an obscure passage in France's earliest legal text, the Salic Law, which stated that a woman could not inherit "Salic" land—they decided that it must refer to the crown itself. The death of the last of Philip IV's sons, though, reopened the issue: should the throne go to Philip's daughter Isabelle, who had recently rebelled against her husband King Edward II of England and probably arranged his death? Or should the heir be Isabelle's son, the teenaged Edward III of England (1327–77), at the

not be driven home. At heart the issue was one of heiresses. A daughter was generally held to have the right to inherit if she had no brothers. In a number of cases the woman proved to be a strong ruler, like Margaret I of Denmark (d. 1412). She was the heiress of Denmark and was married to Håkon VI of Norway, with the expectation that her husband would rule both realms. But Håkon died young, leaving Margaret to unite Denmark and Norway by force and add Sweden, creating a great North Sea kingdom. Typically, when the heiress married a foreign prince, it was expected that he would rule in her name. It was marriage to heiresses that allowed Aragón to claim Sicily, the Angevin rulers of Sicily to claim Hungary, and Jogaila of Lithuania to unite his country to Poland in 1386. Often subjects resented rule by a foreigner, as when Hungarian nobles rebelled against control by the German Sigismund, who had married their queen, Mary. There was, however, little recourse, as the succession needed

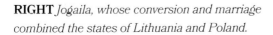

RIGHT *Jogaila, whose conversion and marriage combined the states of Lithuania and Poland.*

ABOVE *Philip IV of France and his family. The king is flanked by his daughter Isabella and son-in-law Edward II of England, along with his sons, the future Louis X, Philip V, and Charles IV.*

time completely dominated by his mother and her lover? Invoking the "Salic" law, the decision was made instead to crown a royal cousin, Philip VI (1328–50).

The matter might have ended there, had Philip VI not decided to exploit the young Edward III's weakness by intruding French royal government into Gascony, a territory of France still held by the English kings. France also supported Scotland in its ongoing war of independence against England. Finally, in 1337, Edward III declared war, soon declaring that he rather than Philip was the true king of France, by right of inheritance through his mother. Since royal honor was then at stake, no easy resolution was possible and the war between England and France ground on, with long pauses due to fiscal exhaustion, minority governments,

and plague, until 1453—the Hundred Years War.

Europe's economy was, quite simply, not sufficiently advanced to sustain an extended international war. The onset of the Little Ice Age lowered crop yields, a problem exacerbated by the massive mortality of the Black Death. Adding to the economic downturn was the fact that by the 1330s the production from Europe's silver mines was declining sharply, worsening Europe's already negative trade balance with Asia. The late 13th century had seen the development of great Italian merchant banks, Italy as always precocious in matters of trade. But all the early banks had failed by 1346 due to a combination of political tensions and economic downturn. Meanwhile, the rulers of Europe were apparently unable to grasp that they could not

LEFT *Jacques de Molay, last Grand Master of the Knights Templar, was executed along with Geoffroi de Charney in March 1314 in Paris.*

of taxation in both lands fell above all on the poor, provoking the largest European peasant revolts of the Middle Ages, the Jacquerie of 1358 and English Peasant Revolt of 1381. Once given teeth by regular use, England's kings soon discovered that they opposed parliament at their peril. Parliament seized control of the government in 1376 and 1388, even deposing King Richard II in 1399.

Inspired in part by shortage of money, Edward III pursued an innovative course in warfare. For two centuries, European armies had depended on highly trained elite heavy cavalrymen—knights—as the decisive factor to win battles. But France dominated the chivalric world of the late Middle Ages, and although Edward established the Order of the Garter in 1348 to encourage knights, he could never hope to equal French numbers on the battlefields. Instead, he considered the growing evidence that

simply wring more money from their subjects, as when Edward III imprisoned his whole council for failing to keep money flowing to him as he campaigned in France. The war had a devastating effect on the economy of England, France, Scotland, Flanders, Italy, and parts of Spain.

The state of endemic war between England and France in 1337–1453 played a major role in shaping each country's national identity. Edward III of England and his successors raised money by consenting to assemblies not just of nobles but of gentry and townsfolk who would authorize taxes in return for redress of grievances, regularizing the summoning of parliaments in continuation of an experiment already begun in the 13th century. The French kings at first raised money by the simple expedient of devaluing their coinage. After King Jean II was captured at the Battle of Poitiers in 1356, however, the need to raise his ransom became the basis for France's first regular taxation system since the Romans. The burden

BELOW *English gold noble, struck in 1340 to celebrate Edward III's great naval victory at Sluys.*

RIGHT *A harder-fought battle because the French men-at-arms advanced without their vulnerable horses, the Battle of Poitiers was the Black Prince's great victory.*

trained infantry could defeat cavalry, for example in William Wallace's victory at Stirling Bridge in 1297 or the triumph of the Flemish town militias over a French army in 1302 in the Battle of the Golden Spurs. So the English king took a disproportionate number of longbowmen with him to France. They proved their worth in the naval Battle of Sluys (1340) and then at Crécy in 1346, when 15 French cavalry charges failed to break the carefully placed archers, whose arrows inflicted catastrophic losses on Philip VI's force. The victory was repeated at Poitiers in 1356, and the Treaty of Brétigny in 1360 granted the English king possession of about one-third of the territory of France. The aging king could not hold onto his conquests, however, as good commanders and a new tax base enabled a major French recovery. And so the war continued.

The Greatest Explorer

Abu Abdullah Muhammad ibn Battuta (1304–1368/1369) was a North African scholar from Tangiers who in 1325 set out on the pilgrimage to Mecca. This proved to be only the beginning of 24 years of travel, Ibn Battuta clearly filled with a longing to see the world. From Mecca he went to Iraq, then Iran. His adventures included time among the Ottoman Turks and in the employ of the Delhi sultanate. The learned wanderer was welcomed wherever he went in Muslim lands, frequently finding employment with local rulers as a judge or ambassador. He reached Southeast Asia and China, Crimea, and even West Africa and Spain after he had returned to his north African home. When Ibn Battuta finally finished his travels (traversing about 73,000 miles/117,482 km) in 1354 he dictated an account of what he had seen, a work commonly known as the *Rihla* ("travels"). It is a precious witness to much of the 14th-century world.

WAR IN CHINA

In its way, the destruction of China's Yuan (Mongol) Dynasty was also a triumph of infantry over cavalry. As long as the Mongols had stayed true to the ways of the steppe, including their distinctive horse archery, they had been unstoppable. The Yuan Dynasty had rapidly sinicized, however, and the hybrid power system its emperors established to rule both native Chinese and Mongols proved to be deeply flawed. The government, corrupt and inefficient at best, had no adequate means to respond to a series of natural catastrophes, including major flooding of the Yellow River and famine in the 1330s and a devasting epidemic (maybe bubonic plague) in 1353–4. Chinese opinion was clear: when disasters struck, it was evidence that the emperor no longer ruled with heaven's favor. Sectarian religious movements began to rebel against Yuan rule in 1351, such as the Buddhist White Lotus Society, which predicted the imminent end of the world. China broke down into a series of civil wars, to a large extent a sequence of districts fighting each other rather than the central government, accompanied by large-scale banditry. Finally, in 1368 a rebel band, the Red Turbans, was powerful enough to invade Beijing and proclaim its leader as the first emperor of a new Ming Dynasty, the last Mongol emperor fleeing to his people's steppe homeland.

The Red Turban leader, Zhu Yuanzhang, was the son of peasants, radicalized after most of his family died in an epidemic and then his mother was executed by being burned alive for collaborating with the rebels. He proved to be a strong and ruthless leader, first eliminating rival commanders within the movement and then as emperor with the regnal title Ming Taizu (1368–98). Ming Taizu actually encouraged Mongol troops to remain in China and was happy to employ them to secure his own borders. But as the emperor's reign continued he became ever-more paranoid. He established a dynastic "house law" forbidding imperial descendants from living in society, following a career, or holding most offices. Instead, they were confined in princely establishments. The imperial kin were thus neutralized as a threat to

BELOW *Members of the White Lotus Society, a group that began as intellectuals gathering to discuss Buddhist theology.*

government stability, but at a heavy cost; by the mid-16th century more than 100,000 members of the imperial family received stipends from the state. More frighteningly, Ming Taizu began a reign of terror in 1376 when he suddenly executed about 1,000 officials, accusing them of corruption. In his 30-year reign he probably executed about 100,000 administrators.

Civil war broke out in China almost immediately after the first Ming emperor died in 1398. Ming Taizu had designated a grandson as his heir, but one of the boy's uncles contested the choice, leading to a civil war that raged for three years. The young emperor and his family probably died in his own burning palace at Nanjing in July 1402 and the evil uncle took the throne in one of China's few full-scale usurpations by a member of the imperial family. His reign was marked by the brutal suppression of all of his critics.

RIGHT *18th century portrait of Zhu Yuanzhang, founder of the Ming Dynasty.*

NEW CONQUERORS

Far to the west of China, the Mongol conquests had caused the Seljuk sultanate in Anatolia to fragment by the 1270s. The end of a central power opened the door to a number of small Turkish emirates, one of which, led by the minor border lord Osman (d. 1324) in time grew into the mighty Ottoman Empire. The early Ottomans, their territory bordering that of Byzantium, were able to take advantage of Byzantine weakness and a civil war in 1341–7. The Turks articulated an ideology of expansionism as *ghazis*, warriors fighting for the glory of Islam. By the 1350s, they had united the emirates of Anatolia and had initiated the conquest of the Balkans, after a major earthquake in 1354 destroyed the Byzantine defenses along the coastline of Thrace. Murad I (1362–89) was an especially successful conqueror, adding Serbia, Bulgaria, and Macedonia to his burgeoning empire. The Turkish triumphs roused alarm in Europe and engendered a new sort of crusade, one intended to protect Europe from the new advances of Islam. In 1396, the Crusade of Nicopolis set out to relieve the Ottoman siege of Constantinople itself. The Hungarian, French, German, and Burgundian crusaders suffered a catastrophic defeat at the hands of Sultan Bayezid's large and well-disciplined army at Nicopolis, however.

It must have seemed inevitable that within a few years the triumphant Ottomans would complete the destruction of the Byzantine Empire. The Byzantines were saved, though, when a new and unexpected enemy emerged to devastate the Ottomans and much of western and central Asia. The West's improbable savior was Timur the Lame, known in Europe as Tamerlane. Timur,

LEFT *Stylized portrait of Osman I, founder of the Ottoman state.*

LEFT *Crusaders besieging Nicopolis, a siege interrupted with catastrophic results when Sultan Bayezid arrived with a relief force (16th-century Turkish miniature).*

a man of mixed Turkic–Mongol blood born to a humble family near Samarkand, had a burning drive to conquer the world. He brought the Turkic and Mongol tribes of Central Asia under his control and in 1385 set out to conquer Iran. From there he invaded India, sacking Delhi in 1398; the Delhi sultanate survived, but was greatly weakened. Timur then lunged westward again, conquering Christian Georgia and Armenia and devastating Iraq. In 1402, he inflicted a massive defeat on the Ottomans in the Battle of Ankara, displaying the defeated sultan Bayezid in a cage as he continued his travels. Timur was planning the conquest of China at the time of his death in 1405. Wherever he went, Timur was determined to sow terror, with horrendous massacres and the mass enslavement of surviving populations, rather than attempting to establish a stable government of his own. Timur's empire fell apart when he died, but its memory lingered for centuries.

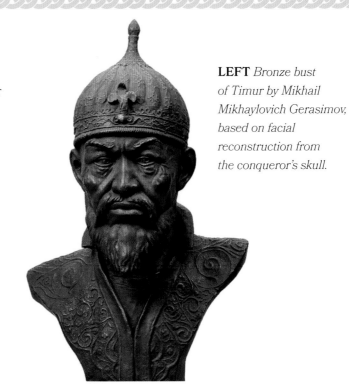

LEFT *Bronze bust of Timur by Mikhail Mikhaylovich Gerasimov, based on facial reconstruction from the conqueror's skull.*

Samarkand, Gem of the Silk Road

The ancient city of Samarkand was ideally situated to dominate the caravan trade across Central Asia. It was a thriving center throughout the medieval centuries and beyond, a focus for Muslim scholarship that was probably the site of the first paper mill in the Islamic world. Despite Chinggis Khan's massacre of much of the populace in 1220, Samarkand soon regained prosperity. When Marco Polo visited he reports that the city was large and splendid, as did Ibn Battuta after he went there in 1333.

When Timur came to power he made Samarkand his capital and spent the rest of his reign making the city into a showcase worthy of his glory. He even made an exception to his usual policy of rampant slaughter in favor of artists and architects, sparing their lives and resettling them in Samarkand.

Bibi-Khanym Mosque, Samarkand (Uzbekistan). One of the most magnificent mosques in the world, it was commissioned by Timur in 1399.

ABOVE *Ruins of the palace constructed by Delhi sultan Firuz Shah. The complex includes a mosque, granary, and noble palaces, all within a major fortress.*

One of the regions most disrupted politically by Timur's aggression was India. The Delhi Sultanate had started the 14th century strongly, Alauddin Khalij (who usurped the throne in 1296) successfully beating back repeated Mongol invasions and conquering much of the Deccan. His rule was harsh, but stability was restored when Ghiyasuddin (1320–5) founded a new Dynasty, the Tughluq. This enlightened ruler made administrative reforms, lightened the tax burden by increasing acreage under cultivation, digging irrigation canals and reclaiming waste lands. Nowhere is it clearer than in the Delhi Sultanate that a ruler's whims could shape a country's fate, however. Muhammad bin Tughluq (1325–51) massively disrupted the society he ruled. He caused an enormous fiscal crisis with the ill-conceived issue of copper tokens intended to be legally equivalent to gold and silver coins— but without removing the gold and silver from circulation. Muhammad also ordered the entire population of Delhi to relocate to a new capital at Devagiri, more than 900 miles (1,448 km) away. The move caused immense suffering for no purpose, as the sultan changed his mind in a few years and allowed a return to Delhi. The next sultan, Firuz, was rigidly orthodox and demolished the temples of his majority Hindu population, including the great temple of Jaggannath at Puri. Peasant rebellions were common, as was famine and probably significant outbreaks of the plague. It is hardly surprising that the Delhi sultanate disintegrated after Timur's 1398 invasion; his sack of Delhi was accompanied by massive looting and massacre. The weakening of the Muslim Delhi state allowed the resurgence of Hindu states further to the south, above all the Vijayanagara Empire, founded by two brothers in *c.* 1330.

THE FLOURISHING OF MALI

Perhaps the greatest success story of the 14th century is that of the Mali Empire of western Africa, a region unaffected by the epidemic disease and climate woes of so much of the world. The empire had started as a small Mandinka kingdom, but expanded as the Ghana Empire (Wagadu) declined. Mali had become a major power in the 13th century under Sundiata Keita, who conquered Sosso in *c.* 1235. Later rulers oversaw further expansion, most notably Sakoura, who after seizing the throne in a successful coup in *c.* 1285 established his rule as far west as the ocean and probably conquered the state of Gao. The state reached its greatest extent under the *mansa* (emperor) Musa (1312–37). He took control of the Middle Niger valley, including Timbuktu, and maybe completed the conquest of Gao. He also pushed north to the salt-producing areas of the Sahara.

Mali was a major mercantile state, its rulers taking vigorous steps to control the trade in gold from Africa's interior and salt from the north. In Mansa Musa's time the capital, Niani, had a population of at least 100,000. It was a syncretist state, Muslim merchants exerting a strong influence on the elites. Much of the elite converted to Islam and by the time of Mansa Musa at least a rudimentary civil service existed, with secretaries

BELOW *Samples of the hundreds of thousands of manuscripts, written in Arabic and several African languages, that still survive from medieval Timbuktu.*

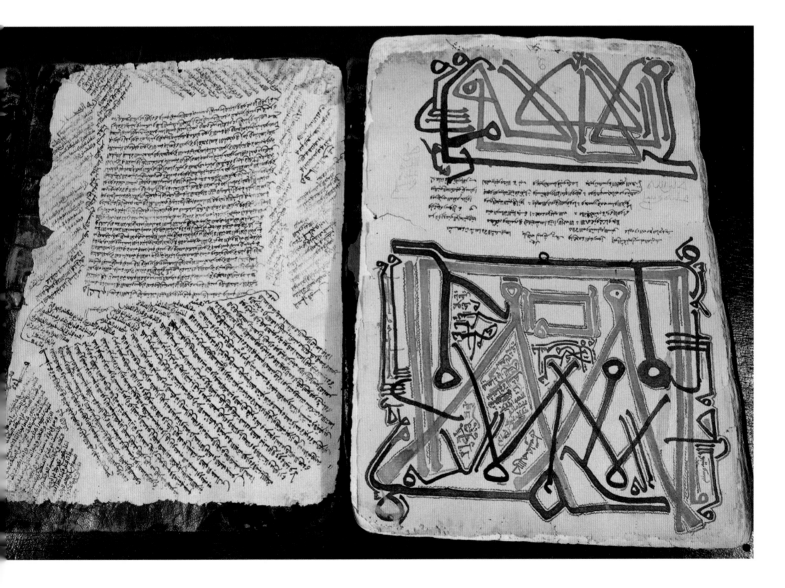

ABOVE *The Great Mosque of Djenné (Mali). First constructed in the 13th century, the adobe structure has been rebuilt several times in the same style. The current building dates to 1907.*

keeping records in Arabic. Timbuktu in particular became a center for Islamic scholarship; starting at the end of the 20th century hundreds of thousands of manuscripts from as early as the 12th century have been recovered from private homes in the city, attesting to a rich literary culture, not just in Arabic but in a number of African languages.

Mali suffered some decline after the death of Musa, its Wolof-speaking provinces breaking away to form the Jolof Empire in the 1360s by taking advantage of a succession struggle in Mali. This Wolof state was a confederation of small kingdoms rather than a strongly centralized unit. Mali itself, however, survived to the 17th century.

The Greatest *Hajj*

A number of West African rulers made the pilgrimage to Mecca. None caught the imagination of the Islamic world—and that of Christian Europeans as well—as the great *hajj* of Mansa Musa in 1324–5. Taking at least 10,000 of his subjects with him, Musa showed the world just how gold-rich Africa was. His gifts and purchases were so great that the value of gold plummeted in Egypt and on the Arabian Peninsula for 12 years. But Mansa Musa's *hajj* was not just for show. The emperor was himself literate in Arabic and clearly appreciative of Islamic culture. On his return to Mali he brought back a number of Egyptian scholars. One, as-Sahdi, designed new mosques at Gao and Timbuktu and built a new palace for this magnificent ruler.

Mansa Musa, from the Catalan Atlas of 1375.

CHAPTER 10

The 15th Century: A Time of Ends and Beginnings

Various non-European cultures have defined their "middle age" both beginning and ending at different times. Europeanists, by contrast, usually mark the 15th as the last medieval century. Was the fall of Constantinople to the Ottoman Turks in 1453 the key turning point? Or was it the ascent of the Tudors to the English throne in 1485? Several possible "end of the Middle Ages" scenarios may have more global validity. The ongoing progress of the Little Ice Age forced significant restructurings of many societies. More immediately shocking for world societies were developments in gunpowder technology in this century, making firearms of all sizes a game-changer in warfare as never before. By the end of the century, the world was also on the verge of being linked together to an unprecedented degree, thanks to the voyages of exploration sponsored by both Portugal and Spain. The result was that the world of the 16th century proved to be very different from that of the medieval millennium that preceded it.

RIGHT *Sultan Mehmed the Conqueror on horseback in the hippodrome of Constantinople.*

LOOKING INWARD

East Asia in 1400 appeared well-situated to dominate the world. China, still the most productive and populous region, had thrown off Mongol rule and its emperors commanded enormous resources. Much less wealthy, Japan was also in a promising position. By the 15th century, most of its economy was market-driven rather than subsistence, and strong shoguns had displayed considerable success controlling Japan's warrior class. Japan, however, suffered serious declines in the 15th century, the centralizing power of the shogunate weakening after Ashikaga Yoshinori was assassinated in 1441. A series of succession disputes followed, creating an age of endemic war; the whole 1450–1600 time span has been dubbed the "warring states period" in the Japanese islands.

The strength of Chinese imperial rule is clear in the years following Ming Chengzu's (originally named Zhu Di) usurpation of the throne from his nephew in 1402. Until his death in 1424, Ming Chengzu consolidated the power of his dynasty, restoring the Grand Canal and developing the city now named Beijing, which had already been the Mongol northern capital, into a great showpiece of his Dynasty that by the year 1500

had a population of 672,000. The emperor also launched five expensive campaigns against the Mongols, personally leading the 1410 expedition after a large Ming army suffered defeat in 1409. These military ventures better demonstrate the wealth of the Ming than their military prowess, however, and they accomplished little beyond emptying the treasury. Ming Chengzu's efforts also included a superbly pretentious scholarly event: the emperor ordered the compilation of a great encyclopedia of all knowledge, the *Yongle Dadian*. More than 2,000 scholars labored on it for over five years. The result was a work 22,938 chapters long, bound in about 10,000 large volumes and amounting to more than 50 million words (for comparison, the present volume is about 65,000 words long). The achievement proved ephemeral, as the encyclopedia had disappeared before the end of the Ming Dynasty. One copy had been made, and about 700 volumes of it still exist.

Ming Chengzu's most famous achievement—and the one that most puzzles modern audiences—was the commissioning of seven great naval expeditions, commanded by Admiral Zheng He. These voyages, in enormous specially built

BELOW *Samurai sword from Japan's Warring States Period.*

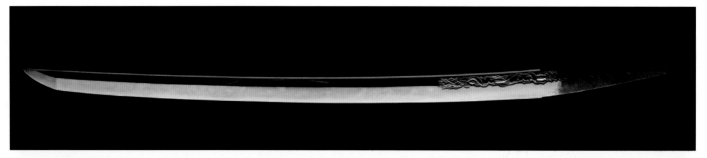

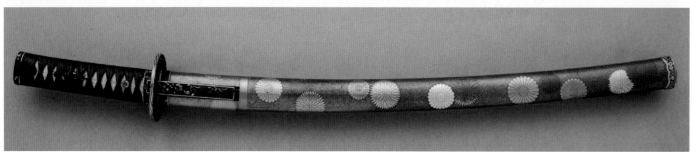

"Treasure Ships" that were as long as 440 ft (134 m) with up to nine masts and able to hold up to 2,500 tons of cargo, took place between 1405 and 1433. Each expedition lasted for two or more years. They were not voyages of discovery; Chinese merchants traded in all the areas the fleet visited. Nor were they voyages of conquest, although each expedition included in excess of 20,000 men, mostly professional soldiers, and they won major battles on Sumatra and Sri Lanka. Zheng He's expeditions are perhaps best described as power projection. They were a demonstration that Ming Chengzu *was* the

ABOVE *Constructed 1406–20, the vast Forbidden City is the imperial palace of Beijing, China. The whole complex includes 8,704 buildings and covers 178 acres.*

ABOVE *Section of the Yongle Encyclopedia.*

A Principled Objection

When Zhu Di usurped the Ming throne, several officials at court protested the attack on the young designated heir to the throne (who died in the fire that destroyed his palace during Zhu Di's seizure of power). One man in particular, Lian Zining, refused to accept the new emperor's self-justification for his actions. He appeared personally before the new ruler to reproach him. The guards knocked Lian down, but from the floor he continued to berate the emperor. The emperor ordered the official's tongue cut out. Unable to speak, Lian wrote an indictment of the usurpation upon the ground in his own blood. Finally, Lian Zining was taken away and dismembered. His principled objection, which he must have known from the start would lead to his punishment and likely death, helps demonstrate the strength of the Confucian moral code of correct behavior in which the Chinese civil service was steeped.

Ming Chengzu may have been unprincipled, but he was at least a strong ruler. After his death, the Ming Dynasty soon faltered, with children succeeding to power, incompetent emperors taking power, or men coming to the throne who were uninterested in ruling. China enjoyed a few fortunate years after the eight-year-old Yingzong became emperor in 1436. His grandmother, the dowager empress Zhang, ruled for him, speaking from behind a screen and winning a reputation as wise and noble-minded. Zhang died in 1442, however, and the emperor, when he came of age, undertook an unnecessary campaign against the Mongols in 1449 that led to the complete destruction of a 50,000-man Chinese army; the emperor himself was taken prisoner. Such expeditions weakened the empire's financial stability, encouraged

BELOW *A 15th-century Chinese helmet.*

ABOVE *Among the tribute Zheng He brought back from his voyages was this giraffe, a gift from Malindi.*

legitimate ruler of China, despite his usurpation, and were designed to intimidate the states of Asia and East Africa they visited into acknowledging the Ming emperor's power and offer tribute. Their mission accomplished, the extravagant and expensive voyages then ceased. Beginning in the 1430s, China's rulers restricted the movement of China-based ships in the Indian Ocean. By 1500, the construction of large ships was forbidden, and in 1525 the emperor ordered all ocean-going ships be destroyed.

conservatism, and reinforced the Chinese elite's fear of foreigners.

China's influence on Southeast Asia also weakened, even during Ming Chengzu's reign. China had intervened militarily in the region early in the century, since Java was unable to control the rising piracy in the Straits of Melaka. In Java's place, China established the rising Malay state of Melaka as the main emporium of the region. The prince of Melaka prospered thanks to his court's special diplomatic relationship with the Ming emperors, so that by 1440 Melaka was the wealthiest port in Asia. After the great Ming diplomatic voyages ended, however, the ruler converted to Islam, finding it more important to encourage Muslim traders than to curry favor with China.

China's intervention in Vietnam was even more ephemeral. In 1400, a usurper killed the king of Annam (northern Vietnam) and declared himself monarch. The Ming court found a surviving member of the Tran Dynasty and tried to

LEFT *Coronation of King Vajralongkorn (2019). The Thai ceremonial still uses regalia seized from Angkor.*

BELOW *Mahanavami Dibba, the "Victory Platform" in the royal enclosure, Vijayanagara, southern India.*

LEFT *As an act of piety, medieval Jain ascetics copied and illustrated religious manuscripts, thousands of which have survived.*

BELOW *Tower of Victory (Vijaya Stambha), constructed by King Rana Kumbha in 1448 to celebrate his victory in the Battle of Sarangpur. It is dedicated to the god Vishnu.*

reinstate him in Annam, only to have the usurper kill both the Chinese puppet and the emperor's envoys. Chengzu responded vigorously, invading to make Annam a Chinese province yet again. Despite a 20-year war, however, the Chinese armies failed in their goal and Annam remained independent. Other regions of Southeast Asia simply acted on their own, without reference to the distant Chinese court. Thus in 1431 the Thai king Trailok sacked Angkor, seizing the Khmer king's regalia in the process, a clear statement of Thai independence.

Other new states in South and Southeast Asia also rose to new prominence. It was a great age for the Vijayanagara Empire of southern India, which expanded especially in the reign of Devaraya II (1432–46). The maharajas of Vijayanagara had learned a number of important lessons from the fading Delhi Sultanate. Although the rulers and most of the populace were Hindu, they enlisted many Turks and other Muslims to develop their army, especially the cavalry, importing warhorses for the purpose. The result was a large and flourishing state. Its capital, enclosed in a series of massive walls, boasted a 15-mile (24 km) aqueduct to supply fresh water and had an estimated population of 300,000–400,000. The state of Gujarat in western India, which won independence from Delhi in 1407, also flourished, the ruler founding the city of Ahmedabad in 1411. Nor should we forget that the Polynesian state of Tonga developed into what can fairly be described as a maritime empire in the 15th century, as the chiefs of the island of Tongatapa centralized control over a large region.

EUROPE'S GROWING PAINS

As China turned in on itself, the states of Europe increasingly looked outward, both waging war within Europe and probing sources of revenue beyond Europe's borders. The reasons are not far to seek. Besides the entangled genealogies of European monarchs, which allowed them to claim each others' lands with dizzying frequency, the downturn of the European economy with the onset of the Little Ice Age, exacerbated by a critical shortage of bullion as veins of silver and gold within Europe were exhausted, made competition for resources worse. Europe simply did not have sufficient infrastructure to pay for its rulers' increasingly elaborate and lengthy wars. This was especially the case as the growing dominance of a new military technology—gunpowder weaponry—developed to the point that it could really be a game-changer in battle.

As we have seen, the Chinese military made significant use of gunpowder by the 10th century. When the Mongols invaded China, they too saw its potential; for example, the ships that invaded Japan carried an early form of gunpowder grenade. The Islamic world learned the hard way to appreciate gunpowder as did eastern Europeans, perhaps first seeing gunpowder weapons deployed by the Mongols at the Battle of Muhi in 1241.

It was apparently Europeans who first experimented with using gunpowder to launch larger projectiles—heavy javelins or rock spheres—from tubes, the earliest cannon (which are first mentioned in Europe in 1327). Early cannon were very slow, liable to explode, and not particularly powerful, although by *c.* 1380 cannon were being crafted that could launch a ball weighing hundreds of pounds. The great breakthrough came in *c.* 1430, when a process was invented to "corn" gunpowder, wetting it with alcohol and then drying it to crystals, which trebled its power. Already King Henry V of England (1413–22) invested heavily in artillery, which he used to reignite the Hundred Years War. From that point to the end of the century and beyond, Europe saw a full-scale arms race, as rulers strove to keep up with their belligerent neighbors.

The high cost of war, as well as the fact that the English kings could not honorably withdraw

BELOW *Mons Meg. Presented to King James II of Scotland as a gift by the duke of Burgundy in 1454, this late medieval bombard shoots 386-pound balls (Edinburgh Castle).*

LEFT *Siege of Orléans, 1429, from the Vigiles de Charles VII.*

BELOW *A masterpiece by the Burgundian goldsmith Gérard Loyet. The kneeling Duke Charles the Bold, protected by St. George, holds a relic of St. Lambert (1467–71).*

their challenge after Edward III had claimed to be rightful king of France, assured that the Hundred Years War ground on for a very long time, with long pauses for bankruptcy, plague outbreaks, rulers going insane, and internal struggles within both France and England. Henry V of England in the Treaty of Troyes (1420) was actually named heir to the French throne, but died leaving an infant heir before the incapacitated Charles VI of France's demise. As Henry VI of England (and supposedly France) grew up, he proved unable to rule, and England eventually broke down in internal dissent. While England struggled to hold onto its conquests in western France, however, Charles VII planned—and invested. Given a leg up by the meteoric career of Joan of Arc (d. 1431), Charles proved to be a strong king. He succeeded in imposing national taxes, and with the income built up both a standing army and a formidable artillery train. He then employed the new technology to drive the English out of almost all of France (England held Calais until 1558); in 1446, French heavy cannon were able to break open English castles in Normandy at the rate of five per month, rather than the month- or year-long sieges that had characterized most of the Middle Ages. The final battle, fought near Castillon in Gascony in 1453, was a triumph of artillery, as English soldiers were slaughtered trying to assault a carefully fortified artillery park.

The conclusion of the Hundred Years War propelled the newly centralized kingdom of France into a leading position in Europe, especially as England immediately descended into the civil strife known as the "Wars of the Roses." The great nobles of France were not willing to give up their independence without a fight, Charles the Bold of Burgundy in particular creating a major army in opposition to French centralization and making a spirited attempt to resurrect the old Carolingian "middle kingdom" of Lotharingia. Charles's death in the Battle of Nancy (January 1477), however, assured that the French kings could continue to grow in strength. By 1483, the French monarchy could mobilize 50,000 men, and in 1494 Charles VIII invaded northern Italy in an effort to dominate a new region.

Everywhere in Europe rulers attempted to consolidate their power, causing desperate upheaval among noble and peasant alike. Monarchies usually won such struggles, but there were important exceptions. Sometimes the institution survived but an incumbent lost, as when both James I and James III of Scotland were assassinated (in 1437 and 1488). It seemed for a time that the power of the popes would devolve into a more representative process, in which the "nobles" of the Church (the cardinals and bishops) would make important decisions. The Council of Constance (1414–18), which finally ended the Great Western Schism, established the principle of "conciliarism"—a return to the early Church's practice of authoritative councils. The popes, firmly adhering to the tradition that they were vicars not only of St. Peter but of Christ himself, strongly opposed conciliarism, and by mid-century the papacy was once again firmly established as a monarchic system.

The most notable noble triumph was the further decline of the Holy Roman emperors of Germany in the 15th century. Centuries of struggle against ecclesiastical authorities and the triumph of the elective principle for choosing new emperors had assured that the German emperors did not have sufficient power to resist the forces of decentralization. In 1400, the German electors succeeded in deposing Wenzel IV as German king after he had colluded in the murder of John of Nepomuk for resisting royal interference in the Bohemian Church, a process comparable to the English nobles deposing Richard II in 1399. By the mid-15th century, the imperial title carried little but a ceremonial role; what power the Hapsburgs, who finally made the imperial crown hereditary, had came from their family lands. Meanwhile, German nobles could wage private war with impunity; for example feuding nobles destroyed about 1,200 villages in the Rhineland and southwestern Germany in the first half of the 15th century.

It was not only nobles who opposed the extension of monarchic power. In far northern Germany, the peasants of Dithmarschen held off their local lords and the kings of Denmark throughout the 15th century. Peasant revolts in Scandinavia, where peasants had traditionally held many more rights, became common; for

BELOW *The structure of the Holy Roman Empire, from the* Nuremberg Chronicle *(1493).*

LEFT *The burning of Jan Hus, from the* Life and Times of Emperor Sigismund *by Eberhard Windeck, c.1440–50.*

example, rebellion broke out in Sweden and Denmark in 1433–4 and in 1436 in Norway, playing an important role in Sweden winning its independence from Danish rule. England in 1450 was rocked by Jack Cade's peasant revolt, and the Remença Revolt in Catalonia (1462–86) won the abolition of serfdom there. Most striking of all was the Hussite Rebellion in Bohemia, which broke out after the popular reformist preacher Jan Hus was executed as a heretic in 1415—an event that brought to a head roiling discontent at German rule over the region. What developed was a war for religious reform, waged by a largely peasant army. Three crusades against the Bohemian "heretics" failed to suppress the rebellion completely; the result was a series of compromises that prefigured the Protestant Reformation.

The preaching of Jan Hus, who attacked traditional Church practices as having no basis in the Bible, helps illustrate the shifting intellectual climate of Europe, usually defined as a "renaissance," a rebirth of classical learning, but that in fact pushed beyond the lessons of antiquity in a number of ways. This learned movement, fueled by studies of the works of Greek antiquity and feeding off both the Carolingian renaissance and the 12th-century renaissance, took off in Italy in the 1320s and

1330s. The most important contribution of the Italian Renaissance was a new method of textual criticism that examined key texts with new eyes, going back to original languages rather than depending on translations. The movement soon caught on with intellectuals beyond Italy, as well as influencing art and music with its "back to the sources" approach that nonetheless created a great deal that was new.

Europeans playing catch-up with the more advanced civilizations to their east also took a major stride forward in about the year 1450, when a process of printing using moveable type was perfected. China had known the printing press for centuries, although most Chinese printing was carried out by carving the text onto woodblocks rather than by setting type. Europeans had known and used woodblock printing for several centuries, perhaps inventing the process independently. Woodblocks are labor-intensive for longer texts, however, so most copying of books continued by hand, copying shops struggling to keep up with burgeoning demand from the schools and an increasingly literate urban populace. Europe's breakthrough came thanks to the inventor Johannes Gutenberg (c.1400–68) of Mainz, who invented a means to cast durable individual letters and a process to fix those letters into a frame and print them cleanly, a method simplified because Europe's alphabetic writing system drastically reduced the number of symbols needed. Gutenberg's invention, flamboyantly demonstrated with a deluxe edition of the entire Bible (printed between 1450 and 1455), was an instant sensation. By the end of the century, a printing press could produce up to 3,600 pages per day and every significant European town had at least one press. Gutenberg's press, combined with paper (whose production had gradually spread from China, reaching Europe in the 13th century), greatly reduced the cost of the written word and literacy rates soon climbed. Europe rapidly became a hotbed not just of the intellectual pretensions of the Renaissance, but of religious dissent and reports of new discoveries.

The Platonic Academy

One of the greatest advances of the Italian Renaissance was to make the works of Plato available to Western Europeans for the first time in many centuries. Plato's reintroduction was enabled by the increasingly dire plight of Constantinople, combined with the aspirations of a very rich Florentine banking company. The knowledge of Plato's dialogues had never been lost in the Byzantine Empire, and as it became increasingly obvious that the Ottoman Turks would take beleaguered Constantinople within a few years, a number of Greek scholars migrated to or visited Italy. Among them was Gemistos Plethon, an important Neoplatonist philosopher. When Plethon lectured on Plato during the Council of Florence in 1439, his fascinated audience included Cosimo de' Medici. One of a number of members of the plutocratic Medici family who invested heavily in patronage of art and culture, Cosimo founded what became known as the Platonic Academy, which effectively reintroduced Plato to Western Europe. Under the leadership of Marsilio Ficino, the academy produced Latin translations of all Plato's works, making them available to Europe's entire educated elite, as well as a number of Neoplatonist works.

The Gutenberg Bible.

LEFT *Quentin Massys*, The Moneylender and his Wife *(1514), portraying a prosperous bourgeois couple from Antwerp.*

THE FALL OF THE ROMAN EMPIRE (PART II)

Most reckonings of the European Middle Ages begin with the end of the *Western Roman Empire* as a political entity in the year 476. But, as we have seen, the Eastern Roman Empire—renamed the "Byzantine" Empire by modern historians—had survived and often flourished for much of the medieval millennium. By the 15th century, however, the Byzantine Empire was but a hollow shell of its former self.

Although a native Greek dynasty in 1261 regained Constantinople itself from the descendants of the crusaders who had taken it, the state was smaller, more divided, and much more economically impoverished than before. Moreover, since the early 14th century the aggressive Ottoman Turkish dynasty had progressively whittled away territory, first in Anatolia and then crossing into Europe, until little of the empire

BELOW *Rumeli Hisar, constructed in 1451–2 by Mehmed II to prepare for the Turkish siege of Constantinople.*

ABOVE *Siege of Constantinople. Turkish ships have entered the Golden Horn along a slipway the sultan had constructed.*

was left but the city of Constantinople itself. Constantinople was granted a breathing space when Timur defeated the Ottomans and captured Sultan Bayezid I in 1402, but a civil war between Bayezid's sons culminated in the ascension of a new, strong ruler, Mehmed I (1413–21). Mehmed restored the Ottoman military, building up the elite corps of janissaries (slave soldiers levied as tribute from the Ottomans' non-Turkish subjects) and equipping them with the most modern firearms available. By 1422, the Ottomans were ready to besiege Constantinople again, and although that siege failed, they did capture Thessalonike in 1430.

Thoroughly alarmed by the Turkish threat, the Byzantine emperor John VIII Paleologus went cap in hand to Western Europe, even agreeing to subject the Orthodox Church to the papacy at the Council of Florence in 1439. The Fourth Crusade and its aftermath had left deep scars, however, and many Byzantines protested what they regarded as a betrayal. Still, in the wake of the treaty, Western Europeans tried to help. The Crusade of Varna in 1444 saw a force of some 20,000 launched against Sultan Murad's forces in Europe—albeit mostly Hungarians under their king, Ladislas, who feared an imminent invasion of his territory. The crusaders were annihilated in a decisive battle and little hope remained for Constantinople.

The final attack came in 1453, Sultan Mehmed II preparing an overwhelming force against which even the great Theodosian Walls of Constantinople could not stand. The Ottomans brought an army of about 60,000 men against perhaps 8,000 defenders. Unable to break the chain protecting Constantinople's harbor, Mehmed ordered his ships to be dragged overland, relaunching them within the Golden Horn. Most importantly,

RIGHT *Armour of Mamluk Sultan Al-Ashraf Sayf ad-Din Qaitbay (d. 1494), who temporarily stabilized the Egyptian state.*

Mehmed bought enormous cannon from a Hungarian engineer (who had first offered them to the Byzantine emperor, who did not have sufficient funds to purchase them), the largest of which fired 1,200-pound balls (544 kg). No walls could have stood up to the 20-day Turkish bombardment, and on May 29, 1453, the Turks broke into the city. The last Byzantine emperor, Constantine XI Paleologus, died fighting on the walls. The Ottoman forces sacked Constantinople for three days, after which Mehmed II devoted years to rebuilding and repopulating the great city, which the Turks called "Istanbul," probably already the local pronunciation of the city's name. The Ottoman Empire had reached even greater heights by the end of the century, including major campaigns against Mamluk Egypt in 1485–91, although the final conquest of Egypt did not come until 1517.

OPPOSITE *Fatih ("Conqueror's") Mosque, Istanbul, constructed on the site of the Church of the Apostles 1463–70 and rebuilt in 1771 after an earthquake.*

The Ethiopians in Europe

Always under threat from the Muslim rulers of Egypt, the Christian dynasty that ruled Ethiopia from 1270 (called the Solomonid Dynasty because they claimed descent from Solomon and the queen of Sheba) sought several times to find allies in Europe. King Yeshaq sent an embassy to Alfonso V of Aragón in 1428, proposing to seal an alliance against the Muslims with a marriage between Alfonso's son and Yeshaq's daughter; he also requested European artisans to teach new skills to his people. We do not know how Alfonso responded, but the embassy ended badly for the ambassador: the Mamluk authorities of Egypt caught the delegates on their return journey and hanged their leader. That unfortunate circumstance did not end Ethiopian outreach. Zara Yaqob sent representatives to the Council of Florence in 1441, who were doubtless puzzled when the council members kept calling their king "Prester John." Another diplomatic mission reached Europe in 1450. None of the embassies bore fruit, but the very fact that they were attempted demonstrates the growing importance of European states on the world stage, and helped to educate Europeans about the broader world.

Letter of Zara Yaqob to Pope Nicholas V.

WHEN EUROPE MET AFRICA

Ethiopia under the Solomonid Dynasty was thriving in the 15th century, as were a number of other states through much of the continent of Africa. Since our sources become rather better in this century, we can see them in sharper focus. Ethiopia flourished with a stable government and a vigorous revival of monasticism. Trade was limited, though, as one can see from the lack of cities. Only the ancient capital of Aksum was a true town, and even it was not a royal center except for coronations; the true "capital" was a peripatetic tent city that relocated

BELOW *A nkisi figure from Congo.*

every three to four months. Further south, the Swahili coast flourished, continuing to exist as a number of independent city-states rather than integrating into a larger state. Sofala on the south coast of Mozambique developed into a main trade link to the interior of the continent, the kingdom of Mwene Mutapa controlling the exchange of gold, copper, silver, iron, ivory, leather, and slaves. The new kingdom, along with Torwa, replaced the empire of Zimbabwe, which broke up in the 1420s and 1430s as trade patterns shifted; by the 1450s Great Zimbabwe was mostly abandoned. The new trade route to the interior, which took advantage of the Zambezi River for easy transport, allowed the kingdom of Malawi in central Africa to develop in the early decades of the century.

For West Africa, the 15th century was an age of transition. Mali was in steep decline by c. 1400. Tuareg nomads had seized Walata and Timbuktu, and a number of vassal regions broke loose, most notably Gao, whose ruler pillaged the Mali capital Niani around the year 1400. Over the course of the century, Gao grew from a small city-state into the great Songhay Empire. Most notable was the reign of Sonni Ali (1464–92), a great military leader who developed an effective cavalry force. He fought off the Tuareg nomads and in 1469 took Timbuktu. Sonni Ali was nothing if not tenacious, as can be seen in his seven-year siege of Jenne. By the time of his death the Songhay state was a major empire. It was not, however the only significant state of western Africa. The kingdom of Benin (occupying part of the territory that is now Nigeria) underwent a major expansion beginning in the 1440s. Tradition tells that Benin's King Ewuare captured 201 towns and villages; he built Benin City into a major capital, improving the fortifications and constructing good roads. Kanem-Bornu, which had declined in the 14th century, also saw a major revival under King Ali Gaji (1472–1504). Ali Gaji conquered some of the Hausa states to the east and regained control of the main northern trade routes.

Very few Europeans had direct contact with sub-saharan Africa before the 15th century. The east coast was only accessible by passing through large Muslim-held territories, while strong currents on the West African coast made access via the Atlantic nearly impossible until ship design improved in the early 15th century with the invention of the caravel. Portugal, facing the Atlantic, took the lead in exploration, embarking on a decades-long quest to establish a sea route to the desirable exports of Asia. The Portuguese conquest of Ceuta (in Morocco) set off a spate of systematic exploration of Africa's Atlantic coast. The Portuguese happily committed piracy, for example fortifying the island of Arguin and using it as a base to raid inland for slaves—a highly desirable commodity, needed to work the large plantations the Portuguese had established on Madeira and the Azores. Soon they were also trading with rulers, for instance establishing contact with the ruler of Jolof by 1450. After a Portuguese captain reached the Bight of Benin, the king of Benin even sent one of his chiefs to Lisbon as an ambassador. By the end of the 15th century, Portugal imported to Europe about a quarter of West Africa's gold production and about 2,000 enslaved people

each year. When Vasco da Gama sailed up the eastern coast of Africa and reached Calicut in May 1498 he opened the door to a massive expansion in Portuguese trade. Unfortunately, he and his successors proved uninterested in working within existing trade systems, instead using their more advanced military technology (including shipboard cannon) to wreak devastation, especially among the Swahili states.

LEFT *One of several thousand bronze plaques that decorated the royal palace in the kingdom of Benin (modern Nigeria).*

BELOW *A Portuguese map of West Africa (1563).*

CREATING A WORLD SYSTEM

The greatest astonishment of the 15th century was when Europeans discovered that advanced civilizations existed in a western hemisphere that had hitherto been barely imagined, and the parallel discovery by the civilizations of the Americas that other parts of the world were not only populated but had also created sophisticated social, political and religious systems. Hitherto, coverage of the Americas has been spotty in this volume. Much of the territory known now as North and South America was sparsely populated, in many regions people living in small villages or as foragers. Where more complex civilizations evolved, as with the Ancestral Pueblo or Mississippi Mound Culture, our understanding is limited by sparse archeological remains and lack of written records. Of the civilizations of the Americas, only the Maya developed a comprehensive written language, but Spanish missionaries destroyed most of the culture's written records before they could be studied. By the 15th century, however, two great civilizations had developed in the western hemisphere, the peoples commonly known as the "Aztecs" and the "Incas." The impressive remains of these civilizations, surviving oral traditions, and the frequently bemused accounts of the Europeans who first encountered them, allow us to develop a picture of the "other" world of the late Middle Ages, a world in many ways more advanced than that of the Europeans who precipitated its collapse.

The central Mexican basin was fertile, able to support a large population thanks above all to intensive maize cultivation. It was thus hardly surprising that over the centuries the region saw a series of migrations from the American southwest. The last to arrive were a Nahuatl-speaking people, the Mexica, who appeared in the late 12th and 13th centuries. Since the best lands were already taken, they hired themselves out as mercenaries, helping the small states of the region with their wars. Their own legends tell that they came from a place called Aztlan, the "Place of the Seven Caves."

The leaders of the Mexica gradually established themselves as rulers of three city-states, Tenochtitlán, Texcoco, and Tlacopan. The chance for empire appeared in 1426, when King Tezozomoc, ruler of Azcapotzalco, the most powerful state of the region, died. Tezozomoc's sons started a civil war for the throne, in the course of which the Mexica king of Tenochtitlán was lured to a feast and murdered. The dead ruler's uncle, Itzcoatl, soon claimed the throne

RIGHT *The founding myth of Tenochtitlán, from the Codex Mendoza, a work in Aztec pictograms with Spanish translation. created c.1541.*

of Tenochitlán, and looked for allies to bring down Azcapotzalco. The result was the creation of the Triple Alliance (or Aztec) Empire in 1428. The combined Mexica armies, under Itzcoatl's leadership, rapidly triumphed, establishing hegemony over a number of central Mexico's small states. This process continued in the reign of Moctezuma I (1440–69), who made Tenochtitlán the capital of a large, militaristic state. As capital of a heavily populated and prosperous state, Tenochtitlán was very much a showcase for Aztec power. Constructed on an island in Lake Texcoco and connected to the mainland with bridges, the whole urban site was laced with canals to facilitate canoe traffic. Two great aqueducts provided fresh water for the inhabitants—with estimates ranging between 200,000 and 400,000 inhabitants in the late 15th century, Tenochtitlán was one of the largest, most complex cities in the world.

At times fielding armies in excess of 300,000 men, Mexica society was very much oriented around war. During the course of their expansion, the forces of the Triple Alliance engaged in terror tactics against people who resisted them. For example, Huaxtecs to the northeast fought back fiercely; its city was sacked and temples burned, the Mexica killing everyone they could in an effort to destroy all traces of Huaxtecs from the earth. Other peoples, when defeated, were subjected to tribute of both food and sacrificial victims, since the gods of the region were propitiated with human sacrifice. Such demands naturally encouraged further warfare, as tributary states preferred not to give up their own people for sacrifice. War provided loot, slaves, and also advancement—good fighters became honorary nobles, with access to wealth and extra wives, despite Moctezuma I widening the gap between nobles and commoners.

By c. 1480 the dominance of Tenochtitlán was unquestioned, as the *tlatoani* of Tenochtitlán had defeated the people of Tlatelolco, who were sick of always being the junior partner in the

BELOW *The Aztec Stone of Moctezuma I, an altar for human sacrifice that originally stood before the Temple of Tezcatlipoca.*

ABOVE *Aztec human sacrifice, from the Codex Azcatitlan, a post-conquest manuscript written in Aztec glyphs.*

Triple Alliance. By the 1480s, the central valley of Mexico was home to about 1.5 million people. To be sure, the Aztec Empire suffered from the growing pains to be expected from its rapid rise. They never controlled the whole region; for instance, the city of Tzintzüntzan, which dominated the western Mexico trade, was strong enough to inflict a major defeat on the Aztecs in c. 1478. Nor could the Aztecs defeat the large city-state of Tlaxcala, so they instituted a competitive semi-war with them every few years, known as the "flower wars." These were highly ritualized events, fought between equal forces, limited to hand-to-hand-fighting, and involving a higher proportion of nobles; scholars debate whether their primary purpose was to show off the Aztecs' martial skill or to seize prisoners for human sacrifice. Still, trade in luxury goods flourished and the Mexica elite grew in wealth, privilege, and number. The excessive size of the royal clan, fostered by upper-class polygyny (where a man has more than one wife), led to a long power struggle after King Axayacatl's untimely death in 1481. A new king, Moctezuma II, only emerged in 1502. He increased central control, establishing administrative provinces with a well-organized bureaucracy and placing permanent garrisons at key locations. All of which proved in vain in 1520, when a combination of the hostile Tlaxcalans,

massive epidemics, and Spaniards brought down his empire.

The South American empire of Tahuantinsuyu, known to modern historians as the "Inca" Empire from the title of its rulers, was even more impressive in its scope and ambition. The Inca Empire enjoyed a meteoric rise in the mid-15th century in the reign of Pachacutec (who may have ruled 1438–71). Pachacutec defeated a number of small states along the Pacific coast and deep into the Andes. His capital, Cuzco, became a major center, as he rebuilt the great shrine of the sun (the sun god was regarded as the ancestor of the royal family) and canalized the city's two rivers. Pachacutec and his successors capitalized on their position as divine rulers, sons of the sun; their role as indispensable intermediaries between the people and the divine served as a justification for imposing their notions of order on a chaotic, dangerous world. The Inca, as divine kings, carried out a massively ambitious program. They were able to demand taxes, above all in the form of labor, from about two million households, in an empire that stretched over 2,000 miles (3,219 km). They engaged in major projects, including the construction of major temples and palaces and the creation of a major road system with two main north-south highways. The Inca royal highways tied their long, thin empire together, the complex of supporting walls, water drainage, bridges, stairways, and in areas paving allowing for trained runners to cover up to 140 miles (225 km) per day, changing in relays at the frequent rest houses along the route.

The *mitimae* system of the Inca rulers was perhaps the most comprehensive control of a civilian populace ever seen in the medieval era. This was a planned program to relocate large portions of the populace—probably as much as a third of their 12 million subjects—to new areas for economic, political, or military purposes. Especially with the conquest of what is now Bolivia, resettlement became a massive enterprise, with a number of groups assigned to cultivate state fields. The laborers were employed

BELOW *The 15th-century Inca fortress city of Machu Picchu, located on a mountain ridge 7,970 ft (2,430 m) above sea level.*

in the massive terracing of mountainsides and other construction projects. The whole system was administered by an aristocracy of natives from the Inca homeland around Cuzco, supported by a provincial bureaucracy drawn from the elites of subject peoples. A massive system of royal estates supported the ruler and his adherents, including the relatives of deceased rulers. The state was complex, maintaining archives of *quipus*, the unique Inca knot-writing system. The whole was a highly ritualized and divinized society, focused on Cuzco as a holy city, surrounded by six sacred mountains. In the year 1500, the peoples of the Andes probably had the most comprehensive authoritative government on the face of the planet.

RIGHT *Inca Figurine from Cerro Plomo, Chile.*

BELOW *The terraces at Pisac still attest to the Inca rulers' vast efforts to shape their empire.*

Imagining the World

Educated people had long known that the world was a sphere, although they differed on the question of its circumference. As Europeans explored, there was ever greater interest in depicting the known world, which expanded into a desire to map the *whole* world. The result was the terrestrial globe. Earlier versions had certainly existed, including one produced by the Sicilian Arab scholar al-Idrisi in the 12th century. But the oldest extant terrestrial globe was produced by the German Martin Behaim in 1492. Behaim, a merchant and cartographer, spent years in the service of the king of Portugal, both as an advisor on exploration and himself exploring the Pacific coast of Africa. When he returned to his native Nürnberg, the city council commissioned the cartographer to construct his globe, known as the *Erdapfel* ("earth apple"). Crafted from papier-mâché, parchment strips were pasted on the globe, showing the location of more than 2,000 places. It was soon outdated, however, because in the same year Christopher Columbus made his first voyage to the Americas, and a whole new hemisphere soon needed to be added as the scope of Columbus's discoveries became clear.

Martin Behaim's *Erdapfel*.

The *Tabula Rogeriana* (note that the South is at the top).

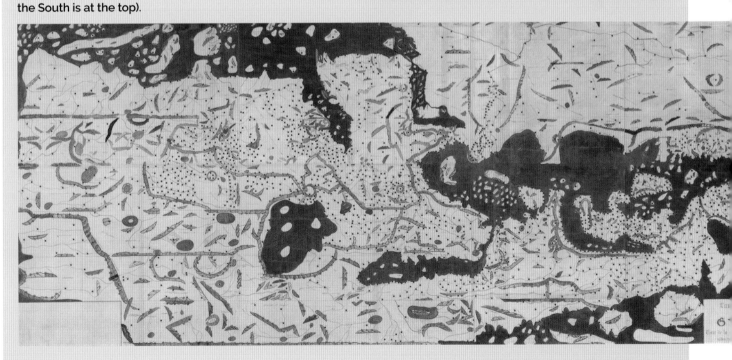